Lord Byron's Marriage

Shakespearian Studies
and
The Christian Renaissance
Atlantic Crossing
The Burning Oracle
Chariot of Wrath
The Starlit Dome
The Dynasty of Stowe
Hiroshima
Christ and Nietzsche
Lord Byron: Christian Virtues
Byron's Dramatic Prose
Laureate of Peace
The Last of the Incas

Lord Byron's Marriage

THE EVIDENCE
OF ASTERISKS

by

G. WILSON KNIGHT

Routledge and Kegan Paul

LONDON

First published in 1957
by Routledge & Kegan Paul Ltd
Broadway House, 68-74 Carter Lane
London E.C.4
Printed in Great Britain
by Butler & Tanner Ltd
Frome and London

Second impression 1957

For
OLIVE HEWETSON
who made the work easy

And if our quarrels should rip up old stories,
    And help them with a lie or two additional,
I'm not to blame, as you well know—no more is
    Any one else—they were become traditional;
Besides, their resurrection aids our glories
    By contrast, which is what we just were wishing all:
And science profits by this resurrection—
Dead scandals form good subjects for dissection.
                              Don Juan, I, 31.

Even now she should speak—or someone else for her . . . and a few
words will suffice. Worse the condition of the dead man's name cannot
be—far, far better it might—I believe it would be—were all the truth,
somehow or other, declared—and declared it must be, not for Byron's
sake only, but for the sake of humanity itself—and then a mitigated
sentence—or eternal silence.
                    John Wilson in *Blackwood's*; XXVII, 828.

The fearless man, in conscious virtue clad,
Endures the persecution of the bad;
Pursues his road by envy's shafts assailed,
Nor reaps renown until his coffin's nailed.
                              Don Leon, 1303.

CONTENTS

vii

ILLUSTRATIONS

PREFACE

THE student of Byron may be forced into biographical enquiries which do not arise in discussion of other great writers. In my previous study *Lord Byron: Christian Virtues* I promised to turn later, if it seemed desirable, to Byron's failings, and the reviews of that work made it only too clear that such a course was demanded. Again and again it was urged that attention must be given to his vices. Though I am myself primarily interested in the great record of his virtues, the promise must be met, and this volume constitutes its fulfilment.[1]

Once again, I disclaim any skill in the art of biography, as the term is usually understood. I find myself ill-at-ease among the great families and social customs of the past, and my memory for facts and dates is untrustworthy. I am only too well aware of the possibility of blunders. And yet it does seem that the thesis presented in the following pages goes far to clear up what is probably the most famous biographical crux in English letters. Whether such a claim is justified may, of course, be questioned; but, if it so turns out, I can, I think, offer certain reasons why such a result has been achieved.

Byron's life and personality possess many of the characteristics and much of the complexity of a work of art. He is, as it were, an incarnation of poetry, and what is needed to elucidate his story and 'pluck out the heart of his mystery' is less the skill of the biographer than the technique of poetic interpretation. During my efforts to untangle the pattern of evidence, I have been strongly aware of using precisely the same faculty of 'spatial' analysis as I have regularly applied to the analysis of Shakespearian, and other, works of art. My book is less a narrative sequence of events than a viewing and reviewing of certain facts from different angles, not unlike the technique employed by Browning in *The Ring and the Book*; you could say that it is less a study of facts than a study of evidence.

[1] See my letter in *The Review of English Studies*, July, 1954.

In my Shakespearian work I found myself continually proving the soundness of Sherlock Holmes' principle that, when attempting to solve a problem, it is above all necessary to face, and indeed concentrate on, what seems queer, what one tends to, and wishes to, neglect, or forget. It happened again and again: with the vagueness of motivation shown in *Hamlet* and *Macbeth*, the cruel humour of *King Lear*, the strangely non-tragic conclusion of *Antony and Cleopatra*, the extraordinary resurrection of Hermione in *The Winter's Tale*, the vision of Jupiter in *Cymbeline*, and the supposedly non-Shakespearian speeches, especially the prophecy of Cranmer, in *Henry VIII*; each in turn proving to be no excrescence or ineptitude, but rather the needed key to a solution. What, then, is there in Byron's story which most steadily refuses to make sense? We think at once of Lady Byron's sudden change of attitude towards her husband, which has seldom received the attention which it demands and is today in danger of being forgotten. And what is there, in the evidence before us, which has been most unwarrantably neglected? Clearly, the *Don Leon* poems. I have accordingly tried to see if these two pieces of evidence could be made to encircle each other, and if the rest can then be made to revolve around them.

It has, once again, seemed advisable to support my statements by a number of exact references. Such a method strongly counters the principles of literary biography in our time, and for this reason the well-loaded text of my previous volume received rough treatment at the hands of the reviewers. In defence I can only say that my own biographical inexperience leaves me peculiarly reluctant to make any assumption for which I can find no tangible evidence. And surely, there is, in certain lines of enquiry, much to be said for such a labouring technique. Let me give an example. Our understanding of Byron's amatory life, and in particular of the famous 'incriminating' letter of 17 May, 1819, often assumed to be addressed to his half-sister, Augusta Leigh, would be seriously modified, perhaps even reversed, could we believe Richard Edgcumbe's uncompromising but unsupported statement, made despite all evidence to the contrary, that Byron visited Mary Anne Chaworth Musters just before finally leaving England. Are we to believe this? He may have had good reason for what he said, but since he has given no reference we shall never know.

There is yet another way in which references may be of value. If my book demonstrates anything for certain, it is this: that, whatever excuses may be offered for Lady Byron's behaviour, her record leaves it clear that none of her statements regarding Byron made after she had left him can be, in themselves and alone, regarded as evidence. And yet Byronic biography has relied almost wholly on Lady Byron for an understanding of the marriage. Since no exact references are given, the reader does not know what is happening. But had each biographer in turn been forced to place beside his detailed account of Byron's domestic wickedness in 1815 such bracketed references as 'Lady Byron's 1816 statement', 'Lady Byron's 1830 statement', 'Lady Byron's 1854 unpublished reminiscences', 'Lady Byron's reported conversation with Lady Anne Barnard (date unknown)', 'Lady Byron's reported conversation with Harriet Beecher Stowe', etc., etc.—well, the story would, to say the least, have appeared, to the reader of discrimination, a little less authentic. But fashion has been against such a technique, and the result has been sad for Byron. We must not forget that his wife did her best during his life to suppress Byron's own defence in the famous but ill-starred *Memoirs*; nor that they were burned by her accredited representative after his death.

The nature of my thesis made me diffident of asking for access to any unpublished family papers, and I have accordingly relied wholly on published work. Should there be any evidence in existence which counters my conclusions, I hope that this book may prove the cause of awaking a more exact revelation.

I would record my gratitude to Mr. R. Caton for important information; to Mr. Alec Craig for advice; to Professor Ricardo Quintana, Miss Patricia Ball, and Mr. B. Taborski, for answering certain questions; to Mr. John Heath-Stubbs for a suggestion; to the Editor of *The Times Literary Supplement* for printing in 1954 a letter of enquiry regarding the *Don Leon* poems; to Professor Samuel C. Chew for pointing, in answer, to his valuable storehouse of bibliographical information, *Byron in England*; and to the Editor of *The Twentieth Century* for printing, in July 1954, my article *Who Wrote Don Leon*, a brief outline of my present argument. I am indebted to all the works listed among my authorities. Among recent general studies, I have been most helped by John Drinkwater's *The Pilgrim of Eternity* and Peter Quennell's *The Years of Fame*, both of which, though in very different ways, have served to clear the ground for my investigations. The collection of my material has been facilitated by generous assistance from the Keeper of Printed Books, and other officials, of the British Museum; the Librarian, Deputy Librarian, and staff of the Brotherton Library, and also the Librarian and staff of the City Library, in Leeds; and the Librarian and staff of both the Roborough Library and the City Library in Exeter.

My thanks are due to Mrs. A. L. Sharber for an interesting study photographed by her son, Dr. Trimble Sharber, from an old cameo discovered by her nephew, Major Archibald Trimble, identified as a portrait of Byron; to Mr. Jeremy F. Bagster-Collins for the picture of George Colman; and to Sir John Murray, both for the portraits of Lady Byron and Augusta Leigh and also for granting me permission to use material under his copyright.

G. W. K.

Leeds, 1956.

LIST OF AUTHORITIES

The editions actually used are named first, and, except when Byron's poems are concerned, the first publication date, if different, follows. Works are listed in the order of their first appearance. The brackets at the right give the designation used in my text.

Journal of the Conversations of Lord Byron; Thomas Medwin; quarto, 1824 [1]   (Medwin)

A Narrative of Lord Byron's Last Journey to Greece; Pietro Gamba; 1825   (Gamba)

The Last Days of Lord Byron; William Parry; 1825   (Parry)

The Life, Writings, Opinions and Times of the Rt. Hon. George Gordon Noel Byron, Lord Byron; 'An English Gentleman in the Greek Military Service, etc.'; 3 vols.; 1825   (see p. 252)

The Life of Lord Byron; John Galt; octavo; 1830   (Galt)

Conversations on Religion with Lord Byron and others; James Kennedy; 1830   (Kennedy)

The Life, Letters, and Journals of Lord Byron; Thomas Moore, 1 vol., 1866 edn. (orig. 2 vols., with variants in title, 1830)   (Moore)

Remarks Occasioned by Mr. Moore's notices of Lord Byron's Life; Lady Byron; privately printed, 1830   (see pp. 76, 109)

Random Records; George Colman; 2 vols., 1830   (see p. 163)

Conversations of Lord Byron with the Countess of Blessington; Lady Blessington; 1834   (Blessington)

The Poetical Works of Lord Byron; variously edited; pub. John Murray, 1 vol., 1837   (*Poetical Works*, 1837)

Memoirs of the Colman Family; R. B. Peake; 1841   (no refs.)

The Life and Letters of Thomas Campbell; ed. William Beattie; 3 vols.; 1850   (Beattie)

Memoirs, Journal and Correspondence of Thomas Moore, ed. Lord John Russell; 8 vols.; 1853   (Moore's *Memoirs, etc.*)

Don Leon and *Leon to Annabella,* as by 'Lord Byron', 1865–1866   (see p. 160)

---

[1] My references to Medwin in *Lord Byron: Christian Virtues* applied to the 1824 octavo edition. In this book I have decided to use the quarto.

LIST OF AUTHORITIES

My Recollections of Lord Byron and those of Eye-Witnesses of his Life; Countess Guiccioli; 2 vols.; 1869 (orig., in French, *Lord Byron jugé par les Témoins de sa Vie,* 1868)   (Teresa)

A Vindication of Lord Byron; Alfred Austin, 1869   (see p. 233)

Lady Byron Vindicated; Harriet Beecher Stowe; 1870   (Stowe)

Contemporary Account of the Separation of Lord and Lady Byron; also of the Destruction of Lord Byron's Memoirs; John Cam Hobhouse, Lord Broughton; privately printed; 1870   (see pp. 51, 233)

Vindication of Lady Byron; anon. (John Fox); 1871   (*Vindication*)

Index Librorum Prohibitorum; Pisanus Fraxi (H. S. Ashbee); 1877   (see pp. 160-1, 232-3)

Records of Shelley, Byron and the Author; E. J. Trelawny; 1905 (orig. 2 vols., 1878)   (Trelawny)

The Real Lord Byron; John Cordy Jeaffreson, 'standard edition', 1 vol., with Appendices, undated, *c.* 1884 (orig. 2 vols.; 1883)   (Jeaffreson)

The Works of Lord Byron; Letters and Journals; ed. R. E. Prothero, Lord Ernle; 6 vols.; 1898–1901   (LJ)

The Works of Lord Byron; Poetry; ed. E. Hartley Coleridge, 7 vols.; 1898–1904   (P)

Astarte; Ralph Milbanke, Earl of Lovelace; 2nd edition, ed. Lady Lovelace, 1921 (orig. 1905)   (Lovelace)

Byron: The Last Phase; Richard Edgcumbe, 1909   (Edgcumbe)

Recollections of a Long Life; John Cam Hobhouse, Lord Broughton; ed. Lady Dorchester, 6 vols., 1909–1911   (Hobhouse)

Byron; Ethel Colburn Mayne; 2 vols., 1912   (Mayne)

The Dramas of Lord Byron; Samuel C. Chew; Gottingen, also Baltimore, U.S.A.; 1915   (see p. 139)

Lord Byron's Correspondence; ed. Sir John Murray; 2 vols.; 1922   (C)

Byron in England; Samuel C. Chew; 1924   (Chew)

Byron: the Last Journey; Harold Nicolson; 1924; and see below   (Nicolson)

The Byron Mystery; Sir John C. Fox; 1924   (Fox)

The Pilgrim of Eternity; John Drinkwater; 1925   (Drinkwater)

The Life and Letters of Anne Isabella, Lady Noel Byron; Ethel Colburn Mayne; 1929   (Mayne, *Lady Byron*)

Byron; André Maurois; 1950 (orig. 1930)   (Maurois)

A Bibliography of the Writings in Verse and Prose of George Gordon Noel, Baron Byron; T. J. Wise; 2 vols.; 1932–1933   (see p. 161)

Byron and the Need of Fatality; Charles du Bos; 1932   (du Bos)

Byron: the Years of Fame; Peter Quennell; 1935   (Quennell)

To Lord Byron; George Paston and Peter Quennell; 1939   (Paston and Quennell)

Byron: the Last Journey; Harold Nicolson, with 'Supplementary Chapter'; 1940   (Nicolson, 1940)

George Colman the Younger; Jeremy F. Bagster-Collins; New York; 1946   (Bagster-Collins)

Byron; C. E. Vulliamy; 1948   (Vulliamy)

My Friend H.; Michael Joyce; 1948   (Joyce)

The Last Attachment; Iris Origo; 1949   (Origo)
Byron: A Self-Portrait; letters, ed. Peter Quennell; 2 vols.;
   1950   (SP)
Lord Byron: Christian Virtues; G. Wilson Knight; 1952   (CV)
Byron's Dramatic Prose; G. Wilson Knight; Nottingham; 1954   (DP)
Laureate of Peace, containing a section on Byron; G. Wilson
   Knight; 1954   (see p. 254)

Also the following journals: *The Academy, The Athenaeum, Blackwood's Edinburgh Magazine, John Bull's Magazine and Literary Reviewer, Macmillan's Magazine. Murray's Magazine, The New Monthly Magazine and Literary Journal, Notes and Queries, The Twentieth Century, The Quarterly Review.*

N.B.—Page-numbers are always given without the letter 'p.', except for references to my own text. Where a confusion might arise, page-numbers are italicized.

I

FRIENDS AND LOVERS

I. FRIENDS AND LOVERS

I

FEW great men puzzle us like Byron. Many biographical problems are still unsolved, our moral valuations are uncertain, and, though his importance both as man and as writer is unquestioned, he remains mysterious. Despite his remarkable record of private goodness and public service, there is firmly printed, at least on the English imagination, the impression of a bad man; and yet no one appears to know why. The heart of the biographical problem is, very clearly, the marriage separation; but why exactly Lady Byron left him remains obscure, and we know no good reason for the social ostracism to which he was subjected. He was, of course, regarded as a political, perhaps a religious, threat; but there seems to have been more than that; and the fog is only thickened when we begin to realize that much that appeared most satanic to his contemporaries is precisely what we most admire, and whose symbol, or final expression, is *Don Juan*. Tastes have changed, and yet the old impression persists.

It cannot have been a question of sexual irregularity of any normal sort, since this has been readily forgiven in such men as Dante, Goethe, Tolstoy, and Burns, and a number of other great men; and Byron himself was no seducer. But it may be a question of abnormal sexuality. As soon as this is mentioned, we think inevitably of incest; and indeed the possibility of an illicit relationship with his half-sister Augusta Leigh has, since the cloud-burst of Mrs. Beecher Stowe's supposed revelation in 1869, drenched Byronic studies to the point of saturation, to leave us in a marshland of biographical imprecision. And yet there is good reason to suppose that this incest-motif has been all the time, whether or not there be truth behind it, playing the part of a peculiarly effective red herring.

It is my aim to counter this insistence with another; to suggest

3

that a more important and more consistently motivating secret of Byron's life lay somewhere within the area of homosexuality; and that this, together with the possibility of an improper relation with his own wife, was one main cause of the marriage separation and is responsible even now for the vague feeling of distaste and horror which, in England at least, sullies the splendour of his name and precludes our recognition of his stature as man and poet.

It may be feared that my present study will merely serve to make bad worse. But before we have done I shall, I hope, have shown that this is not so. With Byron we cannot, if only because of the number of accusations and defences which have already accumulated, avoid the issue. Until we attain so far as may be clarity as to Byron's vices, we shall remain, illogically perhaps but none the less inevitably, unable to focus his virtues.

So much by way of introduction. Let us now glance briefly at Byron's love-life before his marriage.

Byron was born on 22 January, 1788. His early childhood was passed in Aberdeen in close association with his widowed mother, a woman of Gordon descent, occult interests and turbulent disposition; and also with a nurse of strict Calvinistic principles. On his wild father's, 'mad Jack's,' side, his background was ominous: his grandfather, Admiral John Byron, called 'foul-weather Jack'—'He had no rest at sea, nor I on shore', wrote Byron (*Epistle to Augusta*, II, P, IV, 57)—was a grim figure; and so was his grand-uncle, tenant of Newstead and known as 'the wicked lord', a man of erratic habits who had killed a certain Mr. Chaworth, who lived near by, in a duel. Byron's forbears and upbringing alone were enough to predispose him to fears and frenzies. And when in 1798 the title came to the boy, together with Newstead Abbey with all its ghostly associations and appalling state of disrepair, the external honour was really as much a cause for disquietude and anxiety as for satisfaction.

The key to the child's life was nevertheless, as Thomas Moore tells us, affection. This, together with a yearning for its return by another, 'formed the dream and torment of his existence'; it is said that he attributed his later troubles to his mother's rejection of his early caresses (Moore, VIII, 84). His amatory passions were developed soon; so soon, he tells us, that few would believe it were he to 'state the period and the facts which accompanied it'; and he suggests that this premature development lay at the root of his melancholy

(*Detached Thoughts*, 80; LJ, v, 450). At Aberdeen he was already engaged during the year 1797 in a childhood romance with a distant cousin, Mary Duff (*Journal*, 26 Nov., 1813; LJ, II, 347–8); and later, in 1800, when he and his mother had moved to London and he was at Dr. Glennie's academy at Dulwich, he fell in love with another cousin, Margaret Parker (*Detached Thoughts*, 79; LJ, v, 449). After that Byron went to Harrow and in 1803, when he and his mother were living at Southwell near Newstead, he fell in love during his holidays with a third cousin, a little older than himself, Mary Anne Chaworth, grand-niece of the Mr. Chaworth killed by his grand-uncle. This was a romance in Byron's mind of deep significance and fatality. It ended tragically, both for him, and, as it turned out, for her, with the girl's marriage in 1805 to John Musters.

But his affections were not given only to the opposite sex; he could be equally devoted to members of his own. There are two early poems, *To E——* (1802; P, I, 4) and *Epitaph on a Beloved Friend* (1803; P, I, 18), both, it seems, expressing ardent devotion to the same boy of humble birth, son of a Newstead tenant (Moore, III, 22, note; IV, 43), at whose deathbed he appears to have attended. It is worth observing that the original of the *Epitaph* as printed privately in *Fugitive Pieces* and *Poetry on Various Occasions* (for the successive editions of Byron's *Juvenilia*, see P, I, xi–xiii) differs considerably from the version printed in Byron's published collection called *Hours of Idleness* (1807). The later version shows a definite toning down; the title *Epitaph on a Beloved Friend* is changed to *Epitaph on a Friend*; the opening 'Oh, Boy! for ever loved, for ever dear!' is changed to 'Oh, Friend . . .'; and there are other changes, among them the addition of the thought, 'What though thy sire lament his failing line', as though to veil the boy's social status (see Moore, IV, 43; *Poetical Works*, 1837; 377, note; P, I, 18, note). We may assume that Byron was diffident concerning the unorthodoxy of such a passion.

This is not the only instance. We find that his 1807 poem on his Harrow friendships called *Childish Recollections*, which was printed in his first public collection *Hours of Idleness*, had originally, in *Poetry on Various Occasions*, a number of lines considered too bold for publication, with an opening marking an attempt to break free from love of all sorts, 'friends' and 'females' alike, with the statement that 'censure no more shall brand my humble name' (P, I, 84, note). The word 'censure' is interesting, the thought occurring elsewhere (p. 30); and we may suppose that Byron had incurred criticism for his propensities. True, ladies are mentioned first, perhaps as a mask, but the poem once states emphatically (199–208; P, 1, 94) that their charms were weak rivals. Some of the omitted lines are enigmatically vivid:

> Yet, though the future dark and cheerless gleams,
> The curse of memory, hovering in my dreams,
> Depicts with glowing pencil all those years,
> Ere yet my cup, empoison'd, flow'd with tears;
> Still rules my senses with tyrannic sway,
> The past confounding with the present day.
> Alas! in vain I check the maddening thought;
> It still recurs, unlook'd for and unsought . . .
>
> (P, 1, 84, note)

With 'maddening' we might compare the word's use in a similar context in one of Byron's latest poems (p. 218). Even after the publication of the revised version, we find him writing to his mentor, the Rev. John Becher, 'I am sorry—but *Childish Recollections* must be suppressed during this edition' (26 Feb., 1808; LJ, 1, 185). This was, presumably, the next edition entitled *Poems Original and Translated* (P, 1, xii).

That some of Byron's most important male loves should have been social inferiors is not really surprising, since with them the deeply Byronic impulses of care and protection were the more readily engaged. Moore observes, perhaps not quite accurately, that for this reason Byron's best Harrow friendships did not involve those of equal rank (Moore, III, 23); but 'protection' could be involved, apart altogether from rank, especially with those younger than himself. These school friendships were, as Byron himself tells us, 'passions' (*Detached Thoughts*, 91; LJ, V, 455). There were many, including John Wingfield, commemorated by two stanzas of *Childe Harold* (I, 91, 92), in which Byron altered—though there may have been a special reason for this (p. 38)—'beloved' to 'esteemed' (P, II, 83, note); the Earls of Delawarr and Dorset; the Earl of Clare, whose power over Byron's emotions when they met years later he has himself recorded (*Detached Thoughts*, 91, 113; LJ, V, 455, 463); J. C. Tattersall; William Harness, whom he protected at Harrow from bullying; and Edward Noel Long. Some of these appear under pseudonyms in *Childish Recollections*, and there are other such poems. It is possible that both the famous *When we Two Parted* (given as 1808, *Poetical Works*, 1837; as first published 1816, P, III, 411) and *To a Youthful Friend* (1808, P, I, 271–5), poems blaming the loved one, in the manner of Shakespeare's sonnets, for light behaviour, are addressed to a Harrow associate. Again and again these early poems strike a note of moral or heroic fervour and noble idealism entwined with the theme of friendship. *Hours of Idleness* significantly contained a full-length version of the Nisus and Euryalus episode in the ninth *Aeneid* (P, I, 151), together with a prose narrative called *The Death of Calmar and Orla* which, as Hartley Coleridge notes, is derived from the Virgilian story (P, I, 177, note); and Byron's anger at the reception of his first poems may be considered as directly proportional to the intensity of those youthful and ideal passions which formed so large a part of their subject matter.

In 1805 Byron went to Cambridge, and there began his life-long, but quite unromantic—at least on Byron's side—association with John Cam Hobhouse, afterwards Lord Broughton. And here, too, he experienced an ideal romance in the tradition of earlier passions, with the chorister of humble birth, John Edleston. To this, in Byron's words, 'violent, though *pure*, love and passion' (Journal, 12 Jan., 1821; LJ, V, 169) we shall presently give an extended treatment. It was the most important of all Byron's male romances; and it, like his love for Mary Chaworth which it directly succeeded, was probably one of the three most perfect experiences of uncontaminated devotion which he was ever to know, the third being his love for his half-sister, Augusta.

After leaving Cambridge Byron lived for a while in London with a girl, also of humble birth, who dressed as a boy. He took her to Brighton and back to Newstead, sometimes passing her off as his brother (Moore, VII, 70; Jeaffreson, XI, 120).

We are clearly involved in an enquiry of disturbing complexity. But this, at least, is tolerably certain. The young Byron found no satisfaction in ordinary vice. Of his life at Cambridge he wrote, in 1821, the opening sentence witnessing to the utter normality, indeed the propriety, of the process according to contemporary valuations:

'I took my graduations in the vices with great promptitude, but they were not to my taste; for my early passions, though violent in the

7

extreme, were concentrated, and hated division or spreading abroad. I could have left or lost the world with or for that which I loved; but, though my temperament was naturally burning, I could not share in the common place libertinism of the place and time without disgust. And yet this very disgust, and my heart thrown back upon itself, threw me into excesses perhaps more fatal than those from which I shrunk, as fixing upon one [1] (at a time) the passions, which, spread amongst many, would have hurt only myself.'

(*Detached Thoughts*, 72; LJ, v, 445)

Moore observes that, though Byron's indulgences were probably 'less gross' than those of 'any of his associates', his own self-libelling gave him an undeserved reputation, since 'one single indiscretion, in his hands, was made to *go farther* . . . than a thousand in those of others' (Moore, vii, 70). This remark not unnaturally stung Hobhouse, who was one of the 'associates', to make a sharp rejoinder in the margin of his copy of Moore's book (Nicolson, 1940; Supplementary Chapter, 295)! That Hobhouse, who will feature in our narrative as a pillar of all the proprieties, was himself not averse from the *conventional* vices of his day, may be gathered from a remark of Byron's: 'I maintain that he is more *carnivorously* and *carnally sensual* than I am' (Murray, 9 Nov., 1820; LJ, v, 115).

Byron was, indeed, shocked by his contemporaries. In 1811 we find him writing of the affairs with 'a couple of drabs' of the Rev. Robert Bland and Francis Hodgson, who was to take Holy Orders shortly afterwards, and telling William Harness that he was himself 'a monument of prudence' in comparison. 'Yet', he adds, 'I like the men, and, God knows, ought not to condemn their aberrations. But I own I feel provoked when they dignify all this by the name of *love*—romantic attachments for things marketable for a dollar!' (Harness, 15 Dec., 1811; LJ, ii, 91; for the affair in question see LJ, i, 197, note). This is sincere enough. Of set purpose he starved himself partly in order to master physical passion:

'I should not so much mind a little accession of flesh—my bones can well bear it. But the worst is, the devil always came with it— till I starved him out—and I will *not* be the slave of *any* appetite. If I do err, it shall be my heart, at least, that heralds the way.'

(Journal, 17 Nov., 1813; LJ, ii, 328)

[1] *Letters and Journals* misprints 'me'. See Moore, vii, 70.

'I would not,' he once said, 'give the tithe of a Birmingham farthing for any woman who could or would be purchased, nor indeed for any *woman quoad mere woman*; that is to say, unless I loved for something more than her sex' (quoted Quennell, IV, 116; no ref.). Byron had an uncanny capacity for love of all kinds; and he could pass from affair to affair with a rapidity which looks like license, though it is not.

Rumours regarding his relationships with the maid-servants in Newstead Abbey, the 'Paphian girls' of *Childe Harold* (I, 7), are unsupported. Nanny Smith, the housekeeper, told Washington Irving in 1830 that Byron and his friends were not licentious (Teresa, I; x, 406-7), and this is confirmed by Hobhouse (Nicolson, 1940; Supplementary Chapter, 301); William Harness knew of nothing in the way of excess during his visit in 1811 (Paston and Quennell, III, 24); Moore says that no anchorite who knew Byron directly after his return from his early travels could have desired for himself a greater indifference to 'the attractions of the senses' (Moore, IX, 95); Teresa Guiccioli quotes Galt's statement that his excesses were never libertine (Teresa, I; x, 409); Hobhouse tells us that at the time of his marriage he had, except for being 'a man of the world', no vices calling for reformation (Hobhouse, II; xv, 196); and today Maurois supports Byron's own assertion that he 'never seduced any woman' (Medwin, 66; Maurois, II; XIX, 181). We have, moreover, direct evidence that Byron felt strongly about the morals of those under his care. On the way back from the Levant, he wrote to his mother a determined letter concerning the responsibilities of a seducer on his estate (Mrs. Byron, 25 June, 1811; LJ, I, 312). On one occasion, it is true, he appears to have been more personally involved. A servant girl named Susan Vaughan was devoted to her master, and we have records of her devotion (*To Lord Byron;* Paston and Quennell, III, 23-39); but she got into difficulties elsewhere, and was dismissed. Byron was deeply disturbed, telling Hodgson that her behaviour troubled his 'heart', though he wondered at his folly in excepting one of his own 'strumpets' from 'the general corruption' (Hodgson, 16 Feb., 1812; LJ, II, 100; and see 92-3, note; also Rushton, 21 and 25 Jan., 1812; LJ, II, 92, 94). It would be rash to assume from this that she was Byron's mistress, though she may have been; the account in Paston and Quennell's *To Lord Byron* contains evidence of nothing beyond kisses (III, 29, 34), and he was capable of writing in such apparently uncompromising terms even if there had been

9

no more than a sentimental attachment; and, anyway, it is clear both that his interest went deep and that he was *morally* shocked at her light behaviour. He seems to have regarded his servants as part of a family: the familiar tone and reported facts of Susan's letters are in themselves evidence of Byron's informal and friendly relationship with the lower members of his household. Moore deals with the incident, which he regards as wholly creditable to Byron's sense of responsibility, at some length, quoting the letter to Hodgson as evidence of the depth of Byron's feeling (Moore, XIV, 152–3; and see Vulliamy, V, 77).

Byron had a genius for attaching people's affections to himself. It was not merely a question of pretty girls; as we have seen, he could feel equally, or more, strongly about boys, and among these was Robert Rushton (LJ II, 93, note), the page of *Childe Harold*, whose welfare, as I have elsewhere demonstrated, was his consistent concern. Nor was it a question of age, for he was likewise devoted to the old retainer, Murray. Nor of looks: there was the scarecrow of a charwoman, Mrs. Mule, whom, to everyone's amazement, he insisted, because of her devotion, on taking into his household after his marriage; and it is likely that, had she been young and handsome, people would have supposed that he kept her for sexual gratification; and it is equally likely, indeed certain, that he would then have pretended that he did. But I have written of all this already in my account of Byron's various 'protégés', where other instances are given (CV, II).

The truth is, Byron's affections knew no normal limit, and when they were driven to an improper act, that act must at least be seen in its context. He was one, like his own Lara,

> *With more capacity for love than earth*
> *Bestows on most of mortal mould and birth.*
>
> (*Lara*, I, 18)

Unless we realize this in all its stark simplicity, we shall not understand him. With such a man it is always dangerous to assume that a close association of *any* kind must have led to sexual action; and it is equally dangerous to assume that an association of *any* kind was independent of sexual impulse. We can be sure of very little. And behind it all, as I have elsewhere (CV, Index A, IV) shown at length, there was a sense of guardianship, responsibility, and education.

In the year 1809 Byron left England with John Cam Hobhouse

on a visit to the near East. At Gibraltar he was promptly invited to share her apartment by a Spanish lady of attraction, but was induced by his 'virtue', a word Byron underlines, to decline (Mrs. Byron, 11 Aug., 1809; LJ, I, 238). At Malta he had a purely platonic affair with Mrs. Spencer Smith, the 'fair Florence' of *Childe Harold* (II, 30-4; and see Paston and Quennell, II, 10-15). He resisted her charms, and records how she was annoyed to see him 'withstand, unmoved, the lustre of her gaze' with a 'seeming marble heart' (II, 32, 33). Indeed, he sees himself as one who is unconventional enough to despise sexual intercourse:

> *'Tis an old lesson—Time approves it true,*
> *And those who know it best deplore it most;*
> *When all is won that all desire to woo,*
> *The paltry prize is hardly worth the cost:*
> *Youth wasted—minds degraded—honour lost—*
> *These are thy fruits, successful Passion! these!*
> *If, kindly cruel, early hope is crost,*
> *Still to the last it rankles, a disease,*
> *Not to be cured when Love itself forgets to please.*
>
> (II, 35)

The theme is that of Shakespeare's Sonnet (129) on lust, 'The abuse of spirit in a waste of shame'. Ethel Colburn Mayne, speaking for her sex, not very kindly turns the stanza *against* Byron, suggesting that he knew that he was not able to engage in sexual intercourse without his 'baseness' asserting itself (Mayne, I; IX, 160). That may be; but, whatever the views of the ladies, no decent man of, at least, our century should blame him for resisting. Observe that he regards his resistance as, in the society of his day, abnormal. And so it was. Such invitations a gentleman was expected to accept, and these stanzas of *Childe Harold* may best be read as a public apology for his coldness to a lady of fashion. Though he tried to live up to it, Byron was never really attuned to the prevailing code.

So they went on, through Albania to Greece. In Athens he knew a family of whose girls he wrote in flippant admiration: 'I almost forgot to tell you that I am dying for love of three Greek girls at Athens' (Henry Drury, 3 May, 1810; LJ, I, 269). One was celebrated in the poem *Maid of Athens, ere We Part* (1810; P, III, 15-17). There appears to have been little of importance in the relationship beyond the source of some pretty lines.

After they had visited Turkey, Hobhouse returned to England, but Byron remained in Greece, staying at a convent near Athens, and forming a happy companionship with certain boys who were at school there. He arranged games for them, and enjoyed himself immensely. He described it all to Hobhouse on 23 August, 1810, calling the boys 'sylphs' and saying how there was rivalry among them for his attentions. His chief interest was Nicolo Giraud, a boy of French descent, whom he and Hobhouse had met on their first visit to Athens:

'But my friend, as you may easily imagine, is Nicolo, who, by-the-bye, is my Italian master, and we are already very philosophical. I am his "Padrone" and his "amico", and the Lord knows what besides. It is about two hours since, that, after informing me he was most desirous to follow *him* (that is me) over the world, he concluded by telling me it was proper for us not only to live, but "morire insieme".

'The latter I hope to avoid—as much of the former as he pleases.'
(C, I, 15)

Byron used to bathe with Nicolo. He tells Hobhouse:

'I have, as usual, swum across the Piraeus; the Signor Nicolo also laved, but he makes as bad a hand in the water as L'Abbé Hyacinth at Falmouth; it is a curious thing that the Turks when they bathe wear their lower garments, as your humble servant always doth, but the Greeks not; however, questo Giovane e vergognóso.'
(C, I, 17)

The association was close, perhaps passionate, and thoroughly enjoyable. When the mother of Teresa, 'the maid of Athens', Theodora Macri, was 'mad enough to imagine' Byron was 'going to marry the girl', he comments: 'but I have better amusement' (C, I, 16).

Nicolo accompanied Byron on some more travels. Byron had a fever at Patras; so did Nicolo (Hobhouse, 4 Oct., 1810; LJ, I, 301); and Byron, whose strong maternal instincts always enjoyed nursing his favourites, as he nursed his dog, Boatswain, must have been in his element. On his way home Nicolo accompanied him as far as Malta, where Byron made him a handsome gift of money (Jeaffreson, XI, 128). On his return to England Byron drew up a will dated 12 August, 1811, leaving Nicolo £7000 on his coming of age (LJ, I, 328). The amount is impressive.

There was another Greek boy, Eustathius, whose advances Byron up to a point accepted; but the boy was temperamental, and Byron glad to be free of him. In *Lord Byron's Correspondence* (1922) the relevant passages were omitted from the two letters to Hobhouse where they occur, but they have recently been reinstated in Peter Quennell's *Byron: A Self-Portrait* (Hobhouse, 29–30 July, 16 Aug., 1810; SP, I, 74–9; C, I, 10–13). Throughout our enquiry we must be prepared for such omissions: it is only of late that public opinion allows freedom in these matters, and we can assume that most of our original sources come down to us only too thoroughly 'edited'.

Byron once told Trelawny that 'the only place' he was ever 'contented in' was Greece (Trelawny, 15 June, 1823; LJ, VI, 224). Greece appears to have provided a moral atmosphere more congenial to his natural propensities than that of England, and after his return he was always thinking of the Levant and dreaming of again entering those bright areas, and perhaps settling there; and when he eventually returned to Greece in 1823, he had a new favourite in the boy Loukas.

One other Greek incident must be recorded. A couple of years after he returned to England we find Byron getting Lord Sligo to write down what he had heard at second-hand in Athens of a strange occurrence when, finding a girl being taken for drowning in a sack after having been convicted of associating with a member of the opposite sex during the feast of Ramadan, Byron saved her at the pistol's point, and succeeded in getting her away; though it seems that she died of fever soon afterwards. Without giving any details himself, Byron records that he has had Lord Sligo's account shown to Lord Holland, Galt, 'Monk' Lewis, Moore, Rogers, Murray, and Lady Melbourne (Journal, 5 Dec.; Moore, 1 Sept., 1813; LJ, II, 361; 257–8 and note). What was his reason? Was he himself responsible for the girl's plight? According to both Moore and Medwin he as good as said—though without necessarily committing himself to a serious sin, since the law was strict—that he was (Moore's *Memoirs, etc.*, 17 July, 1824; IV, 221; Medwin, 84–6). Galt thought so too (Galt, XXIV, 158). The incident caused him considerable unrest (Journal, 5 Dec., 1813; LJ, II, 361); he said that it was the origin of *The Giaour* and Lord Sligo's note written to counter another rumour (Moore, 1 Sept., 1813; LJ, II, 258; and see the Advertisement to *The Giaour*; also Lady Melbourne, 19 April; 31 Aug.; 28 Sept., 1813; C, I, 149, 177, 183). However, it seems that according to Hobhouse it was one of Byron's Turkish servants who was to blame, and that Lord Sligo said that Byron had never seen the girl before (P, III, 76; John Fox's *Vindication of Lady Byron*, III, 173, note). The girl died soon after of a fever (Medwin, 86). Had Byron's conscience been tormented by any serious offence he would scarcely have been at pains to advertise the exact story; nor would he have written of Lord Sligo's account, 'I think it will make you laugh when you consider all the poetry and prose which has grown out of it' (Lady Melbourne, 31 Aug., 1813; C, I, 177). It seems that we may be here confronted with a peculiarly neat example of his life-long habit of self-accusation: perhaps he was merely trying to add another ray to his satanic halo. But why should he do this? Although all his contemporaries were aware of the trait, no one has ever explained it.

Here is a possible solution. Of his homosexual instincts he was, at least in public, reserved, and could even take pains to suppress the evidence (pp. 36, 217). In Greece he had enjoyed at least one vivid homosexual experience, and how far it went we cannot know for certain; but if it did go to the limit, then that might account for much of his sense of guilt in the years following, and his satisfying of his conscience by accusing himself of crimes of which he was not guilty. Once, when he was being slandered, he refused to answer, saying, 'Am I not in reality much worse than they make me?' (Lady Melbourne, March, 1814; C, I, 247). And there was another advantage. He was simultaneously winning the reputation of a normally sexed man; and I suggest that he was on occasion quite desperately anxious to convince both himself and others of his sexual normality.

II

On his return to England in July of 1811 Byron was confronted with a series of disasters. First, he heard of the death of his great friend Wingfield; soon after, and before he had again seen her, his mother died; then Charles Skinner Matthews, one of the Cambridge friends whose intellect he most strongly admired, was drowned; and, last, he heard that his once-loved Edleston had died whilst he was abroad. Only William Harness remained to fire his imagination; and there was Scrope Davies, to whom he wrote for comfort; Francis Hodgson; and Hobhouse. And he soon had another friend in Thomas Moore, the poet and song-writer, whose support, throughout the rest of Byron's life, was as important as that of Hobhouse.

The next few years make a story of spiritual unrest with hints of mysterious guilt; of political speeches and poetic fame; and a succession of love-affairs. Our concern here is with the love-affairs. These are strange, and we must beware of reading our own conventional suppositions into our understanding of them. We shall not argue that Byron lived a moral life, but it is quite certain that he did not live an immoral life in the spirit of his contemporaries. It was an age of gross immorality. Lord Lovelace puts it well: 'It should be remembered', he writes, 'that all through the eighteenth century, and for the first third of the nineteenth, seductions and all the similar pursuits formed a great, almost the principal, part of the life of rich Englishmen, without any offence being given to the moral feelings of the community' (Lovelace, I, 18). As Ethel Colburn Mayne tells us, 'The morals of the age regarded adultery as the normal occupation of all men and of most women' (Mayne, II; App. III, 333). This was all very well; but it did not really suit Byron.

He had severe moral principles. In *English Bards and Scotch Reviewers* (1809) he denounced (283–94) the licentious qualities of Moore's poetry, and in *The Waltz* (1812; P, I, 475) inveighed violently against the promiscuous public embraces of new styles in dancing. But he was impelled, by birth and fortune, to take his place in the society of his day. He was, moreover, a person of extraordinary magnetism. Throughout his life, young and old, of both sexes, and of all social strata and various nationalities, succumbed to his fascination; and this was caused very often by no actions on his part at all. 'No man ever lived', said Hobhouse, 'who had such devoted friends. His power of attaching those about him to his person was such as no one I ever knew possessed' (Hobhouse, III; II, 41; and see CV, IV, 211). And when women threw themselves at him, he was shocked: 'In all good faith', writes Charles Du Bos, 'he was always surprised, even scandalized, by both his literary and his amorous conquests' (Du Bos, V, 133). And yet it was not always easy to refuse, as he had refused Mrs. Spencer Smith, because he had an unbounded capacity for loving, a fiery temperament, an instinctive trust in sexual delight, and even, in part, an ingrained respect for the society which he simultaneously regarded as immoral, since he believed in the traditional codes of chivalry and gallantry, and these were involved. He wanted love: 'I cannot exist', he wrote, 'without some object of love' (Lady Melbourne, 9 Nov., 1812; C, I, 104). So he tried to get love in the usual way.

Even so, we are left uncertain as to how much actual physical intercourse was indulged. Throughout his life he was ready, indeed anxious, to accuse himself. We cannot be sure of the exact nature of his engagements, since his own innuendoes are utterly untrustworthy and the assumptions of both his contemporaries and later biographers that a close association with a member of the opposite sex must have involved sexual intercourse are, with so extraordinary a bisexual temperament as his, unwarranted. And it often happens that, when amid the mass of suppositions which cloud his story we find an indisputable fact, that fact directly counters the general tendency of the suppositions.

We shall next glance very briefly at Byron's more important affairs. In the year 1812 Lady Caroline Lamb, after reading *Childe Harold*, became passionately anxious to meet the author, and gained an introduction. It was the lady who, in Vulliamy's words, 'launched the attack' (Vulliamy, VII, 94). She was young, volatile, vivacious, erratic, temperamental, and at times pretty nearly mad, and Byron, though at first willing, became soon extremely anxious to withdraw. Here is his own account as reported by Thomas Medwin:

'I was soon congratulated by my friends on the conquest I had made, and did my utmost to show that I was not insensible to the partiality I could not help perceiving. I made every effort to be in love, expressed as much ardour as I could muster, and kept feeding the flame with a constant supply of *billets-doux* and amatory verses. In short, I was in decent time duly and regularly installed into what the Italians call *service*, and soon became, in every sense of the word, a *patito*. It required no Oedipus to see where all this would end. I am easily governed by women, and she gained an ascendancy over me that I could not easily shake off. I submitted to this thraldom long, for I hate *scenes*, and am of an indolent disposition; but I was forced to snap the knot rather rudely at last.'

(Medwin, 212)

The phrase 'made every effort to be in love' is revealing: Byron was *trying* to live up to the usual practice. So he wrote to Lady Melbourne:

'When our drama was "rising" ("I'll be damned if it falls off", I

16

may say with Sir Fretful) in the fifth act, it was no time to hesitate. I had made up my mind to bear the consequences of my own folly. Honour, pity, and a kind of affection all forbade me to shrink, but now, if I can *honourably* be off . . .'

> (Lady Melbourne, 13 Sept., 1812; C, I, 75)

He calls dramatic literature to his support, but it is not quite natural; it is done partly as a *duty* ('forbade me to shrink'); and he adds, 'I soberly say that it would have been want of gallantry, though the acme of virtue, if I had played the Scipio on this occasion' (C, I, 75). Now he is anxious to be 'free'. Possibly it was to keep him up to it that the assiduous lady used to press her attentions on him in the dress of a boy.

Things got worse and worse. At one time Caroline in a fit of desperation ran away, saying she would live with Byron; and Byron's aid was solicited by Lady Bessborough, Caroline's mother, and Lady Melbourne, her mother-in-law, to find her and bring her back, which he did almost, says Maurois, 'forcibly'. It is reported that the Prince Regent was deeply shocked at a collaboration so strongly countering all the traditions of illicit love: 'I never heard of such a thing in my life—taking the mothers for confidantes' (Maurois, II; XVI, 158). The situation was quite extraordinary, Lord Melbourne remarking that Byron must have bewitched the whole family (Quennell, V, 155).

Byron at last cut her off with cold advice not to be a fool. She burned his effigy with a ceremonial of her own devising; forged his name; and when they again met socially, tried to stab herself. As late as the summer of 1814 she was tormenting him. On 26 June he told Lady Melbourne of her persecution:

'You talked to me about keeping her out. It is impossible; she comes at all times, at any time, and the moment the door is open in she walks. I can't throw her out of the window: as to getting rid of her, that is rational and probable, but *I* will not receive her. . . .

'She may hunt me down—it is the power of any mad or bad woman to do so by any man—but *snare* me she shall not: torment me she may; how am I to bar myself from her? I am already almost a prisoner; she has no shame, no feeling, no one estimable or redeemable quality.

'These are strong words, but I know what I am writing . . . She has been an adder in my path ever since my return to this country; she has often belied and sometimes betrayed me; she has crossed me everywhere, she has watched and worried and grieved and been a curse to me and mine.

'You may show *her* this if you please—or to anyone you please; if these were the last words I were to write upon earth, I would not revoke one letter except to make it more legible.'

(C, 1, 261)

That is a good sample of what Byron's love-affairs could come to. Nor is this the letter of a normal man: he was not merely reluctant; when the lady went too far, he was maddened; he felt his soul being violated. But he could not prevent it. He suffered from his own magnetism; he was a candle, the rest moths; and it was all far from easy.

Byron's biographers agree that Caroline was impossible and Byron to be accorded a high measure of sympathy. Whether there was any actual adultery cannot, I suppose, be known. Samuel Rogers seems to have thought that there was not, but it is generally assumed that there was. What is certain is this—that it was all utterly abnormal, the lady attacking and Byron attempting, ineffectually, and only for a while, to succumb. Refusal he found difficult, because he did, indeed, love people, the ladies included; but, in so far as there was love, he loved them more for their personality than for their sex; and that is not necessarily a compliment to the lady. He once put the problem neatly. After saying that his letters had been consistently cold until Caroline's 'endless' reproaches persuaded him to give expression to his affection, he observes that this was 'no great compliment', since

'I could love anything on earth that appeared to wish it; at the same time I do sometimes like to choose for myself.'

(Lady Melbourne, 26 Nov., 1812; C, 1, 111)

Of this tormenting engagement Byron has left us a bitter poetic record, penned in answer to Caroline's 'Remember me', which she had written in Byron's copy of *Vathek*:

> *Remember thee! Remember thee!*
> *Till Lethe quench life's burning stream*
> *Remorse and shame shall cling to thee,*
> *And haunt thee like a feverish dream!*

18

Remember thee! Ay, doubt it not.
Thy husband too shall think of thee!
By neither shalt thou be forgot
Thou false to him, thou fiend to me!

(P, III, 59)

That may serve as a final comment, from Byron's view.

He had better fortune with Lady Oxford, with whom he went to stay in the autumn of 1812, and again in January, 1813. She was a woman of originality and charm old enough to be his mother, who was married to a husband whom no one praises and had already had a number of love-affairs, some of which produced children, which the husband was willing to acknowledge. With her Byron seems to have found, for a while, a satisfying if temporary, retreat from the attacks of Caroline, her affection blending the emotional sustenance of both mistress and mother; and her husband appears in the main to have left the two together without worrying. It may be written off as, according to the manners of the time, a reasonably normal, blameless, and contented relationship for all concerned.

In the summer of 1813 Byron and his half-sister Augusta were in London, and it is sometimes supposed that incest occurred between them at one or more of their many meetings. This is a problem to which we shall shortly return.

After that Byron was staying at Rotherham with Mr. James Wedderburn Webster and his wife, Lady Frances. Of this we have for once a full account in Byron's letters to his confidante and counsellor, Lady Melbourne, a woman of wide experience and broad principles. It is the only one of his affairs of which we have such an exact, day-to-day, account, and its biographical importance is great.

James Wedderburn Webster was a perfect example of all that most irritated Byron in the moral code, or cant, of the time. He would boast simultaneously of his wife's *virtues* and of his own *irregularities*. The lady appeared to be expecting Byron's attentions, but he was not eager, writing: 'I never should think of her, nor anyone else, if left to my own cogitations, as I have neither the patience nor presumption to advance till met half-way.' But the husband continued to irritate with his sexual egotism, and when Byron pointed out the *non sequitur* of expecting to 'do with impunity, it

19

seems, but not suffer', there was a scene (5 and 8 Oct., 1813; C, I, 189, 190). Now, being thus variously tempted by both lady and husband, Byron advanced on, it might be said, moral, or at least dramatic, principle:

'I need not say that the folly and petulance of Webster has tended to all this. If a man is not contented with a pretty woman, and not only runs after any little country girl he meets with, but absolutely boasts of it; he must not be surprised if others admire that which he knows not how to value. Besides, he literally provoked and goaded me into it, by something not unlike bullying, *indirect* to be sure, but tolerably obvious: "he *would* do this, and he would do that", "if any man etc. etc."; and *he* thought that every "woman" was *his* lawful prize, nevertheless. Oons! who is this strange monopolist?'

(8 Oct., 1813; C, I, 192)

Byron's day-by-day accounts of the flirtation's progress and the fooling of the husband make fascinating reading; and nowhere else can we so clearly watch his peculiar way of standing outside his own drama and watching its effect. It is all done for a purpose, like the writing of a satiric drama.

But what of the result? Lady Frances was quickly devoted, and abandoned herself to his will, whilst admitting that she knew she would suffer afterwards. The opportunity—they were all staying now at Newstead—was perfect. Byron writes: 'Was I wrong? I spared her'. Her manner was 'peculiar', and his decision in the nature of a 'sacrifice', though the time was 'two in the morning' and 'the Devil whispering that it'—the lady's supposed anxiety—'was mere *verbiage*'; that is, insincere coquetry (17 Oct., 1813; C, I, 203-4).

From then on Byron was himself in love. He was ready, if need be, to go off with her (19 Oct., 1813; C, I, 206). He wondered whether he had done right in resisting, admitting that he was 'not yet old enough' to be proof against a lady's tears and run the risk of 'making her wretched', since he could never indulge his 'passions' at the cost of another's 'misery'. If he had indeed been her 'dupe', he had at least been fooled by his 'good feelings' (21 Oct., 1813; C, I, 209). He was glad that Lady Melbourne approved of his 'ethics'—that is, perhaps, glad to find her, woman of the world as she was, for once on the side of the angels—and he certainly did 'sacrifice the selfish consideration' to spare Lady Frances' 'self-reproach' (23 Oct., 1813; and postscript; C, 1, 211–12). All this is genuine enough:

'I hate sentiment, and in consequence my epistolary levity makes you believe me as hollow and heartless as my letters are light. Indeed, it is not so.'

(23 Oct., 'Monday'; 1813; C, 1, 213)

A correspondence was for a while kept up after they had parted, Lady Frances passionately devoted, and Byron now both lover and critic, with a number of comments on the morality of it all and particularly on a phrase of the lady's hinting at her anxiety to deceive her husband out of conjugal duty: 'It has enlivened my ethical studies on the human mind beyond fifty volumes. How admirably we accommodate our reasons to our wishes' (22 Nov., 1813; C, 1, 216). On looking back he bitterly regarded his virtue as a weakness and was *ashamed* of such 'Platonics', thinking that it may have been merely a lady's 'coquetry'; yes, he had been a 'fool' (10 Jan., 1814; C, 1, 227). It must be remembered that failure to respond to a lady was always liable to seem like cowardice, since action might lead to death. That is why Byron makes it clear that he was prepared for a duel, and if it came to that would not return the shot, being himself in the wrong (13 Oct., 25 Nov.; Journal, 17 Nov.; 1813; C, 1, 200, 218; LJ, II, 323).

These letters are intensely revealing. Byron was first shocked by Wedderburn Webster's atrocious sense of values, and afterwards by his wife's easy principles. He originally engaged himself as an instrument of judgment, was prevented from driving the matter to a conclusion from regard for the lady's welfare, and finally cursed himself for being a fool. For his own morality was undecided: there were two codes involved, and his code as a gentleman of the time urged him to act the lover and take the consequences. He had in him the sharply opposed traditions of both puritan and gentleman. And behind it all may well have been the consciousness that he was less attracted by, perhaps we should say 'more averse from', heterosexual intercourse than he liked to admit, even to himself; and this may be why he wondered, in characteristic fashion, whether he was really 'attributing to a good motive what may be quite otherwise' (21 Oct., 1813; C, 1, 209). He was not at all sure whether his refusal *was* to be acclaimed, if only, perhaps, since, from the homosexual's standpoint, any sort of normal sexuality is a tribute to morality. Such are the complexities involved in the little drama of which Byron was simultaneously composer, protagonist, critic, and reporter.

Of this affair he has also left us a neat poetic account in the lines *Remember Him Whom Passion's Power* (P III, 67), a comparison of which with the letters throws a valuable light on the relation of Byronic poetry to Byronic prose.

Our last is Clare Clairmont, step-daughter of William Godwin, who started an offensive in the spring of 1816, towards the end of the agonizing proceedings for Byron's marriage-separation, when he was in a state of considerable anxiety. She sent anonymous letters which were unanswered; called at his house and was turned away; but by persistence at last gained an interview. She pretended to be soliciting his interest for a part at Drury Lane, but her real object was personal. Her letters (LJ, III; App. VII, 429–37) make extraordinary reading. Eventually she persuaded Byron to spend a night with her, and after he left England followed him to Switzerland. Writing to Augusta on 8 September, 1816, Byron apologized for continuing the association, saying that he had done all he could to prevent it and had sent her back, though, when a lady comes all that way, he could not exactly 'play the stoic' (Lovelace, XI, 267; see p. 130). The pattern repeats itself. These engagements were undertaken in a spirit of half-reluctant gallantry. The fruit of this liaison was the child Allegra: Clare later followed Byron to Italy, and there was disagreement about the child. The association ended in bitterness; Byron grew to hate her. But the whole affair had been forced on him: 'He did', writes Ethel Colburn Mayne, 'what he was pestered into doing' (Mayne, *Lady Byron*, XIV, 219).

Let us review briefly our findings regarding Byron's main heterosexual adventures before the Separation. There is little firm evidence of vice and much evidence that he was shocked at it in his contemporaries. As for his *liaisons*, the women approached him, not he them. 'In practically all the serious love-affairs of Byron the preludes and advances were the preludes and advances of the women; not of Byron himself' (Vulliamy, VII, 94). He rejected advances in Gibraltar, Malta and Greece; Caroline Lamb pressed him like a lunatic till he joined forces with her mother; Lady Oxford was probably as much mother as mistress to him, and there was nothing in this affair even distantly, according to prevailing manners, reprehensible; to Lady Frances he originally responded out of moral revulsion from her husband's licentious boasts and immoral values, and, when it came to the point, declined; and Clare Clairmont pestered him till he gave way. 'Your *Blackwood*', Byron once wrote to Murray, 'accuses me of treating women harshly: it may be so, but I have been their martyr. My whole life has been sacrificed *to* them and *by* them' (10 Dec. 1819; LJ, IV, 386).

Byron's male relationships were far happier. 'With men,' writes Ethel Colburn Mayne, 'he was delightful'; he could then become 'a merry, happy boy', but with women he was, she says, 'a blighted being', and his vision of them was 'distorted'. She accordingly regards his love-affairs as of 'little importance', saying that 'worthily to write of Byron is to write of all but them' (Mayne, I; XIV, 281, 286, 297). It was, says Peter Quennell, 'in the world of masculine companionship' that he was most 'at his ease' (Quennell, XI, 308). This was not because he did not like women—he always liked to have a woman near him—but because they wanted to possess him sexually and permanently.

And there was more, as Quennell too tells us, than male 'companionship'. We have touched on Byron's romantic feelings for his school friends, for John Edleston, and Nicolo Giraud; and there is some reason, which we shall face later on, to suppose that the last affair was driven to an extreme. Whatever be the exact truth, we can say that these experiences were as harmonious as the others were disastrous. They may have induced a sense of sin, but never of loathing.

It does not take much perspicuity to see Byron as a man whose instincts were abnormal, but who tried to act the part of a normal male. This he did partly because, as persons, he was genuinely fond of women, as he was of everybody who was at all kind to him, though the specifically sexual adjustment may have been less easy; and partly, too, because response was a matter of gallantry. Of the writing of *Marino Faliero* he said:

'I never wrote nor copied an *entire scene of that play* without being obliged to *break* off—to *break* a commandment, to obey a woman's, and to forget God's . . . The lady always apologised for the interruption; but you know the answer a man must make when and while he can.'

(Quoted Mayne, II; VIII, 187; no ref.)

There was a third reason. Though he was in part a feminine type

(CV, II, 81), he certainly was not prepared to regard himself a such, except perhaps when writing poetry (e.g. in *Don Juan* and *Sardanapalus*). His strongly male manner of address in prose alone witnesses the will to assert his, also genuine, masculinity. We can accordingly regard his utterly distorted self-accusations as arising from two sources: (i) his honest desire to expiate and compound with the sin of homosexuality within, together with (ii) a desire to mask that sin. Through such an understanding, much of Byron's paradoxical behaviour becomes clear.

III

For the purpose of my present study it is necessary to select for closer attention three of Byron's loves: they are, Mary Anne Chaworth, John Edleston and Augusta Leigh.

Mary was a distant cousin of Byron belonging to a family whose property at Annesley adjoined Newstead. A detailed account of the relationship is given in a note in *Letters and Journals* (I, 16–17): 'The connection between the families of Chaworth and Byron came through the marriage of William, third Lord Byron (died 1695) with Elizabeth Chaworth (died 1683)'. But there was an ugly incident. Mary was the grand-niece of the Mr. Chaworth who was killed in a duel by William, fifth Lord Byron, on 26 January, 1765; that is, Byron's grand-uncle had killed hers. Mary, the heiress of Annesley, lived with her mother. Byron saw her frequently in his youth. In the year 1803, while still a schoolboy on holiday from Harrow, he fell violently in love with her. She would play and sing a Welsh ditty which gave him peculiar delight, its name 'Mary Anne' being, according to Moore, part of the attraction (Moore, III, 27). His early feelings are recollected in a note set down in 1821 (*Detached Thoughts*, 65; LJ, V, 441; and see Moore, III, 26–9). She was two years older than Byron, and in 1805 married John Musters, whom Vulliamy calls an 'extremely stupid', though 'vigorous', man (IV, 57). Byron suffered severely.

The romance was to him saturated in a certain fatalism descending from the duel. Throughout his life he remembered that 'our union would have healed feuds in which blood had been shed by our fathers' (*Detached Thoughts*, 65; LJ, V, 441). Teresa Guiccioli (II; V, 79) tells us that he had wished 'to efface the stain of blood and hatred through love'—after the manner of *Romeo and Juliet*.

Byron saw Mary, now a mother, in the year 1808, and referred sadly in some lines *Well thou art Happy* (P, 1, 277), and again in a bitter poem written in 1811, from which we shall quote later (p. 122), to his emotions. He seemed to think, or to grow to think, that Mary's rejection of him was the cause of his future mental and spiritual agonies. She remained in his thoughts a dream-image of what might have been, a symbol of purity, to be grouped with Edleston, as an ideal from which he had fallen. Poems were written about her throughout his life; she never ceased to move his imagination. Had he married her, things, he thought, would have been different; he probably even persuaded himself that his homosexual instincts would have been for ever quelled. Moore tells us that 'six short summer weeks' of youthful love were sufficient to lay the foundation of a life-long emotion (Moore, III, 27).

And yet Byron only appears to have seen her once more, on his return from the East (Medwin, 62). The question is of importance, since Richard Edgcumbe in *Byron: the Last Phase* advanced an elaborate theory that Medora Leigh, who was born on 15 April, 1814 and is sometimes supposed to have been the child of Byron and his half-sister, Augusta Leigh, was really the child of Byron and Mary. His theory is fantastic and developed beyond all reason, poems which have no relevance being wrenched into service, and facts regarding meetings stated, as, indeed, is only too usual in Byronic biography, with no references whatsoever. Nevertheless, the book holds considerable suggestive value, and sometimes more than that, and we shall have occasion to return to it.

Mary was soon estranged from her husband, who behaved cruelly, and Edgcumbe believed that Byron and Mary met in 1813, after the estrangement. She had a mental illness, but eventually returned to her husband. We cannot be certain that Byron never saw her, but there is strong evidence to the contrary, of which Edgcumbe was ignorant.

I refer to certain new material first printed in the two volumes *Lord Byron's Correspondence*, published in 1922. We have letters from Mary to Byron dated 24 December, 1813 and 7 January 1814, in the second of which she calls herself one of his 'earliest' and 'still most faithful' friends, expresses her desire to meet him, and describes her unhappy condition: 'You would hardly recognise in me the happy creature you once knew me. I am grown so thin, pale, and gloomy.' She recognizes that her writing to him would be condemned as wrong; but the letter is in the nature of an SOS. She signs herself 'Mary' (C, I, 223–5, note; another undated letter of this period is given by Edgcumbe; II, 267). Byron told Lady Melbourne of Mary's letter on 8 January, calling her his 'old love of all loves' and saying that her husband 'has been playing the Devil with all kinds of vulgar mistresses, and behaving ill enough in every respect'. He adds that he means to see her, though it would be but 'a melancholy interview', since they had scarcely met, and never been on intimate terms, since her marriage. On 10 January he told Lady Melbourne that he had heard that she was about to be reconciled with her husband, while he himself had 'no feelings beyond esteem, etc., now to spare, and she still fewer for me'. He wrote again the following day, saying that he was worried by her persistence and wanted advice, since 'It is impossible I should now feel anything beyond friendship for her or any one else in present circumstances'; he refers darkly to another, all-consuming, passion that has him under its control; and says that he has accordingly 'touched very slightly on my past feelings towards her, and explained what they *now* were'. He is not certain that a meeting might not arouse the old passion, and is reluctant to risk 'this same sickly friendship which is reviving between M and me'. He remains guarded and cautious, and on 6 February says that, though Augusta had tried hard to persuade him to see Mary, he had been too 'sluggish upon the subject' to do so. When Mary was in doubt whether or not to return to her husband, he had avoided giving advice (C, I, 223, 225, 228, 241–2). Edgcumbe quotes two letters of Byron to Augusta on Mary, dated 7 and 12 February (Edgcumbe, II, 267–8); and on 12 February, 1814, Byron wrote to Miss Milbanke, his future wife, about her, saying that he had decided not to see her for fear of reviving his love (SP, I, 270).

In the summer of 1814 Mary followed Byron to Hastings in the hope of a meeting, but it seems that he had left in order to avoid her, and soon after came her mental collapse, which may have been partly caused by her failure to renew his acquaintance (Paston and Quennell, VIII, 174–5). On 25 and 31 October, 1814, Byron wrote from London to Miss Milbanke about Mary's illness, saying that his 'oldest friend' was lying between life and death a few streets away (Paston and Quennell, VIII, 175). Possibly he saw her then, and that would account for the vivid description of her madness in *The Dream* (p. 123 below).

Byron's correspondence shows nothing more until 12 July, 1823, when he wrote to J. J. Coulmann, giving an unemotional account of the duel, mainly in defence of his grand-uncle who had incurred, he said, no particular odium, and kept the sword he had used in his bed-chamber.[1] He goes on to speak of his own association with Mary, noting that 'at one time it was thought that the two families would have been united in us'; that Mary married unhappily; and how, though 'her conduct' was 'irreproachable', there was a separation; that later Byron was about to see her after many years without a meeting when his sister persuaded him *not* to for fear of a passionate renewal; and that Mary later suffered from insanity, but was now, he thinks, reconciled to her husband (LJ, VI, 233–4).

Our present knowledge clearly contradicts Edgcumbe's thesis that Byron and Mary met in 1813, and the tone and tenour of Byron's letters would seem to preclude the likelihood of any renewal of passion. It is, of course not impossible that the letters to Lady Melbourne and J. J. Coulmann which, by the way, bluntly contradict each other as to Augusta's attitude—both Teresa (I; VII, 309)and Byron's account to Medwin (62) corroborate the letter to Coulmann —were cold for a purpose; and that Byron did meet Mary during, or after, her illness in the year 1814. This, however, leaves no scope for Edgcumbe's theory regarding Medora, who was born 15 April, 1814.

Byron always had moods of regret about Mary. As late as 1821 we find him commenting bitterly on what might have been. The union would, he says, have healed the blood-feud; it was suitable in every way; 'and—and—and—what has been the result?' He continues:

'*She* has married a man older than herself, been wretched, and separated. I have married, and am separated, and yet *We* are *not* united.'

(*Detached Thoughts*, 65; LJ, V, 441)

This mood is found often in his poetry; for his love certainly enjoyed a *poetic* perpetuation throughout his life. In his bitter *Epistle to a Friend* (pp. 35, 122) he prophesied that, having seen Mary the husband of another, he was now, in 1811, likely enough to load himself 'with deepening crimes' and be eventually ranked among 'the

[1] For an account of the affair and an exoneration of Byron's grand-uncle, see Hartley Coleridge on *The Duel*; P, IV, 542–3, note.

worst anarchs of the age' (P, III, 28–30). Possibly his subsequent poems about her were inspired less by any still vivid passion than by the ever-present and continuing torment of those more dangerous instincts, both political and homosexual—for the two were closely involved in each other—from which he felt, probably quite erroneously, that Mary could have saved him. Had he married her, he remarked to Medwin, 'perhaps the whole tenour of my life would have been different' (Medwin, 62).

We turn next to Edleston, the young chorister of humble birth whom Byron met at Cambridge directly after his rejection by Mary Chaworth. The romance was started by Byron's saving Edleston from drowning (LJ, I, 130–1, note). Years later he referred to it as 'a violent, though *pure*, love and passion', which was, together with his 'friendship' for Edward Noel Long, the 'romance of the most romantic period of my life' (Journal, 12 Jan., 1821; LJ, V, 169; and see Moore, IV, 31). That his love for Edleston took precedence over his other early friendships is suggested by his rather non-committal statement: 'I don't know what to say about "friendship". I never was in friendship but once, in my nineteenth year, and then it gave me as much trouble as love' (Moore, 22 June, 1813; LJ, II, 225).

Here is his description in 1807 of his 'musical protégé', as given to Elizabeth Pigot: 'He is exactly to an hour two years younger than myself . . . nearly my height, very *thin*, very fair complexion, dark eyes, and light locks.' Byron's usual sense of guardianship is involved: 'My opinion of his mind you already know—I hope I shall never have occasion to change it' (Elizabeth Pigot, 30 June, 1807; LJ, I, 132). Soon after he wrote at greater length, saying that 'Edleston and I have separated for the present and my mind is a chaos of hope and sorrow', and continuing, with a reference to the business prospects which Byron's influence might obtain for him:

'I rejoice to hear you are interested in my *protégé*; he has been my *almost constant* associate since October, 1805, when I entered Trinity College. His *voice* first attracted my attention, his *countenance* fixed it, and his *manners* attached me to him for ever. He departs for a *mercantile house* in *town* in October, and we shall probably not meet till the expiration of my minority, when I shall leave to his decision either entering as a *partner* through my interest, or residing with me altogether. Of course, he would in his present frame of mind prefer the *latter*, but he may alter his opinion previous to that period;—

28

however, he shall have his choice. I certainly love him more than any human being, and neither time nor distance have had the least effect on my (in general) changeable disposition. In short, we shall put *Lady E. Butler* and *Miss Ponsonby* [1] to the blush, *Pylades* and *Orestes* out of countenance, and want nothing but a catastrophe like *Nisus* and *Euryalus* to give *Jonathan* and *David* the "go by". He certainly is perhaps more attached to *me* than even I am in return. During the whole of my residence at Cambridge we met every day, summer and winter, without passing *one* tiresome moment, and separated each time with increasing reluctance. I hope you will one day see us together. He is the only being I esteem, though I *like* many.'

(Elizabeth Pigot, 5 July, 1807; LJ, I, 133)

They did not, as it turned out, set up house together, and Byron in due course went on his travels. After his return in the summer of 1811 he heard from Ann, Edleston's sister, that her brother had died of consumption in May. [2] The news, coming so soon after the deaths of his mother and other friends, including Wingfield and Matthews, affected him deeply.

On receiving the news, he wrote, on 11 October, 1811, to R. C. Dallas from Newstead:

'I have been again shocked with a *death*, and have lost one very dear to me in happier times; but "I have almost forgot the taste of grief" and "supped full of horrors" till I have become callous, nor have I a tear left for an event which, five years ago, would have bowed down my head to the earth.'

(LJ, II, 52; *Macbeth*, V, iv)

On 22 October, on a visit to Cambridge, he wrote to Hobhouse:

'The event I mentioned in my last has had an effect on me I am ashamed to think of. But there is no arguing on these points. I could "have better spared a better being". Wherever I turn, particularly in this place, the idea goes with me. I say all this at the risk of incurring your contempt; but you cannot despise me more than I do myself.'

(SP, I, 124; 1 *Henry IV*, V, iv)

---

[1] For the celebrated 'Ladies of Llangollen' see LJ, I, 134, note.

[2] Ann Edleston's letter is dated 26 September, but Byron had been away from Newstead and apparently did not receive it until his return on 9th October (Quennell, I, 50, and note).

The use of Prince Hal's words marks no aspersion on Edleston; Byron is thinking of the power such friendships exert over him, and is ashamed, the use of 'contempt' neatly serving to indicate one reason at least for his life-long unrest. The letter is, of course, toned for Hobhouse as a representative of normality who did, indeed, as we shall see, most strongly, and perhaps a little *jealously* (see p. 276), disapprove of Byron's male loves. Others have done so too. Indeed, *Lord Byron's Correspondence* (1922) omits from the letter this particular paragraph, which did not appear until Quennell's *Byron: A Self-Portrait* (1950).

To Francis Hodgson, on 16 February, 1812, Byron was more outspoken:

'I believe the only human being that ever loved me in truth and entirely, was of, or belonging to, Cambridge, and in that no change can now take place. There is one consolation in death—where he sets his seal, the impression can neither be melted nor broken, but endureth for ever.'

He adds, with a thought recalling Shakespeare's Sonnets: 'I almost rejoice when one I love dies young, for I could never bear to see them old or altered' (LJ, II, 100). The strength of Byron's feelings will be clear.

Edleston had given Byron a cornelian heart, and the gift was celebrated in Byron's early poem *The Cornelian* (about 1805; P, 1, 66), which tells us that those who 'sneer' at 'friendship's ties' have often 'reproved' him for his 'weakness'. In another early poem, *Pignus Amoris* (date uncertain; P, 1, 231–3), Byron develops a similar trend, thinking of one 'who loved me for myself alone', and defending himself against criticism with the claim that this is a youthful friendship at a time when pleasure contains no 'base alloy', life may be blest without risk of 'crime', and innocence join hands with joy. There is a reference to the Cornelian Heart as 'my simple toy'. The pledge is probably the one referred to as a 'sacred gem' in *The Adieu* (1807), which contains a pretty stanza on Edleston's 'gentle love' (P, 1, 240).

On the day of his letter to Dallas reporting Edleston's death, 11 October, 1811, Byron wrote the elegy *To Thyrza*. That the poem was inspired by his love for Edleston seems quite clear, though he uses, for obvious reasons, a feminine name. Typically, he expresses his regret at not being by to nurse his friend during his last illness:

Could this have been—a word, a look,
  That softly said, 'We part in peace',
Had taught my bosom how to brook
  With fainter sighs thy soul's release.
And didst thou not, since Death for thee
  Prepared a light and pangless dart,
Once long for him thou ne'er shalt see,
  Who held, and holds thee, in his heart?

Here are the concluding lines (Hartley Coleridge gives Byronic authority for not printing the poem in stanzas):

Ours too the glance none saw beside;
  The smile none else might understand;
The whispered thought of hearts allied,
  The pressure of the thrilling hand;
The kiss, so guiltless and refined,
  That Love each warmer wish forbore;
Those eyes proclaimed so pure a mind,
  Ev'n Passion blushed to plead for more.
The tone, that taught me to rejoice,
  When prone, unlike thee, to repine;
The song, celestial from thy voice,
  But sweet to me from none but thine;
The pledge we wore—I wear it still,
  But where is thine?—Ah! where art thou?
Oft have I borne the weight of ill,
  But never bent beneath till now!
Well hast thou left in life's best bloom
  The cup of woe for me to drain.
If rest alone be in the tomb,
  I would not wish thee here again:
But if in worlds more blest than this
  Thy virtues seek a fitter sphere,
Impart some portion of thy bliss,
  To wean me from mine anguish here.
Teach me—too early taught by thee!
  To bear, forgiving and forgiven:
On earth thy love was such to me;
  It fain would form my hope in Heaven!

(P. III, 33)

31

The 'pledge' may be the Cornelian Heart; but this Byron had sent before leaving England to Elizabeth Pigot. He wrote on 28 October to Mrs. Pigot, Elizabeth's mother, to reclaim it. In his letter he refers to himself as having *given* it, but it was returned with the assurance that it was only lent, probably for safe-keeping (LJ, I, 131, note). He would, of course, have had it before the lines were published, but there was perhaps a second pledge.

There are other *Thyrza* poems, and they all surely refer to Edleston. The next is dated by Hartley Coleridge 8 December, 1811. In it the poet feels himself, with perhaps a thought of his experiences in Greece, to have fallen below the purity of the earlier romance:

> *Away, away, ye notes of woe!*
> *Be silent, thou once soothing strain,*
> *Or I must flee from hence—for, oh!*
> *I dare not trust those sounds again.*
> *To me they speak of brighter days—*
> *But lull the chords, for now, alas!*
> *I must not think, I may not gaze,*
> *On what I am—on what I was.*
>
> *The voice that made those sounds more sweet*
> *Is hush'd, and all their charms are fled;*
> *And now their softest notes repeat*
> *A dirge, an anthem o'er the dead!*
> *Yes, Thyrza! yes, they breathe of thee,*
> *Beloved dust! since dust thou art;*
> *And all that once was harmony*
> *Is worse than discord to my heart!*
>
> *'Tis silent all!—but on my ear*
> *The well remember'd echoes thrill;*
> *I hear a voice I would not hear,*
> *A voice that now might well be still:*
> *Yet oft my doubting soul 't will shake;*
> *Even slumber owns its gentle tone,*
> *Till consciousness will vainly wake*
> *To listen, though the dream be flown.*

Sweet Thyrza! waking as in sleep,
 Thou art but now a lovely dream;
A star that trembled o'er the deep,
 Then turn'd from earth its tender beam.
But he who through life's dreary way
 Must pass, when Heaven is veil'd in wrath,
Will long lament the vanish'd ray
 That scatter'd gladness o'er his path.

(P. III, 35)

Our next, *One Struggle More and I am Free*, which is undated and
was originally called *To Thyrza* (editions 1812–1831; P, 36, note),
is valuable for its firm internal evidence—and this may be why the
title was dropped—that 'Thyrza' is to be identified with Edleston:

On many a lone and lovely night
 It soothed to gaze upon the sky;
For then I deemed the heavenly light
 Shone sweetly on thy pensive eye:
And oft I thought at Cynthia's noon,
 When sailing o'er the Aegean wave,
'Now Thyrza gazes on that moon'—
 Alas, it gleamed upon her grave!

(P, III, 37)

Edleston had died on 11 May, 1811 (P. 1, 66, note); Byron left
Athens about 4 May and arrived at Malta about 14 May (C, 1, 31
where '4 March' is a misprint for '4 May'). The dates fit.[1] We have
also a reference to 'my Thyrza's pledge in better days', and the
words 'the heart that gave itself with thee' clearly suggest the Cornelian Heart. In Byron's manuscript there is a variant 'dear simple
gift', recalling the 'simple toy' of *Pignus Amoris* (p. 30). Now the
Cornelian Heart had been returned to Byron by Elizabeth Pigot
broken (Mayne, 1; VI, 92). Therefore he addresses it:

How different now thou meet'st my gaze!
How tinged by time with sorrow's hue!

---

[1] I follow Hartley Coleridge. Peter Quennell gives the date of Edleston's death as
16 May (Quennell, 1, 50, note). If that be correct, Byron's memory must have been
at fault.

He continues:

> *Thou bitter pledge! thou mournful token!*
> *Though painful, welcome to my breast!*
> *Still, still, preserve that love unbroken,*
> *Or break the heart to which thou'rt pressed.*

(P, III, 38)

At every point the evidence is firm.

Euthanasia, published in 1812 (P. III, 39–40), being addressed to a live person, seems to be out of place. Next, the exquisite *And Thou art Dead as Young and Fair*, dated February, 1812 (P, III, 41–4), contains some powerful stanzas playing, just like the conclusion to Byron's letter to Hodgson (p. 30), on one of the key-thoughts of Shakespeare's sonnets:

> *The flower in ripened bloom unmatched*
> *Must fall the earliest prey;*
> *Though by no hand untimely snatched,*
> *The leaves must drop away:*
> *And yet it were a greater grief*
> *To watch it withering, leaf by leaf,*
> *Than see it pluck'd today;*
> *Since earthly eye but ill can bear*
> *To trace the change to foul from fair.*
>
> *I know not if I could have borne*
> *To see thy beauties fade;*
> *The night that followed such a morn*
> *Had worn a deeper shade:*
> *Thy day without a cloud hath passed,*
> *And thou wert lovely to the last;*
> *Extinguish'd, not decayed;*
> *As stars that shoot along the sky*
> *Shine brightest as they fall from high.*

(P, III, 43)

Again, the poet typically wishes that he could have kept at the least 'one vigil' over his love's death-bed.

Our sixth poem, *If Sometimes in the Haunts of Men*, dated 14 March, 1812, repeats the thought of *Pignus Amoris* and also of Byron's letter

34

to Hodgson (p. 30) that Edleston loved him as did no one else. It concludes:

> For well I know, that such had been
> Thy gentle care for him, who now
> Unmourned shall quit this mortal scene,
> Where none regarded him, but thou:
> And, oh! I feel in that was given
> A blessing never meant for me;
> Thou wert too like a dream of Heaven
> For earthly love to merit thee.

(P, III, 47)

Again, the associations are all but divine. There is a seventh poem dated 16 March, 1812 (P, III, 48), *On a Cornelian Heart which was Broken*, which serves to complete the series.

That the various poems of this group are addressed to 'Thyrza' is clearly stated by the editor of the 1837 edition of Byron's collected poems (*Poetical Works*, 1837; 550, note). That 'Thyrza' is Edleston appears unquestionable; and yet it has been questioned. Moore, who could not, or professed not to, understand Byron's romantic attachments to youths of lower status, as his remarks on Nicolo Giraud (Moore, x, 114) make clear, regards 'Thyrza' as a composite of Byron's friendships for Edleston and others and his love of Mary Chaworth. All poetry is, as poetry, necessarily a composite; and it is true that Byron's other friendships of *this* kind may be regarded as a constituent; but the poetry is obviously more 'occasional' than Moore suggests. Indeed, the very perfection of Byron's love for Edleston is exquisitely underlined by his insistence that the poem must include more than one person since no mere friendship could be so passionate and no sexual passion so pure (Moore, XIII, 140-1). Besides, apart from the reference to singing, there is nothing whatever in these elegiac poems to suggest Mary. Not only was she not dead at all, but on the very day that he composed the first *Thyrza* poem, 11 October, 1811, he apparently, for this is its stated date (P, II, 163 note), composed for Francis Hodgson the totally different and bitter *Epistle to a Friend* about his love for Mary (p. 122), prophesying that her rejection of him might yet lead him into anti-social actions of dangerous sort. We have already suggested that Mary was associated in his mind with his own more unorthodox instincts, and that may be why the two poems were composed together on hearing of Edleston's death.

It is necessary to make these points firmly, since even Hartley Coleridge regards, or pretends to regard, the identity of 'Thyrza' as a mystery (P, III, 30-2, note). Richard Edgcumbe, riding his theory to death, naturally insists on Mary, whom he finds in pretty nearly everything that Byron wrote. Scandal-mongers during Byron's life hinted that the poems revealed a perverted love for Byron's pet bear at Newstead (Medwin, 225, note). On the whole, we shall be safer with Edleston.

As we have seen, the news of Edleston's death caused Byron to write to Dallas, on the same day, 11 October, 1811, as the date of *Thyrza*, saying 'I have been again shocked with a death'. This directly follows a request to him to insert some new stanzas at the conclusion to the second canto of *Childe Harold*, which Dallas was then seeing through the press (LJ, II, 52; P, II, 162-3, note); and of these two, 95 and 96, surely refer to Edleston. So does stanza 9, sent either with these or later. The editor, or editors, of the 1837 *Poetical Works* definitely relates stanza 9 to Edleston, and, by implication, the others also (*Poetical Works*, 1837; 17, 27, notes); and Byron himself told Dallas that all these stanzas referred to *the same person* (31 Oct., 1811; LJ, II, 66). Now in sending Dallas some corrections to stanza 9, Byron wrote: 'I think it proper to state to you that this stanza alludes to an event which has taken place since my arrival here, and not to the death of any *male* friend' (Dallas, 14 Oct., 1811; LJ, II, 58). He wished to suggest that the stanzas were not addressed to Edleston, but he was a poor deceiver and had forgotten his own lines. Hartley Coleridge comments:

'It may be noted that the lines 6 and 7 of stanza 95

> *Nor staid to welcome here thy wanderer home,*
> *Who mourns o'er hours which we no more shall see*

do not bear out Byron's contention to Dallas . . . that in these three *in memoriam* stanzas (9, 95, 96) he is bewailing an event which took place *after* he returned to Newstead. The "more than friend" had "ceased to be" before the "wanderer" returned. It is evident that Byron did not take Dallas into his confidence.'

(P, II, 163)

Despite his reserve, Hartley Coleridge appears to be aware of the truth, or at least of something very like it. Here are the last two stanzas:

> Thou too art gone, thou loved and lovely one!
> Whom youth and youth's affections bound to me;
> Who did for me what none beside have done,
> Nor shrank from one albeit unworthy thee.
> What is my being? thou hast ceased to be!
> Nor staid to welcome here thy wanderer home,
> Who mourns o'er hours which we no more shall see—
> Would they had never been, or were to come!
> Would he had ne'er return'd to find fresh cause to roam.
>
> Oh! ever loving, lovely and beloved!
> How selfish sorrow ponders on the past,
> And clings to thoughts now better far removed!
> But Time shall tear thy shadow from me last.
> All thou could'st have of mine, stern Death! thou hast;
> The Parent, Friend, and now the more than Friend:
> Ne'er yet for one thine arrows flew so fast,
> And grief with grief continuing still to blend,
> Hath snatch'd the little joy that life had yet to lend.

(II, 95, 96)

The 'friend' is Wingfield, or Matthews (p. 14), the 'more than friend', Edleston. 'Who did . . .' repeats a thought we have already found in Byron's correspondence and the *Thyrza* poetry. These lines conclude our collection.

On 31 October, presumably sending *To Thyrza*, Byron wrote to Dallas: 'I send a few stanzas on a subject which has lately occupied much of my thoughts. They refer to the death of one to whose name you are a *stranger*, and, consequently, cannot be interested'. He adds that this is *the same person* addressed in the three stanzas to *Childe Harold* (LJ, II, 66). It all holds together, and dovetails with the letters. Though denying, for some unnamed reason, that Edleston is the subject, Hartley Coleridge admits the unity: 'We have Byron's authority for connecting stanza 9 with stanzas 95 and 96, and, inferentially, his authority for connecting stanzas 9, 95, 96 with the group of *Thyrza* poems. And there our knowledge ends. We must leave the mystery where Byron willed that it should be left' (P, II, 105, note). But that, I fear, we cannot, and need not, do.

No one else in Byron's story called forth such memories of unsullied adoration. It is perhaps significant that it was after hearing of Edleston's death that he changed the word 'beloved' in the stanza of Canto I on Wingfield to the word 'esteemed' (Dallas, 25 Oct., 1811; LJ, II, 58). The anonymous editor—or editors—of the 1837 edition of Byron's poetry tells us that once when Byron, years later, was questioned as to Thyrza's identity 'by a person in whose tenderness he never ceased to confide', he 'refused to answer, with marks of painful agitation, such as rendered any farther recurrence to the subject impossible'; and the editor comments: 'The reader must be left to form his own conclusion' (*Poetical Works*, 1837; 549–50, note). But since he very similarly refers to Byron's October correspondence with reference both to *Thyrza* and to the *Childe Harold* stanzas, one of which he relates to Edleston (p. 36), he presumably recognized the truth (*Poetical Works*, 1837; 17, 27, 549, notes; and see 398, 552, notes). So does Maurois (XIV, 133).

This is the high-light of Byron's emotional life, perhaps most perfectly expressed in *The Adieu* in the simple words 'our souls were equal'. If we contrast these poems to Edleston with that stanza in *Childe Harold* which we have already (p. 11) compared with Shakespeare's sonnet on heterosexual lust, we shall, remembering how the Fair Youth was Shakespeare's 'better angel' (Sonnet 144), realize how closely the pattern of Byron's emotional life repeated that of Shakespeare.

We turn last to Augusta Leigh, wife of Colonel George Leigh, the daughter of Byron's father by a former marriage and some years older than Byron. He had met her, before her marriage, as a boy, and during the years 1804 and 1805 he wrote to her frequently. The young Byron found in Augusta one in whom he could confide and who made up for his difficult relationship with his mother; the nature of this youthful correspondence has been excellently handled by Drinkwater (II, 95–104). There was more correspondence, but Augusta does not assume any primary importance in our story until the year 1813. Hitherto they had rarely met; but during July and August of that year both Byron and Augusta were in London, and, though they did not live together (Maurois, II; XVIII, 174), they saw each other frequently; and it is then that it is supposed by many that incest occurred between them. Augusta also visited him at Newstead for three weeks during January, 1814, and again later; and Byron visited her home, near Newmarket.

The attachment has been so thoroughly, if indecisively, worked over that comparatively little need here be said concerning it. In justice to Byron and Augusta, Drinkwater's careful account (III, 227–234) must be followed, and the arguments of C. E. Vulliamy faced. If there were anything in the rumours that certainly arose, it is strange that Augusta's husband, Colonel Leigh, appears to have remained unconcerned; that Augusta's position in society was not affected; and that soon after Miss Milbanke, who was a model of respectability, should have accepted Byron's proposal of marriage (Vulliamy, VIII, 106–13).

At this period our only solid evidence for incest occurs in Byron's letters to Lady Melbourne in 1814, which were not published until they appeared in the two volumes *Lord Byron's Correspondence* in 1922. One of his letters about Mary Chaworth Musters, dated 11 January, 1814, is often supposed to give us a hint:

'I have heard from (what new initial shall we fix upon?) M. again, and am at a loss. You must advise me. I will tell you why. It is impossible I should now feel anything beyond friendship for her or anyone else in present circumstances; and the kind of feeling which has lately absorbed me has a mixture of the terrible, which renders all other, even passion (pour les autres) insipid to a degree; in short, one of its effects has been like the habit of Mithridates, who by using himself gradually to poison of the strongest kind, at last rendered all others ineffectual when he sought them as a remedy for all evils, and a release from existence.'

(C, I, 227)

That may refer to Augusta. On 15 April, 1814, Augusta gave birth to a daughter, who was christened Medora. Byron's fatherhood has been suspected, and a facetious letter of his to Lady Melbourne on 25 April appears, at first sight anyway, to admit it:

'Oh! but it is "worth while", I can't tell you why, and it is *not* an "*Ape*", and if it is, that must be my fault; however, I will positively reform. You must however allow that it is utterly impossible I can ever be half so well liked elsewhere, and I have been all my life trying to make someone love me, and never got the sort that I preferred before. But positively she and I will grow good and all that, and so we are *now* and shall be these three weeks and more too.'

(C, I, 251)

Our third extract, dated 30 April, 1814, opens as follows:

'*You*—or rather *I*—have done *my A* much injustice. The expression
which you recollect as objectionable meant only "loving" in the
senseless sense of that wide word, and it must be some selfish stupid-
ity of mine in telling my own story, but really and truly—as I hope
mercy and happiness for her—by that God who made me for my
own misery, and not much for the good of others, *she* was not to
blame, one thousandth part in comparison. She was not aware of
her own peril till it was too late, and I can only account for her
subsequent "*abandon*" by an observation which I think is not unjust,
that women are much more *attached* than men if they are treated
with anything like fairness or tenderness.'

(C, I, 254)

Later in the letter he says:

'As for my A, my feelings towards her are a mixture of good and
diabolical. I hardly know one passion which has not some share in
them, but I won't run into the subject.'

(C, I, 255)

This is our evidence.

To many it will seem strong. Our first extract might, it is true,
refer equally well to some homosexual engagement, but it corresponds exactly with the use of 'diabolical' in the third. The second
extract is precise, referring to an old superstition that the child of
incest must be a monster; but the passage is pitched on a facetious
note, and refers to a superstition which no one believes. The words
'that must be my fault' do not precisely fit a child of Byron's, since
then the child itself, not just its appearance, would be his 'fault'; and
Byron's most careless prose is exact. A nearer meaning may be: 'If
the child of Colonel Leigh and Augusta is an Ape that must be
caused by my close association with her.' It is difficult to believe that,
had Byron really been the father, Augusta would have done what
she could to drive home the scandal by naming Medora after the
heroine of his recently published narrative, *The Corsair*. The action
does not make sense.

Our third extract, while suggesting as much sin as is possible in a
non-committal way, *simultaneously* asserts that what is meant is a
non-sensuous love. In so far as these extracts are evidence, we find
that not one firmly admits incest, and that the last denies it.

We are accordingly left guessing. The moral aspect is not, per-haps, of overriding importance. Both Lord Lovelace and André Maurois refuse to regard sexual intercourse as between these two as a great sin. Lovelace's view we shall discuss in due course. Maurois calls it 'something of an imaginary crime'; she was only a half-sister, and Byron had hardly ever seen her before the year 1813 (Preface, 12); indeed, 'it could almost be said that it was Byron, and he alone, who, by giving to this quite natural love for an unknown half-sister the name of incest, transformed the lapse into a crime' (II; XVIII, 175); the reference being, presumably, to some reported words of Byron. He is known to have spoken rashly on this, as on all other, matters.

Byron liked arousing people's suspicions. In his diary Moore notes of another lady: 'Lord Byron *did* endeavour to make her think that he murdered some one . . . This at first alarmed ——, but when she came to know him better she saw through his acting * * * Must enquire more about this' (Moore's *Memoirs, etc.*, 10 Nov., 1827; v, 233). So often asterisks appear at the telling moments. On one occasion in Greece he expressed the wish to experience the feelings of a murderer (Galt, XXIV, 156). Both Stendhal and Goethe half believed that he had committed some romantic murder (LJ, III, App. VIII, 440; v, App. II, 506). Hobhouse records that Augusta her-self used to say: 'Byron is never so happy as when he can make you believe some atrocity against himself' (Hobhouse, II; XV, 283). Moore tells us that there was 'hardly any crime so dark or desperate' of which he might not on occasion hint that he had been guilty (Moore, LVII, 648). This was a trait everyone recognised, and evidence of it abounds. Referring to scandals, he once, as we have seen, wrote, 'Am I not in reality much worse than they make me?' (Lady Melbourne, March, 1814; C, I, 247). He perhaps satisfied his con-science, troubled by secrets undivulged, in this way.

There is another possible reason for these incriminating letters to Lady Melbourne. She was a woman of the world whose lax morals Byron probably found both entertaining and shocking. Now when she showed disapproval of his proposal to go abroad with Augusta, who according to Byron (Lady Melbourne, 21 Aug., 1813; and see 26 June, 1814; C, I, 175, 261) wished it, he remarked: 'She is a good woman after all, for there are things she will stop at' (Lady Byron's notes, quoted Lovelace, II, 34). Had Byron's letters to her been written in part merely to *test her response*? Much of Byron's life was, like his affair with Lady Frances—remember his pleasure at

Lady Melbourne's approval of his 'ethics', and his remark on Lady Frances 'it has enlivened my ethical studies on the human mind beyond fifty volumes' (pp. 20–1)—a deliberately controlled dramatic experiment; he had a vivisectional interest in the society of his day, and was always ready, if need be, to cast himself for the role of guinea-pig. Lord Lovelace puts it well: 'When he took a part in the low comedy of bad company, his immutable self, unknown to such bystanders, was watching in tragic contemplation of the ribald nightmare, judging and condemning the transient self with the surrounding crew' (Lovelace, I, 12). 'Anything', Byron wrote, 'that confirms or extends one's observations on life and character delights me' (Lady Melbourne, 1 Oct., 1813; C, I, 187); and again, 'How I do delight in observing life as it really is!—and myself, after all, the worst of any' (Journal, 17–18 Dec., 1813; LJ, II, 378). Was he 'observing' Lady Melbourne's responses?

There appears, however, to be no certain evidence that Lady Melbourne warned Byron not to go abroad at all. All we have is a letter of Byron to her saying that one of hers is 'unanswerable' (31 Aug., 1813; C, I, 177), and the rest has merely been assumed on the evidence of a reported 1817 memorandum by Lady Byron (Lovelace, II, 33–4; Fox, X, 73; Drinkwater, III, 234), whose evidence at that period was, as we shall see, utterly untrustworthy. Lady Byron, who certainly cannot be trusted in this matter, quotes some supposedly condemnatory words spoken by Lady Melbourne and Byron's comments (Lovelace, II, 33). Drinkwater observes that the evidence produced in this instance by the supporters of incest is 'as unimpressive as it has a way of being at crucial moments' (Drinkwater, III, 234). So Byron's remark, if indeed he ever made such a remark, may conceivably have referred to some other matter altogether.

Whatever may have been Byron's reasons for using them, it is hard to accept the phrase 'a mixture of the terrible' and the word 'diabolical' (pp. 39, 40) as adequately defining any important part or aspect of Byron's love for Augusta, since this love is, as we shall see, throughout his life so strongly characterised by thoughts of 'purity' not unlike the 'purity' of his early loves for Mary Chaworth and John Edleston, with Augusta functioning as moral and spiritual support. Here is an early example. On 8 November, 1813, after leaving the Wedderburn Websters, Byron wrote to Augusta from London:

'My Dearest Augusta,

'I have only time to say that I shall write tomorrow, and that my present and long silence has been occasioned by a thousand things (with which *you* are not concerned). It is not Lady C, nor O; but perhaps you may *guess*, and if you do, do not tell.

'You do not know what mischief your being with me might have prevented. You shall hear from me to-morrow; in the meantime don't be alarmed. I am in *no immediate* peril.

'Believe me, ever your,

B.'

(LJ, II, 277)

The reference may, or may not, be to Lady Frances. But is that conceivably the letter of a man to an accomplice in what he himself regards as a criminal love? And what is the relation of this letter to the dark *Macbeth* thoughts contained soon after in a letter to Moore concerning the writing of *The Bride of Abydos* 'to wring my thoughts from reality, and take refuge in "imaginings" however "horrible"' (Moore, 30 Nov., 1813; LJ, II, 293; *Macbeth*, I, iii). We must, too, observe that Zuleika in that poem, whom some have equated with Augusta, is as a guiding 'star', one to 'bless' the hero's 'bark', a 'Dove of peace' and 'the rainbow to the storms of life' (II, 20): she is untainted, and the love a supreme positive. Was it only Byron's extraordinary *conscience* that made him regard it as in any sense evil? And what is the awful 'reality' which it replaces? Does Byron refer to each and all of his love-exchanges, however harmless, in these melodramatic terms? Either way, we are warned not to regard the Lady Melbourne correspondence as certain evidence of incest.

At this period, in his letters both to Lady Melbourne and to Moore, Byron was continually referring to mysterious troubles with a goodly sprinkling of initials, asterisks and crosses. He seemed, indeed, to enjoy the thought of baffling us today, once, well before his association with Augusta, observing to Lady Melbourne that a certain initial would puzzle posterity 'when our correspondence bursts forth in the twentieth century' (6 November, 1812; C, I, 102). He was right in so far as the letters to Lady Melbourne were first published in 1922.

Now, whereas there is once a name which he dared not even write in private (Journal, 14 Nov., 1813; LJ, II, 314; see p. 139 below), Augusta's can be set down freely. Thinking of joining the revolution

43

in Holland, he writes: 'And why not? * * * is distant and will be at * * *, still more distant, till spring. No one else, except Augusta, cares for me'; and his suicide 'would annoy Augusta and perhaps * * *' (Journal 23 Nov. and 10 Dec., 1813; LJ, II, 340, 371). Richard Edgcumbe relates these asterisks to Mary Chaworth Musters; he appears justified in thinking that the name Byron dared not write even in private could scarcely be that of Lady Frances (Edgcumbe, II, 259); but he has a personal theory, and there is, indeed, little that he does not relate to Mary. To these problems we shall return.

Peter Quennell recounts that in 1812, *well before Byron's association with Augusta* and during the difficulties with Lady Caroline, Byron, apropos of his own unresponsiveness to her wayward daughter, confessed something to Caroline's mother both 'terrifying' and 'extraordinary', perhaps admitting to some relationship 'of a more scandalous kind' or hinting 'that his real tastes were more eclectic' (Quennell, v, 157; the Penguin, 1954, edition reads 'more esoteric'; v, 113). Are these strange 'tastes' behind some of our other mysteries and innuendos? And may not that other fearful disclosure to Caroline herself, with which Byron seems finally to have crushed her love (Quennell, x, 277), have been of similar sort? It is perhaps relevant to recall, once again, that Caroline was in the habit of forcing her attentions on Byron in the guise of a boy.

The women who affected Byron most deeply before his marriage appear all to have been relations: Mary Duff, Margaret Parker, Mary Anne Chaworth were cousins, and Augusta Leigh a half-sister. It has been recognized by both Maurois and Du Bos that Byron's 'familial' love for Augusta has a certain metaphysical, or at least psychological, significance. It reflects, we may say, a kind of self-sufficiency in the man of genius, a lack of need to find completion elsewhere; and so, in a rather different way, may his homosexual engagements, too, in that he is there searching for satisfaction in one of similar sex. Both sorts of love can be seen, if we wish, in terms of self-reflection and self-sufficiency; and that is why he wrote of Edleston in *The Adieu*, 'our souls were equal'.

Did Byron himself recognize that the two loves were of the same kind? And is this why he was so interested in themes of incest, in *The Bride of Abydos* and elsewhere, and so eager to make the most, or worst, of his love for Augusta? Did he welcome it as an alternative?

And there were other alternatives. Byron also found his true soulmates in nations, especially subjected nations; or classes, like the cotton-weavers of Nottingham; or any causes which demanded protection and sacrifice. Indeed such impulses were merely extensions of the other. During his many games with the convent boys and his romance with Nicolo at Athens in 1811, he was also composing his grave political commentary on Greece for the notes to *Childe Harold*; and in 1824 at Missolonghi his thoughts during the last weeks of his life were divided between (i) Greece and (ii) the boy Loukas (p. 216 below).

And yet he was not able to live a celibate life; nor was there anything in his *milieu* to encourage, or enable, him to do so. As Peter Quennell brilliantly suggests, he might have been happier, one way or the other, in ancient Greece or, with his strong cloisteral and ascetic instincts (see CV, Index A, IV, XVI), medieval Europe (Quennell, XII, 358). As things were, however, he could not help loving: 'I cannot exist', he wrote, 'without some object of love' (Lady Melbourne, 9 Nov., 1812; C, I, 104); and again, 'It is unlucky we can neither live with nor without these women' (Moore, 22 Aug., 1813; LJ, II, 251). His life was complicated beyond all reason; he wished for peace and respected morality; and that is why he took the conventional step, and married.

IV

In the year 1812 Miss Anne Isabella Milbanke, daughter of Sir Ralph Milbanke and niece of Lady Melbourne, having read *Childe Harold*, desired an introduction to Byron. She was generally considered a girl of great gifts and impeccable virtue. She was a mathematician, a woman of a 'commanding mind,' who had, as Mrs. Beecher Stowe tells us, the soul 'not only of an angelic woman, but of a strong, reasoning, man' (Stowe, II, 136; III, 290). Byron, at first rather tentatively, admired her: 'She is too good', he wrote, 'for a fallen spirit to know, and I should like her more if she were less perfect' (Caroline Lamb, 1 May, 1812; LJ, II, 121). He has listed for us her gifts and qualities: 'She is a poetess—a mathematician—a metaphysician, and yet, withal, very kind, generous, and gentle, with very little pretension. Any other head would be turned with half her acquisitions, and a tenth of her advantages' (Journal, 30 Nov., 1813; LJ, II, 357). He dubbed her 'the princess of parallelograms'.

Some time in October, 1812, Byron got Lady Melbourne to forward a proposal of marriage, but Miss Milbanke declined.

However, Annabella, for so she was called, re-opened the matter in the summer of 1813 by writing Byron a letter of friendly advice (Maurois, II; XXI, 204). Though still little more than a girl, she prided herself, not altogether without reason, on her insight. He wrote back, answering questions concerning himself and his religion (Miss Milbanke, 26 Sept., 1813; LJ, III, 401-4).

Byron the moralist naturally saw in her a woman of principle above the average, and one whose intellect and imagination, for her verses were promising, he respected. She, on her part, was, like everyone else, fascinated by the man of charm and genius, and, though aware of many failings, aware also that they might prove the best possible field for the exercise of her own virtues, of which she seems to have been fully aware, could she only act as the moral reclaimer of this famous and splendid being.

She invited him to stay with her parents. Though he did not at first accept the invitation, she continued to write. His letters gradually gained warmth from hers until, in September, 1814, he was brought to the point of a second proposal. He had, as he once told Lady Blessington, persuaded himself that he 'ought' to marry (Blessington, 109). Both Lady Melbourne and Augusta were in favour of his marrying, though Augusta had doubts concerning Annabella; and it is true that just before writing to her, Byron had tried another lady, who turned him down. The two proposal letters were discussed with Augusta, and now Annabella accepted. Years later Lady Byron told Mrs. Stowe how she had discovered in one of Byron's journals a note made on receiving her acceptance: 'A letter from Bell—never rains but it pours' (Stowe, II, 156). Byron went to stay with the family as a prospective bridegroom.

It is generally recognized that Annabella was throughout the prime mover, as indeed were all Byron's female lovers, if indeed 'love' is the right word to designate the emotions which brought about this strange union. Byron certainly married less for love than as an escape from love. He wanted, or thought that he wanted, peace and security.

He is usually blamed for his choice. But perhaps it was not so foolish. He himself, like so many men of genius, was a bisexual type, with a strong feminine strain, observed by his friends (CV, II, 81); and Annabella was a woman of male intelligence, addicted, like

46

Byron, to passionate friendships with people of her own sex (p. 276). Might not this be a rational match? Bisexual types may be ill-adapted to heterosexual unions; but what if one such marries another? The experiment may have been worth trying.

The marriage took place on 2 January, 1815, with a certain Mrs. Clermont, who had been Lady Byron's governess, in attendance and Hobhouse as best man. After it Hobhouse, who knew, and regularly tried to suppress, most of what there was to know of Byron's real instincts, commented in his diary (Hobhouse, I, 196), 'I felt as if I had buried a friend'.

II

THE SEPARATION

II. THE SEPARATION

I

WE shall now discuss Byron's separation from his wife. In the process we shall rely heavily on Hobhouse's account as published in *Recollections of a Long Life* (1909–1911; p. xiv). This account was originally set down in May, 1816 (Hobhouse, II; xv, 350), directly after the Separation, but was not actually printed until 1870 (p. 233 below). It is a deliberate defence, and must be accepted with caution: factually, we may suppose it to be true, but in tone it may be prejudiced, and we need not assume that it tells the whole truth.

I shall also quote from Mrs. Harriet Beecher Stowe's *Lady Byron Vindicated* (1870) and the Second Edition of Lord Lovelace's *Astarte* (1921).

In discussing Byron's relations with his wife we must be constantly on our guard. No later recollections as to details of behaviour are in themselves trustworthy guides, since it is clear that there was a very serious break of an unknown nature and we can never tell how far this mysterious trouble may have coloured subsequent statements. Certainly rumours as to Byron's actual words as the married couple started for their honeymoon are quite irrelevant. Not only are Lady Byron's, or any one else's, recapitulations of such details untrustworthy, but you can deduce little from a cold transference of the spoken word from its living context into a new one specially prepared to have a certain effect; and least of all with a remark of Byron's, since he regularly spoke out with an almost perverted honesty, and often with a sense of humour or irony which, unless the exact conditions are recaptured, makes deduction hazardous. All we can say is that the honeymoon spent at Halnaby during January 1815 seems to have been reasonably normal. Byron had moods of depression, and Lady Byron afterwards looked back

51

on them, and perhaps on Byron's confession of their cause, in answer to her enquiries, with disquiet (Hobhouse, II; XV, 281). Byron told Medwin that it had its troubles, but was never at zero (Medwin, 39). On 2 February, 1815 he wrote to Moore about his marriage in high satisfaction, calling it 'ambrosial' and looking forward to a happy life (LJ, III, 175). The Byrons visited Augusta at her home at Six Mile Bottom, near Newmarket, in March and, though Lady Byron subsequently hinted that Byron's remarks on this occasion suggested an abnormal relationship, it would be rash to lay any emphasis on that, without a full realization of the nature and purpose of Lady Byron's subsequent actions and endeavours.

Lord and Lady Byron went to London and took up residence at Piccadilly Terrace. Augusta stayed with them awhile, and then went home. On 4 August Hobhouse's diary hints that Byron was in financial difficulties and regretting his marriage (Hobhouse, I; VII, 323). In November Augusta returned to stay with them in London, and remained until 16 March, 1816 (Lovelace, II, 48).

During the autumn and winter Byron was clearly in a distressed state. Finances were in confusion. His wife had brought him prospects, but little more, and yet his creditors assumed that he was now well off. The expenses of married life were beyond his means; he made plans to sell his library; and there were a number of executions in his house. He told Hobhouse that his 'financial embarrassments', which he would have minded far less were he not married, were 'such as to drive him half-mad'; and Augusta said that there was something in his manner when talking of these embarrassments which terrified her and might well terrify his wife (Hobhouse, II; XV, 201, 278–9). It must be remembered that Byron was not one to regard business affairs carelessly. In her comprehensive study Teresa Guiccioli emphasized his horror of debt (Teresa, II; XII, 229); and, even when she had begun to think that Byron really was mad, Lady Byron admitted that he was perfectly 'competent to transact business', and indeed 'particularly acute' (Lovelace, II, 40).

Byron's health at this period was bad and so was his wife's. He had, indeed, excuses of a normal sort for whatever strangeness in his behaviour there may have been.

Our first objective evidence of serious matrimonial trouble is from Hobhouse's diary which notes, under 25 November 1815: 'Called on B. In that quarter things do not go well. Strong advice against marriage. Talking of going abroad' (Hobhouse, I; VII, 324). But this does not, in itself, argue any final incompatibility, since Byron also told Hobhouse that he had no complaint to make against his wife, who was 'the very best woman living', and that with any other wife he could not bear his situation 'for an instant' (Hobhouse, II; XV, 223). And yet there was shortly to be a final and irrevocable break.

Among the possible contributory reasons we may suppose that Lady Byron was, on occasion, jealous. She seems to have disapproved of her husband's visits to Melbourne House where he met his old flame and tormentor, Caroline Lamb (Mayne, I; XV, 317). She was also anxious as to Byron's activities on the Drury Lane Committee. An actress named Susan Boyce was certainly in love with him, and what little is known of her is given in Paston and Quennell's *To Lord Byron*. It is even possible that actors as well as actresses may have been involved. But this is pure hazard. All we really know is that Lady Byron was disturbed by Byron's association with the stage and its people. According to Mrs. Stowe (p. 207 below), she seems to have disliked his going to certain parties where he met, among others, George Colman, the dramatist and theatre-manager. Of Colman we shall have much to say in a later section (V).

At this period, too, as indeed throughout his life, Byron's mind was distraught by political conceptions of a vast and unusual kind; he half felt himself to be a potential leader in a world of change and disruption, and oscillated between assurance and self-abasement—the story of it is written into *Manfred*—in a fashion that might well have militated against domestic peace: it was not until after the battle of Waterloo in June 1815, with the onsequent reinstatement of the Bourbon monarchy, that Byron's unrest seems to have become serious. To this, perhaps the central cause of the trouble, we shall return at the conclusion of my study; but first we shall do what we can without relying on so vast and ill-defined a speculation.

The first eight months of the marriage cannot have borne much resemblance to what Lady Byron was later to make of them. On 5 July, 1815, Augusta had written to Hobhouse saying that Byron was looking 'particularly well'; that 'the only drawbacks to their present happiness and comfort' were 'pecuniary concerns'; and that he was looking forward to accepting his father-in-law's offer to let them occupy his Seaham residence (Hobhouse, II, App. A, 357–8). That is firm evidence from one who understood Byron and had his interest at heart. Again, an American, George Ticknor, who called on the Byrons 'several times' during the summer of 1815, 'was impressed by the poet's simple goodness, gentleness, and vivacity, and by his patent affection for his wife' (Joyce, VIII, 95). At the end of August, 1815, some six months after they were married, we find Lady Byron writing to Byron, who was on a visit to Augusta and had asked for some medicine, as follows:

'Darling Duck—I feel as if B. loved *himself*, which does me more good than anything else, and makes young Pip jump.'

The reference is to Byron's lack of self-consideration in matters of health. 'Duck' was their nick-name for Byron, and she was 'Pip'. She does not like being separated. All his faults are preferable to that. So

'Indeed, indeed, *nau* B. is a thousand times better than no B . . . I dare not write any more for fear you should be frightened of the length, and not read at all, so I shall give the rest to Goose!

'I hope you call out "Pip, pip, pip" now and then—I think I hear you; but I won't grow lemoncholy . . . A—da.'

(Mayne, Lady Byron, XIII, 187–8)

'Goose' is Augusta. 'A—da' may refer to their future child.

Anyone who thinks that this can be the letter of a wife who had already suffered six months systematic and deliberately planned brutality from her husband is, indeed, entitled to think so; but credulity is strained. That is what Lady Byron was soon to assert: to the end of her life she seems to have gone on drawing pictures of her marriage which were false, and which have sadly misled one biographer after another.

She was, as we shall see, worried about his state of mind during the autumn, and wrote to Augusta of it (Mayne, *Lady Byron*, XIII, 194–6). But she and Byron worked together. She copied out *Parisina* for him, probably in November or early December (P, III, 499; and see Murray, 3 Jan., 1816; LJ, III, 251), and wrote to Lady Melbourne on 4 January, 1816, of its approaching publication with *The Siege of Corinth* (LJ, III, 292).

We also have some ably turned lines of hers composed probably during the autumn, which show a playful tolerance that is most revealing. These come in a satiric poem on the Drury Lane Committee, mainly directed against its Chairman and Byron's friend the banker Douglas Kinnaird, as a magpie who

chatters so mal-a-propos
Too foolish the mischiefs it causes to know.

The lines on Byron himself are revealing in their playful mingling of kindly criticism and genuine admiration:

> *Then there's Byron, ashamed to appear like a Poet,*
> *He talks of finances, for fear he should show it—*
> *And makes all the envious Dandys despair*
> *By the cut of his shirt and the curl of his hair.*

(LJ, III, 291)

The lines, written some time before the birth of Ada, were addressed to Augusta. To these verses Lady Byron added the remark, for Augusta:

'I believe B. will go to the theatre tonight; but you seem to have mistaken, for the mischief has not lately taken place *there* but after *his return*—when alone. I grow more unable to sit up late.'

(LJ, III, 291)

The 'mischief' is left undefined. It seems to have something to do with Byron's Drury Lane contacts, but appears, from this remark, to be an inward and mental matter.

Years later Lady Byron, despite her life-long bitterness, admitted freely that Byron had often been loving to her. She told Mrs. Beecher Stowe of his 'pleasant little speeches' (Stowe, II, 144), and that lady reports:

'There were lucid intervals in which Lord Byron felt the charm of his wife's mind, and the strength of her powers. "Bell, you could be a poet too, if you only thought so," he would say. There were summer hours in her stormy life, the memory of which never left her, when Byron was as gentle and tender as he was beautiful; when he seemed to be possessed by a good angel: and then for a little time all the ideal possibilities of his nature stood revealed.'

(Stowe, III, 289)

'My dear', she would say to Mrs. Stowe, 'there was an angel in him' (Stowe, III, 299). We may suppose that these remarks, reported by one hostile authority from the conversation of another, fall well below the facts.

As we have seen, they called each other by nicknames, with Byron as 'Duck', his wife 'Pippin', and Augusta 'Goose', and we have every reason to suppose that they were often enough happy. On the evidence we may say that the relationship at its best was a *playful* relationship: that is the word for it. That, too, may have been what Byron wanted; perhaps she was there mainly, in his thoughts, for moments of relaxation. But Lady Byron was not quite the type for that; she was, as Mrs. Stowe tells us, a woman of 'commanding mind', with the soul 'not only of an angelic woman, but of a strong reasoning man' (Stowe, II, 136; III, 290). Such a woman might well find it impossible to go on playing the part of a relaxation, and there may be a trace of Ibsen's *Doll's House* in our story.

On 10 December the child was born, Augusta Ada, named after Byron's half-sister, who was still staying with them. Lady Byron and Augusta were fast friends, almost lovers—for Lady Byron, like her husband, had strong homosexual propensities (p. 276)—and they were jointly anxious about Byron. Both of them, as well as Byron's cousin Captain George Anson Byron, were aware that he was in a strange mental state (Hobhouse, II; xv, 207, 348–9; Augusta to Hobhouse, 21 May, 1816; 364). Lady Byron consulted a physician.

On 15th January she left London for Kirkby Mallory in Leicester-shire to stay with her parents, now Sir Ralph and Lady Noel, the name 'Milbanke' having been dropped and 'Noel' adopted on the death of Lady Milbanke's brother, Lord Wentworth, according to the terms of his will. It is not quite clear who first suggested her going, since we have different accounts. Lovelace prints a note of 6 January from Byron referring to the urgent need for 'the dismissal of the present establishment' and directing his wife's departure (Lovelace, II, 39), but this tells us nothing of the previous arrange-ments, and its—to us—curt style may be merely a characteristic of the authoritarian manners of the period. According to Hobhouse, Byron admitted sending her a note saying that he wished her to go before the establishment was broken up, and that there was a short altercation, after which she was satisfied and they lived together on 'conjugal' terms up to the last moment (Hobhouse, II; xv, 210, 215). Byron's solicitor, John Hanson, later regarded this living on 'conjugal terms' as an important piece of evidence (Hobhouse, II; xv, 290; and see 278, 350). On her arrival home she wrote to Augusta saying: 'On the whole I am satisfied to have come here. I am sure it was *right*, and must tend to the ultimate advantage of *all*' (LJ, III, 295). She had not liked London, and as early as August had written to Augusta, 'O that I were out of this horrid town, which makes me mad', longing for the country (*Athenaeum*, 18 Aug. 1883; 207; Jeaffreson, App. II, 474). She, like Byron, was suffering from ill-health, and in a state of nerves. Anyway, both Byron and Lady Byron appear subsequently to assume that she had left him willingly, (pp. 61, 63, 65 below), and it had been agreed that he should follow.

What we hear afterwards about an agonised marriage must not prevent our facing the quite solid evidence that the relationship had been, often anyway, normal, and even happy: Byron was soon to recall to his wife their *daily* interchanges of married companionship (p. 61 below). Now Lady Byron's letters directly after her departure exactly fit such a supposition. Of the first, written from Woburn, on the journey, we have a fragment only, which runs:

'We arrived here safely—the child is the best of travellers. Now do leave off the abominable trade of versifying, and brandy, everything that is nau . . .'

(Hobhouse, II; xv, 238)

The rest, says Hobhouse, is lost. Hobhouse takes the word 'naughty' to refer to an act of infidelity admitted by Byron (p. 67 below). This was no major offence in Regency England, and his wife obviously, if this be the reference, regarded it as venial; but the reference may be different, and involve some less acceptable fault, which Hobhouse may be intentionally veiling. The word 'nau', which had already appeared in her August letter (p. 54), may hold some special significance lost to us.[1] Our second letter, written on her arrival at Kirkby Mallory, is even more revealing:

Kirkby, January 16, 1816.
'Dearest Duck,
    'We got here quite well last night, and were ushered into the kitchen instead of drawing room, by a mistake that might have been agreeable enough to hungry people . . . Of this and other incidents Dad wants to write you a jocose account, and both he and Mam long to have the family party completed . . . Such . . .! and such a *sitting*-room or *sulking*-room, all to yourself. If I were not always looking about for B, I should be a great deal better already for country air. *Miss* finds her provisions increased, and fattens thereon. It is a good thing she can't understand all the flattery bestowed upon

[1] Sir John Fox quotes another version of this Woburn letter given as from Lord Lovelace's papers. This we shall quote in due course (p. 207).

her. "Little angel" . . . and I know not what . . . Love to the good
goose, and everybody's love to you both from hence.

    'Ever thy most loving,

Pippin . . . Pip . . . Ip'.
(Hobhouse, II; xv, 203)

Lady Byron wrote simultaneously to the 'good Goose', Augusta,
whom she had left to care for her husband, urging that Byron should
come on (LJ, III, 295). The Noel family were all anxious for his arrival,
Lady Noel writing also. One of Lady Byron's letters to Augusta
contains the words 'God Bless you and *him*' (undated, LJ, III, 298).

These were the last gestures of friendliness made by Lady Byron.
Soon after, she and her parents were irrevocably hostile.

Lady Byron claimed afterwards, both in a letter of 13 February
1816 and in her *Remarks on Moore's Life of Byron* (pp. 61, 75 below),
that she at first wrote brightly to her husband merely because the
doctor had told her to avoid 'all but light and soothing topics'.
Hobhouse observes that the letter scarcely reads 'as a prescription
against a paroxysm'; and says that, if it was 'written by an injured
and terrified woman' to 'soothe the insanity and play with the pernicious propensities' of her lord, it was 'as little admirable for its
artifice as for its composition'; and wonders if Sir Ralph Noel's
'jocose account' was to have been penned 'with the same charitable
purpose' (Hobhouse, II; xv, 204-5, 247).

It is, however, true that Lady Byron had indeed been acting on
the supposition that Byron was insane. She, or someone else for her
(see p. 102), had searched his papers and his drawers, and found an
indecent book hidden away. She consulted a medical journal and
discussed symptoms with the doctor (Hobhouse, II; xv, 250). But
now, soon after her arrival home, she heard from one of the two
doctors whom she had consulted and who had, according to her
arrangement, visited Byron under false pretences, that her husband
could not be called insane, and on hearing that decided that she must
see him no more. We cannot be sure that this *was* the reason for her
decision, but it is the reason given afterwards by her (p. 61). She
appears to have told her parents something concerning her husband
which affected them deeply.

On 20 January Lady Noel hastened to London. There she would
have discussed matters with the enigmatic Mrs. Clermont, former
governess of Lady Byron, who had been staying with Byron and his

wife, had inside knowledge of the household, and appears to play a controlling and none too pleasant part in our story. That she had not gone to Kirkby Mallory with Lady Byron seems clear from the latter's own statement (Fox, XII, 103), though she must have gone there later (p. 70), presumably returning with Lady Noel. She was a peculiarly strong-minded woman who from the days of Lady Byron's childhood had been in the habit of giving 'harassing displays of character' which held the whole household in awe (Mayne, *Lady Byron*, I, 2–3). A defence of her actions is printed by Lady Lovelace (Lovelace, Note IV, 322–5), and Lord Ernle asserts that she wrote 'several sensible letters, deprecating extreme measures' (LJ, III, 268, note). That may be; but Byron had little doubt that it was she who was mainly responsible for the Separation, poisoning Lady Noel's mind against him (Medwin, 42). It seems that she was coldly and unemotionally efficient in helping to force the issue (Hobhouse, II; XV, 207).

Taking with her a statement made by her daughter, Lady Noel sought legal advice from an ecclesiastical lawyer, Dr. Stephen Lushington, and on 2 February Sir Ralph Noel, who had come to town on his wife's return, wrote to Byron saying that 'very recently' facts had come to his knowledge which convinced him that in view of Byron's 'opinions' a separation was necessary. He referred to Byron's 'dismissal' of his wife and, vaguely, to his treatment of her in general, and continued with a threat of public proceedings, calling on 'facts capable of the clearest proof' and asserting that his own action would 'bear the test of the most rigid public investigation', were a private arrangement not negotiated (Hobhouse, II, XV, 209).

In reply Byron wrote on the same day stating firmly that he and his wife had parted in 'apparent', and on his part 'real', harmony and against his immediate inclinations 'at that particular time', since he had wished them to go together. He further took the opportunity to assure her father that he himself had no complaints whatsoever regarding his wife:

'Neither in word or deed, nor (as far as thought can be dived into) thought can I bring to my recollection a fault on her part, or hardly even a failing. She has ever appeared to me as one of the most amiable of human beings, and nearer to perfection than I had conceived could belong to humanity in its present state of existence.'

(Hobhouse, XV; II, 211–12)

He also wrote to his wife, but got no answer. On 5 February he wrote again:

'Dearest Bell,

'No answer from you yet; but perhaps it is as well; only do recollect that all is at stake, the present, the future, and even the colouring of the past. My errors, or by whatever harsher name you choose to call them, you know; but I loved you, and will not part from you without your express and expressed refusal to return to, or receive me. Only say the word that you are still mine in your heart, and

'Kate, I will buckler thee against a million.
Ever, dearest, your most, etc., B.'
(Hobhouse, II; xv, 219)

The quotation is from *The Taming of the Shrew* (III, ii).

But from now on Lady Byron was firm. On 3 February we find her writing to Augusta, who had remained in London to look after Byron and send on reports to his wife, with a request that she remind him of his admitted dislike of marriage (LJ, III, 302). On 7 February she replied to Hobhouse, who had written twice in attempt to pacify her, saying: 'If my determination were not founded on such grounds as made it irrevocable, its adoption would be inexcusable' (Hobhouse, II; xv, 230), thereby admitting that on any *ordinary* supposition she was behaving unreasonably. On the same day she answered Byron's letter with a reference to the 'misery' she had experienced 'almost without an interval from the day of my marriage', and concluding: 'Every expression of feeling, sincerely as it might be made, would here be misplaced' (Hobhouse, II; xv, 236). Observe that she does not deny the continuance of her affection, but finds it her *duty* to crush all those emotions so clearly present in her first playful letters. The admission is important. On 28 January, after specifically asking to be left in ignorance as to Byron's emotions, she had told Augusta, 'I dare not *feel* anything now'; and on 14 February, after referring to her love for him, she pulls herself up with, 'I must not remember these feelings' (LJ, III, 302, 311). When Byron's friends were anxious at his evident suffering and Augusta told Lady Byron that if she did not return she could not answer for Byron's life—for they feared suicide —Lady Byron merely answered that 'she could not help it', and 'must do her duty' (Hobhouse, II; xv, 260).

Byron could not make it out. On 8 February he answered his wife:

'Were you, then, *never* happy with me? Did you never at any time or times express yourself so? Have no marks of affection of the warmest and most reciprocal attachment passed between us? or did in fact hardly a day go down without some such on one side, and generally on both? Do not mistake me: I have not denied my state of mind—but you know its causes—and were those deviations from calmness never followed by acknowledgments and repentance? Was not the last that recurred more particularly so? and had I not—had we not the days before and on the day we parted—every reason to believe that we loved each other? that we were to meet again? Were not your letters kind? Had I not acknowledged to you all my faults and follies—and assured you that some had not and could not be repeated? I do not require these questions to be answered to me, but to your own heart . . . You are much changed within these twenty days, or you would never have thus poisoned your own better feelings—and trampled on mine.'

(Hobhouse II; xv, 239)

She replied on 11 February with a curt note saying that 'the language of feeling' ought not to be brought into the matter (Hobhouse, II; xv, 242). It was now to her a matter of cold, objective, duty. Hobhouse thinks Byron's letter had disturbed her, showing her that she was acting wrongly and leaving her with no real justification, either then or for the rest of her life (II; xv, 243). On 13 February she wrote again, saying, in apparent contradiction of her father's remark as to her 'dismissal', that her absence had been recommended on 'medical' grounds in order to avoid causing irritation; that her playful letter had merely been devised to get him to her home for proper treatment; that, though she had been prepared to nurse him had he been really ill, the report as to his sanity had altered everything; reminding him of her remonstrances in the past and of his 'determination to be wicked', and attributing his state of mind to a '*total* dereliction of principle, which, since our marriage, you have professed and gloried in' (LJ, III, 309–10; Hobhouse, II; xv, 244–5). Observe that Byron was being accused of immoral principles and behaviour. Part of the substance of this letter was repeated in her 1830 *Remarks on Moore's Life of Byron* (LJ, III, 287).

Let us again emphasise our main discrepancy. On the one side we have Byron writing on 7 February 1816 to Sir Ralph Noel:

'Lady B. left London without a single hint of such feelings or intentions—neither did they transpire in her letters on the road, nor subsequent to her arrival at Kirkby. In these letters Lady Byron expresses herself to me with that playful confidence and affectionate liveliness which is perhaps a greater proof of attachment than more serious professions; she speaks to her husband of his child, like a wife and a mother. I am therefore reduced to the melancholy alternative of either believing her capable of a duplicity very foreign to my opinion of her character, or that she has lately sunk under influence, the admission of which, however respected and respectable heretofore, is not recognised in her vows at the altar.'

(Hobhouse, II; xv, 237)

Two of the letters Byron refers to we have studied, and there were apparently others in similar strain. His account to Medwin in 1821 tells the same story: the parting on good terms, Lady Byron's playful letter, the following bombshell from Sir Ralph Noel, his astonishment, the staggering corroboration from his wife. 'There can be no doubt', he told Medwin, 'that the influence of her (my?) enemies prevailed over her attachment to me' (Medwin 40–1). And here we may record Byron's letter to his wife of 15 February, saying:

'The trial has not been very long—a year, I grant you—of distress, distemper and misfortune; but these fell chiefly on me, and bitter as the recollection is to me of what I have felt, it is much more so to have made you a partner of my desolation.'

He complains of being left in ignorance of the charges against him, whilst being 'exposed to the most black and blighting calumnies of every kind'. He insists

'that I love you, bad or good, mad or rational, miserable or content, I love you, and, shall do, to the dregs of my memory and existence.'

(Hobhouse, II; xv, 257–8)

We need not regard this as necessarily an overstatement. Certainly Byron continued throughout his life to deplore the separation, and his very bitterness may be regarded as a sign of, at the least, affection.

Against all this we have Lady Byron's letters after her change of tone, referring to the 'misery' endured by herself and the wickedness of her husband (pp. 60–1). She puts it clearly in a letter to Byron's friend, Francis Hodgson, dated 15 February:

'I married Lord B. determined to endure everything whilst there was *any* chance of my contributing to his welfare. I remained with him under trials of the severest nature. In leaving him, which, however, I can scarcely call a *voluntary* measure, I probably saved him from the bitterest remorse. I may give you a general idea of what I have experienced, by saying that he married me with the deepest determination of revenge, avowed on the day of my marriage, and executed ever since with systematic and increasing cruelty which no affection could change. My security depended on the total abandonment of every moral and religious principle against which (though I trust they were never obtruded) his hatred and endeavours were uniformly directed. The circumstances, which are of too convincing a nature, shall not be generally known while Lord B. allows me to spare him. It is not unkindness that can always change affection.'

(LJ, III, 313)

Of this we may make what we can. But how, we must ask, does it dovetail with her previous letters? On her arrival at Kirkby Mallory, she had referred merrily enough to Byron's darker moods, offering him a 'sulking-room' (p. 57); and wrote, on the next day, 17 January, 1816, to Captain Byron, saying that her leaving for home was a good move for her husband's sake, since she regarded a change as advisable for him, and her departure was likely to make him leave London the sooner (Fox, XII, 100). She certainly assumed that he would be anxious to follow her. These letters utterly contradict her later descriptions of the marriage as one of undiluted misery and torment.

Some of Lady Byron's earlier letters may help us to understand the transition. Things had started getting bad during August and September. During September Lady Byron wrote to her mother that they dared not leave London in case their move precipitated trouble from their creditors. She says, thereby leaving evidence of her belief at this time of Byron's consideration for her, that he 'is in great anxiety about me and would have me go by myself—which I *will not*' (Mayne, *Lady Byron*, XIII, 190). A house infested by bailiffs was, certainly, no place for a wife. Byron was in a state of torment, but our evidence as to its exact nature is uncertain, since those of Miss Mayne's statements which are drawn from Lady Byron's subsequent reminiscences are, as we shall in due course show, worthless; and, in view of her method of giving references you cannot always tell which come from this source and which from authentic letters. Nor, indeed, are any letters to be trusted if they come from copies among Lady Byron's papers. With this reservation, we may next notice an undated letter from her to Augusta, written probably in October or November, recording a serious outburst of Byron's. He is said to have upbraided her for having married him and blamed her for the vicious courses to which his despair was driving him, though what these vices are is not stated. This unkindness seems to be a new thing, a reversal:

'It seemed impossible to tell if his feelings towards you or me were the most completely reversed; for, as I have told you, he loves or hates us together.'

(Mayne, Lady Byron, XIII, 195)

That is interesting. It is as though Byron was chafing against any or all of those whose regard for him was hampering his course. She adds: 'All is inexorable pride and hardness' (variant below).

Two points may be noticed. First, this is a passionate outbreak at a time of severe financial anxiety, for the bailiff sleeping in the house was an agony to him, Lady Byron telling Augusta of 'his excessive horrors on this subject, which he seems to regard as if no mortal had ever experienced anything so shocking'; and the day after he was kind to her again (Mayne, *Lady Byron*, XIII, 194–5: with variant, 'It is incurable pride and madness', in *The Quarterly*, Jan., 1870; Vol. 128; *223*). Second, the word 'pride' suggests some course of action on Byron's part either vicious, or, as we shall later (p. 270) suggest, political. At this period Byron seems to have felt that his wife and Augusta were together in some way hampering him. We do not know what prompted the outbreak, and Byron may, of course, have had good reason for it. Our study is complicated by the fact that so many of our reports come from Lady Byron. He himself never, until long after the separation, had anything but good to say of his wife.

Whether the account is exaggerated or not, we can say that it helps us to understand the basis of Lady Byron's later *reconstructions*. It was on a reading of such *moods* of Byron's that she later developed the thought of a *consistent and planned* hostility.

Her own letters during January 1816 give us a further insight into

LORD BYRON
from a cameo in the possession
of Mrs. A. L. Sharber

the workings of her mind. On the day of her arrival at Kirkby Mallory, 16 January, 1816, she asked Augusta how Byron was affected by her absence, suggests that in his 'morbid' state he will not be minding it, and that his writing to her would do him good. She was clearly fearing that he might be missing her. And she missed him. In a brief and distracted, undated, note written at this time, we have: 'I have been endeavouring to write off some of my agonies, and have addressed them to B in the enclosed, which I wish you to read attentively . . . God bless you and *him*!' The following thirteen words are erased: 'Tell B (if you think fit) that I am unwell, but not seriously.' She concludes: 'No; I won't send this today.' This letter appears to mark a conflict and a transition, and was probably written before our next. She had presumably been *discussing things with her parents*, and on 19 January we find her writing to Augusta: 'Such is peculiarly the character of Revenge—a passion you know he is capable of feeling, and which has so long formed the *principle of conduct* towards me (as all my retrospections prove) that a change is impossible unless the whole mind were renovated and restored.' Observe that this is presented as a *new thought*; 'capable of feeling' suggests a newly fabricated diagnosis; and 'retrospections' shows that it is a new interpretation, or rationalization. She is *trying* to believe it. On the next day we have: 'All my recollections and reflections tend to convince me that the irritability is inseparably connected with me in a greater degree than with any other object' (to Augusta, 16, undated, 19 and 20 Jan., 1816; LJ, III, 295, 298, 297, 298). Again, we watch her *retrospective* views being *re-shaped*. 'Tend to convince' is a revealing phrase. It is only now that she suspects, or pretends to suspect, that she personally has anything to do with Byron's 'irritability' at all. These are quite certainly *not the words of a wife to whom her husband had been from the first day of the marriage directly and consistently cruel*. This is the transition; once taken, she maintained her course.

II

It may be as well to pause here to record what faults on Byron's side are generally admitted. It is only too likely that Lady Byron did, sometimes, irritate him, even if he seldom showed it. He admitted 'being occasionally much annoyed, on lifting up his head, to observe his wife gazing at him with a mixture of pity and anxiety' (Hob-house, II; xv, 255). Her very consideration may have been an irritant. 'My wife', he would say, after things had begun to grow difficult, 'is perfection itself—the best creature breathing, but, mind what I say—*don't marry*' (Hobhouse, II; xv, 201). But that may, of course, refer mainly to impersonal matters, and it was certainly not the whole story. According to Lady Byron's subsequent reminiscences, which make the most of her sufferings, he used to tell her that if any woman could have rendered marriage endurable to him, she was that woman; that if he had known her from the age of five he might have been happy; and that he feared it was his destiny to ruin all he came near (Mayne, *Lady Byron*, XIII, 190).

Byron's habits were, of course, shockingly unorthodox. Even Teresa Guiccioli admits Lady Byron's difficulties. Byron ate little, his breakfast being the yoke of an egg swallowed standing, and 'a cup of green tea without sugar'; if he dined it was a 'cenobite's meal', while it was 'a real pain to him to see women eat at all'; and he went to bed at dawn. 'Not one of his young wife's habits was shared by him'. Married life was in sharp contrast with 'his beloved solitude', 'his fasts', and his 'hours for study and rest' (Teresa, II; XII, 237, 239). Byron told Medwin in 1821 that his wife did not respect his pre-judices against the sight of women eating, nor his dislike of inter-ruption during work (Medwin, 41). Hobhouse says that his posses-sion of a bottle of laudanum and the keeping of loaded pistols by his bedside, both among Lady Byron's causes of anxiety, were old customs (II; xv, 250, 253).

During the weeks of crisis, Hobhouse, disturbed by the scandals being rumoured, questioned Byron carefully and drew from him a confession. This he reports in his account. We cannot be sure how far he exactly reports Byron's words, or whether he reports them all. Had there been any fact which he regarded as unpublishable he would, as we know from his practice on other occasions, have been capable of slurring it over. But we need not suppose that he was guilty of lying.

He tells us that Byron confessed freely to having been a difficult husband. 'I made', he said, 'no secret of hating marriage'—an avowal Lady Byron not unnaturally, in a letter to Augusta of 3 February, 1816, regarded as cause for complaint (LJ, III, 302)—'but was equally explicit in avowing my love for her'. He also admitted to having been on occasion frantic, sullen, and morose; but his violence was never directed against his wife, and he was as often loving, holding her on his knee and confessing—and here his wisdom may be questioned, since for Byron confession meant admitting responsibility for every secretest thought and impulse—all his sins to her and leaving out nothing: 'Even those errors which must have been most offensive to herself', he said, 'whether in word or deed, were communicated with an unreserve which may have been mistaken for insult, but which was not meant for such'. His assurance of her veracity, he said, even made him think she must have some foundation for her charges; 'and I am therefore inclined at times to believe that at some periods of my married life I might have been deprived of reason, for I solemnly protest that I am unconscious of the commission of any enormity which can have prompted Lady Byron to desert me thus suddenly, thus cruelly' (Hobhouse, II; xv, 277). He admitted many subsidiary instances of disagreement and incompatibility, among them a single example of infidelity, which he had immediately confessed and for which he had received her pardon. He had also refused to meet certain of Lady Byron's friends, and talked of going abroad, or living alone in London. Hobhouse concludes that he had indeed been guilty of 'some inexcusable indiscretions' and foolish behaviour, but says that he and Byron's other supporters came to the conclusion that he 'had not been guilty of any enormity', and that the charges against him were of a sort normal enough in ill-sorted marriages (Hobhouse, II; xv, 281–3).

Byron never denied that he had been difficult. According to Medwin he recalled, in 1821, making only one harsh remark to her, but Lady Blessington says that he admitted, in 1823, that he had been in a general way 'gloomy', 'violent', and 'personally uncivil', and had accordingly 'disgusted' his wife, though had she really loved him all might have been well (Medwin, 42; Blessington, 163). As for his supposed insanity, he told Medwin that the doctor secretly employed by his wife to test his sanity 'could not conscientiously make me out a certificate for Bedlam', though he felt that his habit of looking down when he met his wife's eyes was a serious symptom, recalling George III (Medwin, 45). Lady Byron had indeed, when questioned whether she had been afraid of her husband, answered: 'Oh, no, not in the least; my eye can always put down his' (Hobhouse, reporting Hanson, II; xv, 253).

George Finlay, writing in June 1824, says that, in discussion of the matter towards the close of his life, Byron 'gave his denials and explanations with the frankness of an unconcerned person' (Edgcumbe, I, 99). But to the end he maintained his original position; that is, that 'unless a total oblivion had surprised him of all that had happened during his marriage, it was absolutely false that he had been guilty of any enormity—that nothing could or would be proved by anybody against him, and that he was prepared for anything that could be said in any court' (Hobhouse, II; xv, 291).

Much of the trouble appears to have derived from Byron's conversation. Lady Byron's statement to the doctor referred to her husband's strange 'sayings' and 'singularities of manner and look' (Hobhouse, II; xv, 251). His talk, as all our authorities observe (CV, Index A, IV, 'Self-Accusations'), showed an extraordinary tendency to self-accusation. Hobhouse considered that Lady Byron was temperamentally incapable of understanding his peculiarities, quite apart from any real faults which he may have confessed in the 'warmth of confidence or passion' (II; xv, 248, 347–8). What exactly the confessions were, we are not told. Hobhouse preserves a certain vagueness:

'He was in the habit of communicating all his passing notions, paradoxical or not, to her; and the more she expressed her surprise the more highly did he colour his sentiments, and to clench his doctrine sometimes represented his principles as being deduced from his own practice. His friends had long been acquainted with this singular love of the marvellous in morals which Lord Byron evinced in his conversation and his compositions, but which he was so far from carrying into his own conduct that no man was ever more commonplace than himself in an habitual display of kindness, generosity, and all the every-day virtues of civilized life. He had the habit of marking in his books traits of singular depravity, and poor Lady Byron mistook these marks for notes of admiration. His sister has more than once said, half jokingly, "Byron is never so happy as when he can make you believe some atrocity against himself."'

(Hobhouse, II; xv, 282)

We must remember that Sir Ralph Noel's original complaint involved Byron's 'opinions'; and Hobhouse was insistent, from the evidence of this first statement, following so soon after Lady Byron's letter of endearment, that what turned the balance was some thing or things Lady Byron told her parents that Byron had *said* (Hobhouse, II; xv, 206, 214–15). His general conclusion is that Lady Byron had 'fatally mistaken' her husband (II; xv, 353).

Such is Hobhouse's more formal statement. Michael Joyce, using presumably some unpublished papers, quotes from a part of Hobhouse's diary giving a rather different account of his questioning of his friend. On 12 February he records that, having learned from both Byron's cousin, Captain George Byron, and Augusta of 'very great tyranny, menaces, furies, neglects and even real injuries, such as telling his wife he was living with another woman, and actually in fact turning her out of the house', he began to fear that Byron was deceiving him, and taxed him with it. The record continues:

'I got him to own much of what I had been told in the morning. He was dreadfully agitated, said he was ruined and would blow out his brains. He is indignant, but yet terrified sometimes, says "and yet she loved me once", and at other times that he is glad to be quit of such a woman . . . I took leave of my poor friend—Alas! what a ruin.'

(Quoted Joyce, VIII, 101)

Michael Joyce concludes that Hobhouse 'determined to conceal Byron's admissions', and did so 'a few months later'; that is, in the formal account from which we have been quoting.

This at first seems true. But notice that there is no factual discrepancy of any great significance. The charges are still general, or refer to words which may have been spoken in momentary anger. Most of them are covered by Hobhouse's more formal and softened account. And when he says, in *that* account, that neither Augusta nor Captain Byron were 'aware of *any individual fact* tending to prove the least violence' (II; xv, 279), the italics make precisely this point. The later statement reads as a more cool and considered survey written after the event, when passions and fears were in abeyance. So we are again left guessing. Hobhouse says that the various complaints show every sign of being 'fictitious and put on to serve a present purpose' (Hobhouse, II; xv, 260). But there is probably more to it than that. We shall, I think, find that we have good cause to suspect that *the real trouble was not being faced openly, or even perhaps privately, by either party*, and we must accordingly distrust everything but the most tangible and water-tight evidence. Much was probably being said by *both* sides in the way of both accusation and confession, in order less to reveal than to veil the truth.

There is clear objective evidence that the marriage was not the systematic torture which Lady Byron, *after her change of attitude*, insisted that it had been. When questioned, Byron's servants were at a loss, saying 'What! Is not my Lady coming back? Is anything the matter?' They attributed the cause of the trouble, as did Byron later, to the mysterious Mrs. Clermont, Lady Byron's governess, who had been staying in the house (Hobhouse, II; xv, 275). Especially important is the official 'Deposition' of Mrs. Fletcher, the wife of Byron's valet, dated 8 March, 1816 (Hobhouse, II; xv, 263–6; a less legally phrased version is given at LJ, III, 320–1). She was serving as lady's maid to Lady Byron and had travelled to Kirkby Mallory with her mistress, and neither then, she said, nor on their arrival, had any reason from Lady Byron's words or actions to suspect a disagreement with her husband. Her mistress was, however, sometimes depressed, and later most deeply troubled at the thought of Sir Ralph's letter, and indeed at one time 'almost insensible', thinking of hastening to town herself, but saying that she was prevented, and not allowed to act 'from her own will'. Mrs. Fletcher goes on to state that Mrs. Clermont, whom, according to Byron's solicitor, Hanson, she called 'that demon' (Hobhouse, II; xv, 263), had 'told deponent not to mind her' (i.e. Lady Byron) 'or pity her, that it was to be expected, and her Ladyship would often be in that low way'; that afterwards Lady Byron never mentioned the matter of going to town, as though forbidden to do so; that Lady Noel pointedly suggested to Mrs. Fletcher that she had told Mrs. Clermont that her mistress had been in danger of her life, saying 'You know it was so', whereas she had to reply that this was what Mrs. Clermont had said to *her*; and that Lady Noel was consequently in 'a great rage', repeating, 'You know it was so.' Mrs. Fletcher herself 'never saw or heard anything unpleasant pass between her master and mistress'. Finally:

'And the deponent further saith, that she has frequently heard Lady Byron express herself in terms of great affection for Lord Byron, and has heard her say that if a separation was to take place between them she would be a wretched creature, and never more be happy; and she has also heard Lady Byron say that her father and mother had insisted that there should be a separation, and that she had passed her word to them that she would herself insist on it, but that she had desired her father and mother not to be too hasty; that the deponent

then asked her Ladyship if she would not retract it. She replied,
"No; it was impossible." '

(Hobhouse II; xv, 266)

When Lady Noel first realized the danger of Mrs. Fletcher's statements, she was in a rage; but subsequently, 'from motives of policy',
as Mrs. Fletcher thought, treated her with especial consideration.
Lady Byron kept her in service, which she would scarcely have done,
says Hobhouse, 'if she had believed her guilty of perjury'; and when,
in April, she spoke to Lady Byron, saying that she hoped she was not
angry with her for saying what was true, her Ladyship replied, 'she
was not, and that it was true' (Hobhouse, II; xv, 267-8). Much later,
we find Byron writing on 20 July, 1819, to Lady Byron, who was
apparently refusing to give Mrs. Fletcher a reference, urging the
injustice of such a course (Lovelace, XI, 291).

The Deposition is corroborated by a letter of Mrs. Fletcher to
her husband saying that her lady was at one time 'rolling on the floor
in a paroxysm of grief' at having promised to separate from her
husband (Hobhouse, II; xv, 220); and Byron told Medwin that he
had heard from Fletcher's wife that Lady Byron tried to withdraw
her letter from the post (Medwin, 41). Hobhouse, after observing
that Mrs. Fletcher's evidence blankly contradicts Lady Byron's statement in her letter to Byron of 7 February, together, we may add,
with her *Remarks on Moore's Life of Byron*, that she had been an
independent agent, supposes that she was either 'the victim of undue
influence' or 'of a sense of duty which made her consider her having
passed her word to her parents a perpetual, irrefragable, obligation'
(Hobhouse II; xv, 268). There is another possibility: that Lady
Byron's parents had opened their daughter's eyes to what she herself
next recognized as a duty; and that, in the performance of that duty,
she was willing to sacrifice her instincts, and even so colour the truth
that it became a series of lies.

That Lady Byron, who was herself far from well at this period,
could exaggerate is clear from the matter of the soda-water bottles.
One of her complaints was that, after she was brought to bed,
Byron 'had made such a noise during *the whole night* by throwing up
soda-water bottles against the ceiling of the room above which she
slept, as to deprive her of her sleep'. But during their investigation
Byron's supporters found no marks on the ceiling at all; the truth
was, Byron had merely been knocking off the heads of the bottles for

71

a reasonable purpose. Hobhouse and others accordingly thought that a woman who could complain that Byron had done this 'in order to disturb her and her child' might have encouraged 'a thousand other extravagant suspicions' (Hobhouse, II; XV, 279, 349; italics Hobhouse's). Byron was always fond of children (CV, II, 75–81), and of his love for his own child we have even Mrs. Clermont's word: 'She had', she said, 'never seen a man so proud and fond of his child as Lord Byron'; Lady Byron had 'more than once said to Lord Byron that he was fonder of the infant than she was', adding 'and fonder of it than you are of me' (Hobhouse, II; XV, 280). Lady Byron herself had never as a child liked dolls, and was not, by nature, a maternal type (p. 276).

Mrs. Fletcher's account of Lady Byron's emotional break-down suggests that she was acting on principle in direct opposition to her instincts. According to Michael Joyce, she wrote to Augusta from Kirkby Mallory: 'O that I were in London if in the coal-hole' (Joyce, VIII, 99). Her cold letters to Byron were written at a severe cost. We have Mrs. Harriet Beecher Stowe's authority for believing that Lady Byron did indeed love Byron and after his death sent for Fletcher, walking about the room in sobs as she tried to elicit from him the meaning of Byron's dying words (Stowe, III, 299).

In Mrs. Fletcher's Deposition we certainly have evidence of a high, objective, order tallying precisely with the general trend of Byron's assertions and Hobhouse's conclusions and utterly contradicting Lady Byron's main contentions after her change of policy. It must be remembered that while men of Hobhouse's rank were always liable to suppress the truth in the name of 'honour', a noble concept which could apparently cover a multitude of otherwise dubious actions, a woman in Mrs. Fletcher's position was under no such constraint. She would probably have regarded any sort of tampering with the truth as a great evil.

In all matters of literary detection, whether in elucidating a work of art or trying to settle a biographical problem, we shall do well to follow Sherlock Holmes' advice to concentrate above all on what appears strange, inexplicable and meaningless; for there especially shall we be likely to uncover the essence, the quiddity, of our problem, which, once found, will throw the rest into pattern. It is fatal to fall back on one of the many techniques which suggest themselves in order to gain a superficial coherence at the expense of the disturbing elements, since we shall thereby probably find ourselves to have ruled out the activating principle behind the whole. So here we must beware of ignoring the sharp incompatibility between Lady Byron's original attitude and that which so suddenly took its place. We must keep firmly in mind the contrast of those playful letters of August and January (pp. 54, 57) and the accusations of systematic torture *from the first day of her marriage* which followed. Hobhouse reiterates his certainty that 'Lady Byron, when she left Lord Byron, had *no notion whatever of a separation*' (Hobhouse, II; xv, 216). Lady Byron's explanation may be logically coherent, but it is humanly insufficient. It does not fit; and Hobhouse was right in rejecting it (II; XV, 247).

That the adverse party were aware of this particular incompatibility is suggested by the rumours that got about saying that the playful letter had been sent to the doctor to show Byron, for purely medical reasons, and that Byron himself had demanded it for evidence. Hobhouse is at pains to insist that it bears Byron's address and 'the Hinkley post-mark' (II; xv, 203). The attempt apparently made to discredit the evidence of this letter is, I think, highly significant.

What, therefore, we have to ask is simply this: what caused the sudden change? Even though the question of madness played its part, that by itself gets us little further until we know what exactly was the nature of this 'boundless and impious pride' (Lady Byron to Augusta, 25 January, 1816; LJ, III, 300), this 'determination to be wicked' and 'total dereliction of principle' (p. 61), what Augusta herself at this period referred to as 'all that is wrong' (to Hodgson, 9 Feb., 1816; LJ, III, 305), and made Lady Noel say that it was 'not fit such men should live' (Hobhouse, II; xv, 207); and which was forgivable in the insane but otherwise abhorrent? Moral values are implied, and we shall, of course, not regard these violent phrases as referring to any such simple Regency vices as marital infidelity of a normal kind. They suggest rather either some Satanic political or theological challenge or, if sexual vice is involved, then vice of some 'perverted' variety. We should, moreover, realize that much of the talk of Byron's cruelty and violent behaviour is probably merest camouflage. Once Hobhouse jotted down beside a passage of Moore's *Life of Byron*, 'This is wrong. There was nothing fierce about Lord Byron' (Nicolson, 1940; Supplementary Chapter, 298). But that is not to say that there was nothing terrifying. Whatever it was, explanations had to be found and phrased by both sides; but the real trouble neither party seems to have been willing to name.

What part did Lady Byron's parents and the enigmatic Mrs. Clermont, her old governess, whom Byron suspected of intriguing against him and denounced in his bitter poem entitled *A Sketch* (1816; P, III, 540), play in all this? That she was closely, and even authoritatively, involved in the negotiations is clear from an incident reported by Hobhouse when Sir Ralph Noel appeared to be weakening, but said that he must first consult Mrs. Clermont, only to return with the statement that it was too late—the step was taken (Hobhouse, II; xv, 256).

Of this, at least, we can be sure. The solution is not to be reached by reference to any suspicions which Lady Byron may have had of an incestuous relationship between Byron and Augusta. She and Augusta were fast friends, her own letters to her sister-in-law being almost those of a lover. The baby was called after her. Augusta had been staying with them for months, and she regarded it as tending to the happiness of all to leave brother and sister together (p. 88). It is firmly substantiated that suspicion of incest was in no sense the cause of Lady Byron's behaviour. We shall return to this question later. Meanwhile, we must recognize that at this period she and Augusta were working together, both of them being, or pretending to be, anxious as to Byron's state of mind, with Augusta sending regular bulletins to his wife.

III

Let us now return to our story. Byron's party showed no signs of fear. Sir Ralph Noel had started by threatening public proceedings with a view to intimidation (Hobhouse, II; xv, 228); but, since so many lurid rumours were afoot, spread, or encouraged, or at least not denied, by the opposition, Byron's advisers counselled a public investigation, and every preparation was made for going into court (Hobhouse, II; xv, 261–2, 269–71, 284, 342, 350). Hobhouse observes that, as soon as Byron and his advisers had showed that they were unafraid, the 'hints and menaces' were 'dropped'; the opposing party now 'sued for a private arrangement' and 'left no stone unturned to obtain one'; and Lady Byron and her supporters 'talked of the cruelty of dragging her into a public court', although it was her own father who 'had been the first person to talk of such a measure' (Hobhouse, II; xv, 270).

Here are some details in sequence. On 21 February Sir Ralph Noel asked Byron's solicitor, Hanson, if Byron had come to any determination upon his proposal for an amicable separation, and Hanson answered on the same day:

'Mr. Hanson presents his compliments to Sir Ralph Noel, and he has Lord Byron's directions to acquaint Sir Ralph that his Lordship cannot accede to Sir Ralph Noel's proposal for a separation from Lady Byron.'

(Hobhouse, II; xv, 272)

That is direct evidence of their stand.

The next day marks an important event in our story not included by Hobhouse, who may have preferred to suppress it. Lady Noel had, as we have seen, already visited Dr. Lushington with a statement made by her daughter. But now, on 22 February, Lady Byron herself joined her father in town (Fox, I, 3; Hobhouse, II; xv, 271), visited Dr. Lushington, who had previously been inclined towards a reconciliation, and told him, apparently under the seal of uttermost secrecy, *some fact or facts hitherto withheld even from her parents*. Hearing this, Dr. Lushington now ruled that Lady Byron should never return to her husband. If she did so, he said, he would himself be no party to such an arrangement. All this was first publicly revealed in Lady Byron's 1830 *Remarks on Moore's Life of Byron* (LJ, III, 290; full title, p. xiii above), which included a letter written for the occasion by Dr. Lushington (p. 110 below). This visit of Lady Byron is of primary importance.

She refused to see her husband during her visit, being reluctant to face so 'distressing' a 'trial' (Hobhouse, II; xv, 287). Instead Lord Holland assumed the part of mediator. A proposal was drawn up and submitted to Byron. On 4 March Byron wrote concerning it to his wife as follows:

'I know of no offence, not merely from man to wife, nor of one human being to another, but of any being almost to God Himself, which we are not taught to believe would be expiated by the repeated atonement which I have offered even for the *unknown* faults (for to me, till stated, they are unknown to any extent which can justify such persevering rejections) I may have been supposed to commit, or can have committed, against you. But since all hope is over, and instead of the duties of a wife and the mother of my child, I am to encounter accusation and implacability, I have nothing more to say, but shall act according to circumstances, though not even

75

injury can alter the love with which (though I shall do my best to repel attack) I must ever be yours.

B.

'I am told that you say *you* drew up the *proposal* of separation; if so, I regret to hear it; it appeared to me to be a kind of appeal to the supposed mercenary feelings of the person to whom it was made— "if you part with, etc., you will gain *so much now*, and so much at the death of" etc., a matter of pounds, shillings, and pence! No allusion to my child; a hard, dry, attorney's paper. Oh, Bell! to see you thus stifling and destroying all feeling, all affections, all duties (for they are your first duties, those of a wife and a mother), is far more bitter than any possible consequences to me.'

(Hobhouse, II; xv, 288)

This plea had no effect.

Whilst showing a cold exterior, however, neither Lady Byron nor her father were willing to face a public investigation. Lady Byron told Augusta and Captain Byron that, 'even if worsted in court', nothing but force would make her return; and also 'hinted, in pursuance of her former style, *that something had passed which she had as yet told to no one and which nothing but the absolute necessity of justifying herself in court should wring from her*', while adding that it was cruel to force her to a public investigation (Hobhouse, II; xv, 290; italics Hobhouse's). This was presumably that fact which she had withheld from her parents but told Dr. Lushington. Such a blend of threat and plea was hard to meet, the more so for the absence of exact statement.

Hobhouse's record of Byron's willingness and Lady Byron's reluctance to face a public examination is firmly set down, and fully supported by his own (p. 147), and other (p. 77), evidence. And yet we have Lady Byron, in her 1830 *Remarks on Moore's Life of Byron*, stating the exact reverse. These *Remarks* not only blankly contradict the facts presented in Mrs. Fletcher's Deposition regarding the part played by her parents in forcing her decision, but falsify the truth on the more important issue too. She is discussing her father's original request for an agreement:

'Lord Byron at first rejected this proposal; but when it was distinctly notified to him that if he persisted in his refusal recourse must be had to legal measures, he agreed to sign a deed of separation.'

(LJ, III, 290).

Either Lady Byron is right here, or Hobhouse is; there appears to be no alternative to regarding one of them as guilty of lying, or at least of gross self-deception after the event.

But indeed, we have clearest documentary evidence of Lady Byron's reluctance. She answered Byron's letter of 4 March on the next day, as follows:

'Without doubting the justice of my cause, I have no hesitation in acknowledging my reluctance to have recourse to any other mode of redress, whilst a possibility remains of obtaining the end with your consent. And after your repeated assertions that when convinced my conduct had not been influenced by others, you should not oppose my wishes, I am yet disposed to hope those assertions will be realised.'

(Hobhouse, II; xv, 296)

Compare that with Lady Byron's statement in 1830: the discrepancy, already observed by Drinkwater (I, 54), is highly significant. Hobhouse observes, and Drinkwater (I, 47) agrees, that this, his wife's final letter, was far milder than the others; the tone of aggression had been dropped; 'and her Ladyship, instead of menacing judicial proceedings against a person anxious to avoid them, was here rather a suppliant for a private arrangement with one who had given every demonstration that he should prefer a public investigation of the whole affair'; but, since 'his Lordship had done enough to show that *he was afraid of no exposure*', he was now 'justified in weighing the *petition* of his wife'; he had, through Augusta, made some such informal promise as his wife referred to, and, since she now 'appealed to his honour for a *private* arrangement', he felt himself 'at liberty to consult the wishes of Lady Byron', being especially, and indeed primarily, induced thereto by news of her bad health (Hobhouse, II; xv, 297–8). Lady Byron's false statement fourteen years after the event may be called a poor return for her husband's consideration in meeting her wishes.

According to Lord Lovelace, it was Hobhouse who persuaded Byron to agree to this arrangement, which was only carried through 'in the teeth of opposition and obstruction' from Byron's legal adviser, Hanson (Lovelace, II, 49).

Before finally committing themselves, Byron's party, with Wilmot Horton, a cousin of Byron's but one who from now on figures as a close associate and adviser of Lady Byron, acting as mediator, asked for a denial of the two main charges being rumoured. One was the old suspicion of incest which had now been reawakened; the other is not defined for us, but characterized in Hobhouse's words as even more 'enormous', and by Henry Brougham as 'something too horrid to mention', which Hobhouse says that he thought should nevertheless *be* mentioned, for the sake of everyone concerned (Hobhouse, II; XV, 301, 349–50). Lady Byron's party did not explicitly deny the truth of these rumours, but agreed to a modified statement asserting that neither would have been among their charges if public proceedings had been forced (Hobhouse, II; XV, 299–303; Fox, XII, 111–12). In Hobhouse's view honour was now satisfied, and Byron free to accommodate his wife. It is important to realize that she had pleaded with him for a quiet separation, since Byron's opposers have used his acquiescence to argue his guilt (p. 234). Hobhouse unequivocally tells us that Byron 'up to the moment of his departure from England, encouraged the immediate disclosure of the whole case' (Hobhouse, II; XV, 350); and Byron's later statements say the same.

The Deed of Separation was signed by the parties concerned on 21 and 22 April, Byron remarking: 'This is Mrs. Clermont's act and deed' (*Quarterly*, Oct., 1869; Vol. 127; *418*); and then, amid a general vituperation, not unlike the outcry raised against Oscar Wilde, Byron left England.

All the concrete evidence so far reviewed points one way; the way of Byron's own assertions; and against it we have only the enigmatic silence and vague innuendoes of the opposing party. The actions and words of Byron and his supporters appear open, simple, and on the face of them honest, with many quite serious failings freely admitted. There is, moreover, evidence that both before and throughout these proceedings Byron spoke nothing but good of his wife (Hobhouse, II; XV, 318–21). On 8 March, 1816, he wrote to Moore:

'I do not believe—and I must say it, in the very dregs of all this bitter business—that there ever was a better, or even a brighter, a kinder, or a more amiable and agreeable being than Lady B. I never had, nor can have, any reproach to make her while with me. Where there is blame it belongs to myself, and, if I cannot redeem, I must bear it.'

(LJ, III, 272)

In strong contrast the behaviour of the opposing party was mysterious, secretive and, in technique at least, suggestive of blackmail, with the scarcely attractive addition of a parade of rectitude and principle. We must lay, moreover, the very greatest emphasis on Lady Byron's patent reversal of the truth in her 1830 *Remarks* as to which party was ready for public proceedings and which party it was that feared them. All Byron's assertions, in writing and reported conversation, both during the crisis and throughout his life, his remarks to Hobhouse, Medwin, Lady Blessington, Kennedy and Parry, together with all his actions, appear from first to last simple and consistent, squaring both with each other, with Hobhouse's account, and Mrs. Fletcher's deposition; and all dovetail perfectly with Lady Byron's first playful and loving letters. Byron admitted to sullen and morose behaviour; and Lady Byron's letter of 16 January (p. 57) referred to a 'sulking-room' for him. Similarly the Woburn fragment makes a facetious comment on his poetry, Kinnaird's brandy-parties and, as Hobhouse supposes, on his admitted lapse from fidelity (see p. 57). All this belongs to one simple world, the world of Byron's confessions, the world of the marriage, with all its troubles, which Byron recognized and Lady Byron, at least on the evidence of her playful letters, had been willing to accept, though she may genuinely have suspected her husband of insanity. None of this by itself can possibly account for her irrevocable about-turn following the unwelcome news—if indeed this was the reason, for we can be sure of very little—that her lord was sane; for her refusal to see him and implacable attitude to all future advances; or for her extraordinary insistence that emotions must not now be allowed to enter the discussion. We must, of course, remember that Lady Byron was herself far from well, as a letter to Augusta written on 16 January, 1816, indicates:

'My looks have disappointed my Mother, but *you* have had little to answer for in regard to them. My mind is altogether so over-strained and my body so weak in comparison, that if it were not one thing, it would be another. I think much worse of my prospects of health than I usually avow; when I tell you there are seldom two hours in a day when my head is not burning, you will conceive there must be a perpetual waste of constitution. I sometimes feel as if this could not go on long . . .'

(LJ, III, 294)

We have seen how Mrs. Fletcher reports her as 'rolling on the floor' and suffering from a 'paroxysm' at the crisis. But she, like Byron, remained acute enough in all matters of 'business'.

Of Mrs. Clermont, we shall have more to say hereafter. Of her Byron wrote to his wife in a letter which, on his friend's advice, he did not send: 'She was *your* stranger, and I made her our inmate; she came as a guest, she remained as a spy, she departed as an informer, and reappeared as an evidence; if false, she belied—if true she betrayed me—the worst of treacheries, "*a bread and salt traitress*"; she ate, and drank, and slept, and awoke, to sting me'. Dr. Le Mann, one of the two doctors consulted by Lady Byron, said that the impression he had received was that she had been 'introduced into the family *to watch Lord Byron*' (Hobhouse, II; xv, 327–8); though she herself claimed that she had been called in by Augusta to help control him (Lovelace, Note IV, 322). Byron himself said later that he had heard that she had 'employed herself and others in watching' his movements about London (Medwin, 42; *Quarterly*, Jan., 1870; Vol. 128; *234*). The public outcry against Byron was conducted mainly on party lines (P, III, 534–5), and if indeed Mrs. Clermont was some sort of spy, it is even possible that scandal was being sought for political reasons (pp. 267, 274 below).

The neatest description of the whole affair, at least in its domestic aspect and as it appears from the evidence so far reviewed, occurs in *Don Juan* (I, 10–22). Here Donna Inez is clearly drawn from life, a 'learned lady', making clever people ashamed and even the good groan with envy, with many of Lady Byron's qualities:

> *Her favourite science was the mathematical,*
> *Her noblest virtue was her magnanimity . . .*
>
> (I, 12)

She is a positive 'prodigy', whose 'thoughts are theorems' and 'words a problem'. Her silent criticism is noted:

> *Some women use their tongues—she* looked *a lecture,*
> *Each eye a sermon, and her brow a homily,*
> *An all-in-all sufficient self-director*
> *Like the lamented late Sir Samuel Romilly.*[1]
>
> (I, 15)

She was 'a walking calculation', 'morality's prim personification', 'perfect past all parallel', going like a clock, with a virtue rather

---

[1] Sir Samuel Romilly was a lawyer who held a retainer for Byron, but roused his anger by going over to the other side. See Hobhouse, II, App. I and K, 365–6; also my *Byron's Dramatic Prose*, 19–22.

JOHN CAM HOBHOUSE
afterwards Lord Broughton de Gyfford
from a miniature by Sir William J. Newton

LADY BYRON
from a miniature by
Charles Hayter

'insipid in this naughty world of ours', but with 'a great opinion of her own good qualities'. Her husband was a simple, erring, man. So:

> Don José and the Donna Inez led
>   For some time an unhappy sort of life,
> Wishing each other, not divorced, but dead;
>   They lived respectably as man and wife,
> Their conduct was exceedingly well-bred,
>   And gave no outward signs of inward strife,
> Until at length the smother'd fire broke out,
> And put the business past all kind of doubt.
>
> For Inez called some druggists and physicians,
>   And tried to prove her loving lord was mad.
> But as he had some lucid intermissions,
>   She next decided he was only bad;
> Yet when they asked her for her depositions,
>   No sort of explanation could be had,
> Save that her duty both to man and God
> Required this conduct—which seem'd very odd.
>
> (1, 26–7)

The poem continues with relevant hints; the keeping of a journal of her lord's faults, the opening of his private letters, the supposed 'magnanimity' of the lady whilst getting her own way, the quarrel raising up 'old stories' with a 'lie or two additional', friends working for a reconciliation, and relations too, and everyone making things worse (1, 28–32).

Byron practically denied the reference to his wife in his *Blackwood's* Defence (LJ, IV, 477–8; p. 147). He indeed seems often to have been strangely unaware of the autobiographical basis of his fictions. To Augusta he wrote, after referring to the supposed 'magnanimity' of his wife in preserving silence: 'People accused somebody of painting her in "Donna *Inez*"; did it strike you so? I can't say it did me; there might be something of her in the outline, but the Spaniard was only a silly woman, and the other is a cut-and-dry, made-up character, which is another matter' (Augusta, Oct., 1820; SP, II, 529). That is scarcely convincing and recalls his first refusal to acknowledge his identity with the hero of *Childe Harold* (Dallas, 31 Oct., 1811; LJ, II, 66). But there he agreed that Harold was a *part* of himself, and here he admits a certain relation. What he apparently means—that is, if he is speaking in earnest—is that *Don Juan* offers a parody ('silly woman'), whereas Lady Byron was an appalling reality. Strangely, though Teresa Guiccioli objected to this quite obvious reference to his wife, and partly for that reason made him promise to discontinue the poem (Augusta, 5 Oct., 1821; Lovelace, XI, 308), a promise he kept until relieved of it, yet Lady Byron, who herself had a gift for humorous verse, appears to have accepted the caricature in a friendly spirit, liking *Don Juan*, which raised such bitter revulsion elsewhere, better than she had expected, and remarking: 'I must however confess that the quizzing in one or two passages was so good as to make me smile at myself—therefore others are heartily welcome to laugh' (Mayne, *Lady Byron*, XIX, 283). Those who are most inclined to blame Byron for his caricature and Lady Byron for her coldness should observe this witness to the redeeming powers of comedy. These stanzas, which *Blackwood's* (Aug., 1819; Vol. 5; *514*; LJ, IV, 385, note) wrote off as 'the wilful and determined spite of an unrepenting, unsoftened, smiling, sarcastic, joyous sinner,' constitute our one ray of light in the whole painful business.

We may conclude this section by quoting an important passage from a review in 1869 of the Countess Guiccioli's book on Byron in *Blackwood's* which, after Byron's 1820 letter which I call his '*Blackwood's Defence*' (p. 147) written in reply to the review just quoted, became from then on and throughout the century his—on the whole —kindly supporter. The writer sums up the problem of the Separation from a viewpoint favourable to Byron, as follows:

'She lives with her husband for more than a year without communicating to her own parents, or to anyone else, any cause for discomfort. She leaves him without the slightest indication of her displeasure. She tries to prove him mad; failing that, she declares her determination never to return to him. Through her mother she lays before Dr. Lushington a statement of her case. He (no doubt very wisely) advises a reconciliation; failing with Dr. Lushington, as she had with Dr. Baillie, she seeks a personal interview, and then, in the secrecy of his chambers, under the seal of a confidence stricter than that of the confessional, she imparts to him *something* which he was bound to assume on her sole assurance to be true—which he was, without investigation or enquiry, to accept as the basis of his opinion—which he was, under no circumstances whatever, without her express authority (an authority which death has now put it out of her power to give), to divulge, upon which she obtains his opinion that a reconciliation was impossible. What that something was we shall probably never know, but, save in the case of the victims who were sent to the guillotine on suspicion of being suspected, we know no condemnation so monstrous, so revolting to every principle of justice and common-sense, as that which has been passed on Lord Byron.'

(*Blackwood's*, July, 1869; Vol. 106; *31*)

The passage is of value for its high-lighting of our central problem as Lady Byron's revelation to Dr. Lushington on the occasion of her personal visit to London (p. 75), together with its emphasis on Lady Byron's insistence then and thereafter on absolute secrecy regarding this mysterious revelation.

III
LADY BYRON'S CAMPAIGN

III. LADY BYRON'S CAMPAIGN

I

FOR the rest of her life, writes C. E. Vulliamy, Lady Byron 'devoted herself to what are known as "good works" ' and to 'the elaboration of the Byronic scandal' (Vulliamy, x, 146). We shall now examine the strange attempt on Lady Byron's part to get proof that Byron had committed incest with Augusta before his marriage. This policy was continued by her and also by Byron's grandson, son of Ada, Lord Lovelace, whose *Astarte*, written in defence of his grandmother, came out in 1905, and was reissued with additional material by his widow in 1921. We shall quote freely from the opinions and documents put forward in *Astarte*.

The behaviour of Lady Byron's party had been from the start questionable, at the best baffling, and at the worst bordering on blackmail. There appeared to be a deliberate intention of branding Byron as a monster, and all normal methods were in their view, as Hobhouse tells us, inadequate (Hobhouse, II; xv, 232-3). After the Separation, when *The Morning Chronicle* said there had been 'a conspiracy against the domestic peace of Lord Byron', Sir Ralph Noel set himself to suppress all public support of his son-in-law (Hobhouse, II; xv, 332-7). One suspects that certain *public* interests had been involved.

What part did the old rumour of incest, which seems to have been spread mainly by Lady Caroline Lamb, play in all this? It was formally denied that incest would have been among the charges had matters come to court (p. 78). On her arrival at Kirkby Mallory on 16 January, 1816, Lady Byron wrote to Augusta that her looks were poorly, but 'you have had little to answer for in regard to them' (LJ, III, 294). Her earliest written statement of her marriage troubles, composed for her mother to take to London on 18 January, 1816, contained a long and minute account of Byron's words and actions,

87

which corroborates Byron's statement in *Don Juan* (I, 28; and see Hobhouse, II; xv, 322), but nothing to incriminate Augusta; the main emphasis was on insanity (Lady Lovelace's note, Lovelace, I, 21). Augusta had apparently been urged by Lady Byron to stay at Piccadilly during her confinement, though Lady Byron afterwards denied it (Correspondence of Lady Byron and Mrs. Villiers, 12 and 18 May, 1816; Lovelace, IX, 203, 205); and during the weeks leading up to the Separation she was functioning as Lady Byron's colleague, Lady Byron writing to her on 16 January, 1816, 'My dearest A., it is my great comfort that you are in Piccadilly' (LJ, III, 295). Augusta was entreated, as her 'one consolation', to send daily reports of Byron's mental health (Augusta to Hobhouse, 21 May, 1816; Hobhouse, II, App. H, 364); though later, when incest had become her theme, she tried to explain away her behaviour (Lady Byron to Mrs. Villiers; 6 May, 1816; Lovelace, IX, 200). Her expressions to Augusta were regularly marked by strong affection, as when on 25 January, 1816, she asks: 'Shall I still be your sister?' (LJ, III, 300). Had any serious fears of an incestuous relationship at this period been present, her behaviour would be hard to understand; as though Othello were to leave Desdemona to Cassio's care with a request for regular bulletins as to her progress. Looking back on Lady Byron's intimacy with Augusta, we find it quite natural that the baby should have been christened 'Augusta Ada'.

Nothing in either Byron's or Augusta's behaviour during the marriage period shows any hint of a guilty secret. In a letter to Hobhouse on 21 May, 1816 she refers frankly to herself as one who 'doats upon dear Byron' (Hobhouse, II, App. H, 363); and Byron himself, on leaving England, specifically commended Augusta to his wife's care (to Lady Byron, 14 April, 1816; Lovelace, II, 51-2, probably authentic; with variants, Hobhouse, II; xv, 328-9; LJ, III, 280-1).

Though Lady Byron was aware of the old rumour, it played no part in her decision to leave her husband. Her conviction, she wrote on 12 May, 1816, had not been her 'principle of conduct' since it was only 'lately fixed' (to Mrs. Villiers; Lovelace, IX, 203). Lord Lovelace tells us that during the libels on Lady Byron in 1870 Dr. Lushington 'repeated emphatically' that when she 'was driven to the decision of parting from Lord Byron she had cogent reasons on account of cruelty and adultery'; and 'that there was nothing else at that time, for she was still determined to repel from her mind all belief in incest' (Lovelace, VII, 159). That is uncompromising: the charge 'cruelty' is vague and perfectly fits Byron's own confession; so does that of adultery, as we have seen (p. 67), though Byron claimed to have had his wife's forgiveness for the single lapse in question (Hobhouse, II; xv, 281). Lady Byron always denied that either she or her family had been in any way responsible for the reawakening of the old scandal (to Augusta, 11 July, 1816; Lovelace, x, 232; and see Lovelace, II, 43). Ethel Colburn Mayne, in her *Life of Lady Byron*, quotes a letter of Lady Byron to her mother during the latter's visit to London in January, 1816, saying of Augusta: 'I very much fear that she may be supposed the cause of separation by many, and it would be a cruel injustice' (xIV, 207).

Nevertheless, as the proceedings developed, she appears to have become keenly interested in the thought of incest having occurred before her marriage, and the use which might be made of it. During the Separation negotiations, on 14 March, 1816, she made an official but private statement before Dr. Lushington and others, wherein it is clearly shown that incest was not one of the charges, partly through absence of proof, and partly since 'the crime, if committed, might not only be deeply repented of, but never have been perpetrated since her marriage'. That is, she was willing to pass it over. She does, however, record suspicions aroused by certain 'intimations' made to her during the marriage—she does not say by whom—and observes that she has detected in Augusta signs of what she says that she 'interprets' as some form of 'deep remorse', though she will not go so far as to state that this remorse relates to the 'dark' crime of incest. It is abundantly clear from this statement that incest had nothing to do with Lady Byron's earlier, and different, revelations to her mother and Dr. Lushington. It is treated as a new, and very tenuous, support to her original complaints.

The statement goes on to say that, though Lady Byron means for the sake of Augusta's reputation to continue her friendship with her, yet she also wishes to record her suspicion in case 'any circumstances should compel or render it necessary for Lady B. to prefer the charge, in order that Lady B. may be at full liberty so to do without being prejudiced by her present conduct'. It concludes with the paradoxical assertion 'that this Paper does not contain nor pretend to contain any of the grounds which gave rise to the suspicion'. There may be a veiled reference to some confession, or supposed confession, by Byron which she and her advisers thought that she, as a wife, could not, at this stage, set on paper. The extraordinary statement, witnessed by her advisers, Robert Wilmot Horton, Colonel Francis Hastings Doyle, and Dr. Stephen Lushington was first printed by Lord Lovelace (II, 46–8).[1]

The meaning is this: Lady Byron intended to continue playing the part of Augusta's friend, whilst preserving to herself the right to use her suspicions for some future purpose, and even 'prefer the charge' should she be able to get any firm evidence. And from now on she sought strenuously to get evidence, using her friendship with Augusta as a means.

This is the first of a series of actions of similar tone. Of these later actions Vulliamy writes: 'It would seem that she was either a scribbling, gossiping, delusionary, or the blackest of hypocrites; and there are depths of hypocrisy which only a woman can reach'. Again, 'The minds of women', he says, 'do not operate in accordance with an intelligible system, and it would be foolish to apply to their dealings the usual standards of logic and honour. But at least they have motives' (Vulliamy, X, 146; XVII, 252). What, we must ask, were Lady Byron's motives?

It seems that she was genuinely anxious to keep control of the child, Ada (see Fox, 'The Custody of the Child', XV); and the threat of blackening Augusta's name might have been useful to this end. She certainly wished to keep the child in her care, and Byron was, provisionally, willing that she should do so. This was all natural enough. What is not quite so natural is the ease with which she engaged in legal subterfuge. Here is a letter written by her to Mrs. George Lamb on 1 April, 1816, where, though she is referring to her 'advisers'—she had herself first suggested a more direct approach (see Fox, XV, 150)—her phrasing remains characteristic:

'In regard to the child, it appears to my advisers most advantageous that it should not be made a subject of discussion at present, or in any way suggested to him as such, because it is highly improbable that he would resign the power *in a formal manner*; and, by not making any particular provision for it, if he goes abroad, he will virtually, to a certain extent, acknowledge my guardianship. To let him know

[1] Wilmot Horton's signature appears as 'Robert John Wilmot'; the name was later changed to Wilmot Horton; later still he was knighted, becoming 'Sir Robert'.

A rather stronger, though brief, note regarding her suspicions exists among Lady Byron's papers as a private 'memorandum' (Fox, XII, 113). Though dated March, 1816, we cannot know whether or not it was composed later.

these reasons would be to defeat them. I am glad that you think of *her* with the feelings of pity which prevail in my mind, and surely if in *mine* there must be some cause for them. I never was, nor never can be, so *mercilessly* virtuous as to admit *no* excuse for even the worst of errors.'

(LJ, III, 327)

The concluding reference is to Augusta. Now the scheme adopted was, no doubt, clever; and we shall later observe Byron straining vigorously under the control she exercised, though he was normally, without ceasing to love his child with intensity, willing to leave her in her mother's care. We may, however, draw attention to the technique of Lady Byron's party; from first to last it was indirect, and depended regularly on keeping the opposing party mystified. As for her 'pity' for Augusta, we shall shortly have reason to question it. Nor was anxiety for the child the only reason for her actions.

When Byron was safely out of England, his wife started to follow up her March statement by a prolonged attempt to substantiate the charge of incest. For this purpose she joined forces with a certain Mrs. Villiers, a close friend of Augusta's, who appears to have enjoyed the scandal and urged Lady Byron to tax Augusta with the crime. Two of Lady Byron's advisers, Colonel Doyle and Dr. Lushington, very naturally 'saw no necessity for this step' (Lovelace, III, 58), but Lady Byron went ahead in the attempt to elicit a confession. She and Augusta had recently been fast friends—'the two women', writes Lady Lovelace, 'appear to have been irresistibly drawn to each other' (Lovelace, IX, 198)—but Lady Byron's manner now quickly developed from ostentatious protestations of affection to a series of half-formulated threats. Much of it was done by letters; Mrs. Villiers was kept posted of every development; and the three-cornered correspondence, which is printed in the second edition of Lovelace's *Astarte*, makes extraordinary reading.

Lady Byron was not concerned with the years of her marriage. All she wanted was proof that incest had at some time occurred. What evidence she had, she says, rested chiefly on Byron's 'words and manners' and Augusta's 'assent and submission to both', but from Augusta's own letters to her during this correspondence she thinks that the sin cannot have been repeated: 'Surely by these assertions she must mean that she has been *innocent* since my marriage'. There was not, she says, enough to justify any greater suspicion. Indeed, one of Augusta's letters 'thoroughly convinces me of her innocence in regard to all the period with which I was concerned' (to Mrs. Villiers, 12 May, 11 and 17 July, 1816; Lovelace, IX, 203, 229, 237; and see Lovelace, 220, 226, 230). Never in all her life, says her grandson, did she have reason to suppose more than that (Lovelace, VIII, 179–80). It is clear, too, that Lady Byron did not particularly *want* to believe it; but she was most keenly anxious to get proof of its earlier occurrence. She appears to bear no particular resentment on this score, but just wants the proof for her own purposes, partly as a justification, since 'it would alone have proved sufficient ground for the step I took' (to Augusta, 11 July, 1816; Lovelace, X, 231), but also as a threat to hold over Augusta, and through her Byron, in order to prevent some revelation of which she stood in fear.

Outwardly she pretends anxiety as to the state of Augusta's soul. To Mrs. Villiers she writes on 6 May, 1816:

'My great object, next to the security of my child, is, therefore, the restoration of her mind to that state which is religiously desirable.'

(Lovelace, IX, 199)

Mrs. Villiers takes the same line, hoping that, with Lady Byron's assistance, Augusta will make herself more fit for the next world (to Lady Byron, 9 July, 1816; Lovelace, X, 228). Such phrases need not mislead us. There was a more immediate purpose at work. Following the example of her father and advisers during the Separation proceedings, we find Lady Byron engaging in a kind of blackmail. Here is an extract from a letter to Mrs. Villiers of 23 May, 1816, outlining her plan of working on Augusta by the use of half-threatening yet non-committal hints:

'The measure which I propose to take appears to me to unite the following advantages—that it will make *herself* acquainted with my real opinions and feelings, without binding me to avow them publicly, should she be desperate in the first impulse—that it will nevertheless suspend this terror over her, to be used as her future dispositions and conduct may render expedient—whilst it leaves her the power of profiting by my forbearance, without compelling the utterly degrading confession of her own guilt.'

(Lovelace, IX, 208)

That is written by a girl of twenty-four about a woman eight years her senior as part of an attempt only thinly veiled by the pretence of forwarding Augusta's spiritual salvation. She had all she wanted, had gained her separation and seen her husband publicly humiliated and ostracized; and might well have remained content. She knew that she was likely to cause suffering. She claims to have stated her conviction to Augusta whilst saying 'everything that could soften the blow', being afraid of causing pain. 'I think', she writes, 'her first feeling will be terror—her second pride . . .' (to Mrs. Villiers, 4 June, 1816; Lovelace, IX, 212). The slow torment continues: 'I feel it would be a false delicacy that might lead me to abstain from probing the wound. My tenderness will however naturally increase with the pain I give, and will, in her present temper, obtain forgiveness for my motives' (to Mrs. Villiers, 11 July, 1816; Lovelace, X, 229). It is done subtly and by carefully considered degrees:

'This is all well and I am now leading her on to promise that she will never renew a confidential intercourse by letter—or any personal intercourse—I find it necessary to gain step by step, and to disclose my views less abruptly than with some . . .'

Again,

' . . . it has only been from consideration for her good, which may be best promoted by *withholding* something, that I have not yet promised to see her.'

(To Mrs. Villiers, 28 July, 1816;
Lovelace, X, 245–6)

It was very carefully planned.

It seems that Lady Byron was afraid of some revelation which Augusta might make. On this Mrs. Villiers herself is more outspoken. She notes frankly how Wilmot Horton intended to tell Augusta that if she heard any talk to the effect that Lady Byron was 'cold-hearted' and 'unforgiving' towards her husband, he 'advised her to put a stop to that sort of language whenever she heard it in any friends of hers, or it would be the worse for her'. Mrs. Villiers' comment runs: 'I see no objection to this—but he promises to do it in a kind way' (Mrs. Villiers to Lady Byron, 18 July, 1816; Lovelace, X, 240). Augusta did, probably, know much regarding both Byron and his wife which Lady Byron and her advisers did not wish to come out. In a postscript to a letter to Hobhouse of 21 May, 1816, Augusta wrote: 'Say not *one* word to anybody of what I may express to you about B., etc. etc. I have made it a rule to *be silent*

AS LONG AS I CAN' (Hobhouse, II; xv, App. H, 365). This may refer to some secret which Lady Byron did not wish to be exposed.

Though Lady Byron writes that 'to me duplicity is the most unpardonable crime' (to Mrs. Villiers, 6 May, 1816; Lovelace, IX, 199), we cannot exonerate her from a goodly strain of it herself. Her mind works tortuously. 'Her letters', Byron told Medwin, 'were always enigmatical, often unintelligible' (Medwin, 46). Our present examples should be compared with Byron's outspoken remonstrance starting 'Oh, Bell . . .' (p. 76), in which he shows himself aware of the propensities we are discussing. We are, I think, in a position to appreciate what lies behind his remark, in a letter to Augusta of 17 September 1816: 'I do not think a human being could endure more mental torture than that woman has directly or indirectly inflicted upon me within the present year' (Lovelace, XI, 272).

Whatever be the truth of Byron's words, a subtle variety of 'mental torture' was now being inflicted on Augusta. Lady Byron appears to have mesmerized her, if not into confession, at least into an abject submission. Her letters at this period to Lady Byron show a confusion quite uncharacteristic of her normal epistolary style (e.g., to Hobhouse; Hobhouse, II, App. A, 357–8; and see p. 111 below), making a morass of muddled and semi-emotional protestations and assurances, though about what, it is hard to say. If she confesses nothing, that may be because there was nothing to confess; but if not, why not say so?

The correspondence as a whole is extraordinarily obscure. Often the writers appear to be at cross-purposes. Lady Byron is apparently concentrating, though without ever naming it, on incest, while Augusta generally seems to be defending herself against charges of some quite different form of disloyalty to Lady Byron. Certain earlier letters of the two women show references of the same kind: 'If all the world', wrote Lady Byron on 16 January, 1816, 'had told me you were doing me an injury, I *ought not* to have believed it. My chief feeling, therefore, in relation to you and myself must be that I *have* wronged you, and that you have never wronged me. You will wish to contradict this . . . etc.' (LJ, III, 294). What exactly the 'wronging' is is not clear. Again, on 14 February, 1816, 'Heaven knows you have considered me more than one in a thousand would have done . . . God bless you, from the bottom of my heart' (LJ, III, 311). But things have now changed, and we find Augusta insisting that she has always considered and consulted Lady Byron's happiness and done her 'duty' by her friend (6 June, 1816; Lovelace, IX, 213–14); and again, 'I have not wronged you', and 'intentionally I have never injured you' (3 July, 1816; Lovelace, IX, 224). Sometimes Lady Byron appears to think that Augusta has been speaking of her own behaviour as 'cold and cruel' (Lady Byron to Augusta, 11 July, 1816; Lovelace, X, 232); and in reply Augusta is at pains to assure her that she has regularly let it be known that Lady Byron had indeed been the irritant behind Byron's supposed insanity (to Lady Byron, 15 July, 1816, Lovelace X, 234); which, whether true or not, was the story which Lady Byron was demanding. Byron appears to be referring to the same, or some similar, matter when he wrote his farewell letter (p. 88) to his wife assuring her that Augusta 'has never spoken nor acted towards you but as your friend'. Provisionally we may suggest that these disclaimers refer to the very danger against which Lady Byron is trying to safeguard herself. Augusta may have known things which she did not want revealed, and the more Lady Byron hints threateningly at incest, the more Augusta, terrified by the blackmail, asseverates her loyalty and good faith.

Incest could, of course, be covered by some of Augusta's passages, but it is not mentioned and sometimes cannot be meant, as in the typically confused letter to Lady Byron of 15 July 1816:

'The *delusion* to which I alluded—was an *entire unsuspicion*—that *you even suspected*—that I caused or added to your misery—which *every* thing on *your* part and many on that of *another* tended to confirm—as I now remember "some things" to which you allude—you may also some which could not but deceive me—it is still like a *horrid dream* to me my dearest A—that *I* caused your sufferings whose whole anxiety was at least to mitigate them—I felt it as my only consolation to do *all* I could, and indeed to the best of my judgment I *did* it. Many a time I should have felt it one to have confided unreservedly in you—but concealment appeared a duty under such circumstances—and you know I am of a sanguine disposition and to the very last had hopes of better for you—and for him.'

(Lovelace, X, 233)

Later we have:

'I must not forget—and I write so uncomfortably I fear I shall half I would and *could* say—that I am equally surprised and hurt at what

95

you quote as the language of any friend of mine—I must say that I could no longer consider any one in that light who could say such a thing *of* not *to* me—and I declare to you no one ever even hinted it —on the contrary—the few to whom I could not help speaking always manifested surprise at the part I took—not knowing circumstances—when I had told as much of *them* as I *could*, I always replied to arguments *"if you knew all you would think differently"*—but my situation was so difficult I *ought* not to be surprised at having incurred censure—and *only* feel it because I never met with it *openly*.'

(Lovelace, x, 234)

When such passages are explained, we shall know a lot.

Against what charge is Augusta here defending herself? There is reason to suppose that Lady Byron thought that Augusta should have warned her in good time of certain irregularities in Byron's life which, she says, Augusta knew about (p. 210 below). There may be a hint in that: Augusta is there being regarded as an *accomplice*.

Augusta's letter of 15 July was answered by Lady Byron on 17 July. She says:

'I am now thoroughly convinced that if from the hour we first met *all* your conduct had been open to me *I* could not have found in it any thing to reproach you with—for that your errors of judgment, however to be regretted, were *perfectly innocent*—God knows what satisfaction I have in making this acknowledgment—and in resigning doubts as to *those* parts of your conduct which have but transiently existed and will never return to wrong you. Tell me if this is satisfactory?'

(Lovelace, x, 235)

Can that refer conceivably to incest? It scarcely sounds like it.

Augusta confesses to nothing. She is always, vaguely it is true, but consistently, on the defensive, as when she wrote earlier, on 6 June; 'The time may come when your present convictions and opinions will change—in the interim I feel how hopeless would be every attempt to defend myself' (6 June, 1816; Lovelace, IX, 214). On 23 July she wrote: 'I have said but little of *him*, my dearest A—fearing you might mistake the *nature* of my feelings—I am certain they are and ever have been such as you could not disapprove—I I did but know how to contribute to his *ultimate* good!' (Lovelace' x, 243). That, it is true, looks like a recognition of Lady Byron's suspicion of an incestuous relationship, but there is no sign of any *confession* whatsoever. Indeed, the reverse.

And yet Lady Byron had already persuaded herself that Augusta was confessing to incest; or perhaps she just wanted to work up the correspondence, which she meant to keep, to *look* like this. So we find her writing to Mrs. Villiers on 12 May, 1816: 'During her last visit my suspicions as to *previous* circumstances were most strongly corroborated—above all by *her* confessions and admissions when in a state of despair and distraction. They were of the most unequivocal nature possible, unless she had expressly named the subject of her remorse and horror' (Lovelace. IX, 203); on which Vulliamy aptly comments, 'Is it possible for nonsense to go any further?' (XVII, 258). Again on 8 July 1816 Lady Byron says, with reference to one of Augusta's letters, that Augusta 'admits respecting what preceded my marriage as much as she could do on paper', and 'maintains her *innocence* since' (Lovelace, X, 226); 'as much as she could do' meaning, as Drinkwater (I, 62) observes, and as a reference to the letter in question shows, precisely nothing. On 11 July, she is still angling, writing to Augusta: '*That we may never mistrust each other again*, it is necessary that we should now be perfectly confidential . . .' A little later, we have: 'As you do not, and never have attempted to deceive me respecting previous facts, of which my conviction is unalterable, I rely the more on your simple assertion of having "never wronged me" intentionally . . .' But if Augusta had confessed, why reassert her own 'conviction' like this? And a little later she herself says openly: 'When I speak of the necessity of confidence, do not suppose I wish to exact any confession . . .' (Lovelace, X, 229–31).

When Lord Lovelace tells us that Lady Byron claimed to have received a full personal confession from Augusta in September, 1816 (Lovelace, III, 65; IX, 198; and see I, 21, note), we have no reason whatsoever to believe it, the more so since she was still apparently trying, as we shall see, later in the century. Lovelace himself appears to admit that Augusta never considered herself to have confessed to incest, since he tells us that at her death she left behind 'all ready and arranged, a small selection of carefully selected documents calculated to rebut the charge that had been expected and prepared for all through her life' (Lovelace, VII, 146).

Throughout this queer and unpleasant correspondence 'incest' is never mentioned. Indeed, John Drinkwater suggested that we lack 'some forgotten or concealed key-word to the problem', some secret whose 'clue' is 'lost'; and in discussing the utter unintelligibility of Augusta's behaviour, he wonders if the central trouble, 'so freely discussed in the correspondence by all parties to it, so plausibly taken to be incest, though always just failing by the turn of a word to declare itself explicitly to be so, may, after all, be a yet more obscure secret than is commonly allowed' (Drinkwater, III, 245; I, 64; I, 70).

That is suggestive. But Lady Byron clearly means incest when she is writing to Mrs. Villiers, though her letters to Augusta are vague. It would almost seem as though she was deliberately writing in such a way as to make posterity assume a meaning which she knows that Augusta does not subscribe to, as when Iago stages a conversation with Cassio to deceive Othello. Her March statement shows that she regarded the substantiation of the incest as an important implement for the future, and it seems that this correspondence was to be kept for a similar purpose. On 19 June, 1816, we find Mrs. Villiers writing: 'I consider that what has passed must be conclusive with respect to your greatest object—the safety of your child—the production of this correspondence should it ever become necessary, and her quiet acquiescence in your proposal must be sufficient for your purpose'. Augusta, she says, will not now bring 'absolute and immediate ruin upon herself by an *éclat*'; and she goes on to consider ways of putting her against her brother (to Lady Byron, 19 June, 1816; Lovelace, IX, 217). They felt that their grip was firm.

Her rights over Ada were not the only, nor probably the main, reason for Lady Byron's actions, since her will to establish the incest continued after Byron's, and even after her daughter's, death. She and her advisers were, indeed, very seriously afraid. There was a secret which they did not want divulged, and this sword of Damocles over Augusta was the means of keeping her, and Byron, silent. This is clear from Colonel Doyle's letter to Lady Byron of 9 July, 1816. He had previously been against Lady Byron's correspondence with Augusta, but now writes: 'Your feelings I perfectly understand. I will even whisper to you I approve . . . But you must remember that your position is very extraordinary'. The dots of the Lovelace text may be significant. He continues:

'We should not neglect the means of fully justifying ourselves if the necessity be ever imposed upon us. I see the possibility of a contingency under which the fullest explanation of the motives and grounds of your conduct may be necessary. I therefore implore you to suffer no delicacy to interfere with your endeavouring to obtain the fullest *admission* of the fact . . .'

More dots. 'Conduct' probably refers to the Separation. If, he says, Lady Byron's motives (i.e. ostensible motives, soul-saving, etc.) are 'properly appreciated' (i.e. believed in), they will all eventually have reason to 'rejoice' at the success of her campaign:

'The step you have taken was attended with great risk, and I could not, contemplating the danger to which it might have exposed you, have originally advised it. If however your correspondence has produced an acknowledgment of the fact even previous to your marriage I shall be most happy that it has taken place.'

(Lovelace, III, 58–9)

That is, it would have been nicer to know that incest had occurred during the marriage, but a previous engagement would be better than nothing. On 18 July he wrote again:

'I must recommend you to act as if a time might *possibly* arise when it would be necessary for you to justify yourself, though nothing short of an absolute necessity so imperative as to be irresistible could ever authorise your advertence to your present communications. Still I cannot dismiss from my mind the experience we have had, nor so far forget the very serious embarrassment we were under from the effects of your too confiding disposition, as not to implore you to bear in mind the importance of securing yourself from eventual danger. This is my first object—and if that be attained—I shall approve and applaud all the kindness you can show.'

(Lovelace, III, 59)

That is, our actions in the matter of the Separation contain a secret; you were, and are, all through your "*too confiding disposition*'—an all-important phrase to which we shall return (p. 196)—in great danger; you are now playing with fire; but if you can get away with it, by all means keep up the pretence of being Augusta's friend, and trying to serve her spiritual interests, in order to establish the blackmail.

Am I reading too much into this letter? Hardly. Lord Lovelace himself admits that the establishment of the incest was a vital necessity to Lady Byron's advisers. What they now wanted was for her to go abroad with Byron for all the world to take note. It was, he says, Lady Byron's nobility that preferred the other course. This saved Augusta's reputation:

'Her return to outward respectability was an unmixed misfortune to the third person through whose protection it was possible. For if Augusta fled to Byron in exile, was seen with him as *et soror et conjux*, the victory remained with Lady Byron, solid and final. This was the solution hoped for by Lady Byron's friends, Lushington and Doyle, as well as Lady Noel; who all rightly wished to prevent or end false and intolerable relations. Their triumph and Lady Byron's justification would have been complete, and great would have been their rejoicing. But with her the romance of self-sacrifice was all-powerful. She dreamed of miracles, of Augusta purified from sin . . .'

(Lovelace, III, 63)

That is written by Lady Byron's grandson and staunchest supporter. But whether 'self-sacrifice' is really the word to characterize her actions (e.g. 'suspend this terror over her', p. 92) may be questioned. Nor have we any certainty that either Byron or Augusta were so anxious to commit incest as were Lady Byron's supporters to urge them on to it.

Augusta's behaviour is mysterious. She certainly appears for 'some reason' to be 'desperately anxious to stand well with Lady Byron' (Drinkwater, I, 70). But why? Why did she allow Lady Byron to dominate her? Why does she keep Lady Byron guessing, playing up, as it were, to her suspicions without ever actually, so far as we can see from the correspondence, satisfying them? Was she really terrified of exposure on grounds of incest? If so, why not deny the charge firmly rather than by innuendo? Or was she, on her side, terrified of Lady Byron giving away some secret regarding her loved Byron, and did she deliberately play up to the suspicion of incest so far as was possible short of actual confession in order to keep this strange woman in a state of doubt? One thing is clear: Lady Byron and her supporters passionately wanted to know for certain that her husband had committed incest with her best friend; and it is conceivable that Augusta was doing what she could, for reasons of her own, and that probably means for the sake of Byron, to keep her, provisionally, satisfied, without finally damaging her own reputation. There may have been something which she, on her side, feared more.

Whether or not she went farther in confession in her conversation with Lady Byron in September 1816 we cannot know. Lady Byron said so, but that means nothing. *Not a word of Lady Byron's evidence subsequent to her leaving her husband can be trusted.* This has already been recognized by Drinkwater (III, 251), though a number of biographers have been deceived. After the supposed September confession, Augusta, according to Lady Lovelace, 'entered into the compact with Lady Byron under which for years she sent her Byron's letters to herself regularly as she received them, and undertook to act in all things regarding him by Lady Byron's advice' (Lovelace, IX, 198). This indeed sounds like an arrangement on Augusta's part peculiarly disloyal to Byron, and there must have been some very cogent reason for her submission to it. Byron was to be allowed to write letters which were later shown, without his knowledge, to his enemy; for Lady Byron wished him to be kept in ignorance of the plan. On 17 July 1816 she wrote to Augusta advising silence to Byron regarding her own detective work and supposed knowledge:

'I have a difficulty in advising as to the communication, from being so ignorant of his present dispositions—I conceive that his *fear* of my penetration would as in other cases create *hatred*—and I do not see the evils of *postponing* the disclosure—but if the evils are to *you*, act so as to avoid them, and you will fulfil my wishes—I will reflect farther on this point.'

(Lovelace, X, 236)

She reports on 28 July 1816 to Mrs. Villiers:

'She says that in her last letter she has only mentioned respecting me that I had shown her "the greatest kindness"—This is all well and I am now leading her on to promise that she will never renew a confidential intercourse by letter—or any personal intercourse—I find it necessary to gain step by step, and to disclose my views less abruptly than with some.'

(Lovelace, X, 245)

'Confidential' apparently means a correspondence not shown to Lady Byron; and the later, September, arrangement met her wishes perfectly. She quite shamelessly led up to this arrangement by putting

Augusta against Byron on 30 July 1816 in a most dishonourable, Iago-like, fashion:

'His feelings towards you have varied—and they were seldom suppressed with me—Sometimes he has spoken of you with compassion—sometimes with bitter scorn—and sometimes with disposition still more reprehensible.'

(Lovelace, x, 247)

Lady Byron and Mrs. Villers correspond continually on the necessity of persuading Augusta that Byron has, presumably in conversation, 'betrayed her' (Lovelace, IX, 218; x, 255, 258–60), Mrs. Villiers boasting of having told her that she has been 'the victim to the most infernal plot that had ever entered the heart of man to conceive' (to Lady Byron, 15 Sept., 1816; Lovelace, x, 259). All this must be balanced against Byron's poems to Augusta, together with his repeated statements, throughout a number of years, that her love was his greatest consolation. The misrepresentation is patent. But what right had Lady Byron, whatever he had said, to put Augusta against him? She admits regularly that she does not suppose that incest had occurred after the marriage; and she had originally been willing not to enquire too closely as to the rest. Why now this slow torment? These Iago intrigues? When Lady Byron denies having used 'clandestine means to obtain information' (to Colonel Doyle, 29 Jan., 1820; Lovelace, v, 106; and see Fox, XVI, 154–5) before the Separation negotiations, she may have been telling the truth. Hobhouse was later uncertain (P, VI, 22, note), and Byron told Medwin (42) that it was Mrs. Clermont's doing. But Lady Byron's instinctive technique was certainly 'clandestine'. Nor did she behave honourably. Byron returned her letters, but, he writes, 'She had not the courtesy to restore me *mine*; but never mind; though they were too much to my credit for her to give them back, we can do without them' (Murray, 28 Sept., 1821; LJ, v, 380).

II

Consideration for the child does not account for Lady Byron's actions. There was some secret which she and her advisers were terrified of coming out; and that is why they were so afraid of Byron's *Memoirs*—the papers which were burned after his death. About these he wrote to his wife on 31 December, 1819 (Lovelace, v, 101; XI, 299), saying that, since they dealt with his marriage troubles, he wished her to read and mark them with her own comments, which would not be erased. In answer she composed a reply, saying, though she had herself been doing all she could to work up evidence on incest, that such memoirs were unjustifiable; that no doubt—since she realized the danger of Byron's plain-speaking—they were 'affectedly candid', and hard to refute by mere contradiction; that she wished to avoid all future publicity; that, though his talents gave him a great advantage, his duplicity would eventually be recognized; and, finally, though wishing his welfare, she would 'lament any proceedings on your part which may render it impossible for me to persevere in a passive conduct'. This letter, on the advice of Dr. Lushington, was not sent (Lovelace, v, 102–3); but the general principle of threat and intimidation was approved, and it was agreed that Lady Byron should refuse to read the *Memoirs*, and that all communications on the matter should go through Augusta.

It was, of course, against just such an eventuality as this that evidence for incest had been so assiduously sought. So now Colonel Doyle wrote to Lady Byron on 27 January, 1820, saying that Dr. Lushington thought that if it were made clear to Augusta that any circulation of the *Memoirs*, with all the controversy that must follow, would only lead to the open disclosure by Lady Byron's party of what everyone would wish concealed, it was fairly certain that she would write to Byron in such a way as to silence him. Byron should be made '*aware* of the *extent* of the *information*' possessed by Lady Byron, and it is suggested that Augusta be made 'the instrument of conveying' to him 'that sort of intimidation' which might 'deter him from the course he is about to enter'; and also that Augusta's personal feelings should not be considered (Lovelace, v, 104). Dr. Lushington composed an outline of the proposed letter from Lady Byron to Augusta. 'His first idea', writes Lord Lovelace, 'was to convey a sort of threat to make a full and unreserved disclosure to the world of all those circumstances which would at once establish Lady Byron's justification, "and involve Lord Byron and others in infamy"' (Lovelace, v, 104). Observe that Augusta was to be made the implement of a threat risking her own ruin by the disclosure of her supposed confidences originally wrung from her—if they ever were—ostensibly on soul-saving grounds.

The *Memoirs* were Byron's defence against the calumnies to which he had been subjected, devised in order to safeguard his name for posterity. But it was precisely such a defence that Lady Byron and her advisers feared, and they resorted to blackmail in reply. There was no proper excuse now for any talk of incest at all. The old suspicion was long past, and Lady Byron had no reason to suppose that anything had gone wrong since her marriage (pp. 91–2). On this Lord Lovelace, with all the family records to hand, is himself definite (VIII, 180). Dr. Lushington 'emphatically' stated in 1870, what we already know, that it was not the cause of the Separation (Lovelace, VII, 159). Therefore the proposed reply to Byron ran, in effect: 'We will not read your account of the Separation which you have composed for the sake of posterity, nor answer its charges; but if you do not suppress it we propose to unearth the old and irrelevant scandal concerning Augusta, which we are in a better position to do than ever, since Lady Byron has reduced her to the condition of a nervous wreck and has her utterly under control'. That it was an effective line to adopt may be seen from one of Byron's letters, to be quoted later (p. 134), where he admits to being afraid of causing trouble for Augusta.

But Lady Byron had an acute and logical mind and knew that it would not quite do. She probably knew, too, that the evidence she claimed to have drawn from Augusta was far less solid than she had led her advisers to suppose. She saw, very clearly, certain weaknesses and wrote a long reply to Colonel Doyle on 29 January, 1820, taking up Dr. Lushington's points in turn. She thought, if it ever had to be disclosed to others, that people would not readily understand, as well they might not, the nature of her own confidential relationship with Augusta. She was also reluctant to allow Augusta to come into the open and tell Byron what had been going on. She feared

'that, an unreserved disclosure from her to him being necessitated, they would combine together against me—he being actuated by revenge—she by fear—whereas, from her never having dared to inform him that she has already admitted his guilt to me with her own, they have hitherto been prevented from acting in consort.'

(Lovelace, v, 106)

Of course, it is extremely doubtful if Augusta *had* confessed anything germane to the blackmail, and that is why innuendoes were employed. Lady Byron never wanted an open disclosure of anything; her power depended on avoiding it. She continues:

'The transmission of the cursory observation suggested in Dr. L's *note*, and the equivalent of what I *have* said to her, would not in my opinion have any effect. Lord B— is not intimidated by terms so general. The addition which you suggest of the paragraph—"*Lord B— is probably by no means aware of the extent of the information of which I was possessed before our separation*, nor of the additional proofs, as well as new facts, which have since come to my knowledge"— would render the communication more pointed (bringing it perhaps into the same case with the *first*) but I perceive objections to the clause underlined. For, my information previous to my separation having been derived either directly from Lord B— or from my observations on that part of his conduct which he exposed to my view—the expression "he is probably not aware" would seem a contradiction, at least unless guarded by something to this effect— "As the infatuation of pride may have blinded him to the conclusions which must inevitably be established by a long series of circumstantial evidences" . . .'

(Lovelace, v, 106)

Observe the phraseology into which she is forced and the extraordinary volutions of her mind. She wishes to keep Byron in ignorance of what she had, if she had, learned from Augusta, whilst simultaneously threatening him with it. But she sees clearly her central weakness. She seems to mean that Byron had, by implication, admitted to incest. If so, she cannot well say: 'If you are not careful I shall reveal to the world that I now know to be true what I gathered from certain hints and actions of yours when we were living together as husband and wife, but which my legal advisers assured you were not part of our case during the Separation when we were so anxious for a quiet arrangement.' She cannot say this. But she wants to *hint* that she is *thinking* of such a course. Or perhaps she just knows that her deductions are purely hazardous, but wishes him to think that they are not. She goes on to suggest a letter to Byron by her father saying

'that, reluctant as I (i.e. Lady Byron) have ever been to bring my domestic concerns before the public, and anxious as I have felt to save from ruin a near connection of his, I shall feel myself compelled by duties of primary importance, if he perseveres in accumulating injuries upon me, to make a disclosure of the past in its *most* authentic form.'

(Lovelace, v, 107)

This last sentence, she says, 'requires very great caution'. She thinks that such an allusion to Augusta by her father will not be so likely to force a disclosure to Byron of her own machinations as would any threats transmitted by Augusta herself. She was very afraid of Byron getting to know of her intrigues with Augusta. She had reason to be afraid. She was not only half-purposing to reveal her husband's confidences—if such there were—but also those of Augusta wrung from her with the supposed purpose of advancing her spiritual and moral welfare. Lady Byron, moreover, knew that she had no real evidence: 'I do not conceive', she says, 'that such a communication would absolutely bind me at this time to publish my case, if he should (relying on the advantage of an intervening sea) return an answer of defiance' (Lovelace, v, 107). She wanted to use her father, that is, as a mask, with herself left free to repudiate his letter.

But Colonel Doyle on 1 February, 1820, urged that a letter from her would be best, since 'the threat of a third person may make it incumbent on his pride to revolt' (Lovelace, v, 108). They were all afraid of their bluff being called. Why, we may ask, these tentative proposals of letters by Augusta, Sir Ralph Noel, or Lady Byron? Why, instead of urging the use of Augusta (Lovelace, v, 104), could not her legal advisers have written direct to Byron in legal terms saying what they really meant? Presumably they dared not; it is doubtful if their action would have been legal; and they knew that they had no case. Eventually Lady Byron wrote a brief letter containing a veiled threat (p. 150).

On the news of Byron's death in 1824 the *Memoirs*, which had been written for posthumous publication, were destroyed after Hobhouse and others had got the agreement of Augusta as Byron's nearest blood-relation. Augusta's official statement, in her own writing, tells us that she herself had never read a line of them, 'shrank from the responsibility', and felt 'dread and unwillingness to be an agent in the business'. She was finally overruled and gave her sanction; but Ethel Colburn Mayne agrees that she seems to have shown no eagerness whatsoever for the destruction (Augusta's Statement, *Athenaeum*, 18 Aug., 1883; 205; Jeaffreson, App. II, 495; Mayne, II; App. II, 326). Despite this, and other, evidence, Maurois, thinking of incest, makes the fantastic statement that the 'everprudent Augusta' was behind it all, and even gives his readers the impression that *at the last moment* it was an 'impassioned protest' from

Augusta, who was not in fact present, which turned the scale (Maurois, Epilogue, 417). This is sheer, and misleading, fiction.

It is often assumed that Lady Byron's influence was at work. So it evidently was, though Colonel Doyle denied it. Lady Byron had already told him that it was 'very desirable' to 'obtain' the manuscript from Moore and had 'requested' him to act for her if necessary, but he claimed that his presence at the burning was accidental and due to a last moment invitation from Wilmot Horton—who was, however, as we have seen, another of Lady Byron's advisers—and that he regarded himself only as a witness, and not as a party, to the proceeding (Lovelace, quoting a letter of his to Wilmot Horton, App. A, 327; VI, 122–3; Mayne, II; App. II, 324, note, and see Fox, XVI, 180–4, 195–6). According to John Murray, the son of Byron's publisher, Colonel Doyle was functioning as Lady Byron's friend (*Academy*, 9 Oct., 1869; Vol. I, 8); and Wilmot Horton, though known to have helped Augusta in business matters, was there, says Jeaffreson, 'as much in the interest of Lady Byron as in the interest of Mrs. Leigh' (Jeaffreson, XXVI, 427). Colonel Doyle and Wilmot Horton together, both friends and supporters of Lady Byron, who had been joint witnesses with Lushington to her March 1816 statement, actually *did the burning*, Colonel Doyle saying, though himself holding no authority from Augusta, 'On the part of Mrs. Leigh I put them into the fire' (Hobhouse, III; App. I, 342). Despite his approval of it, Hobhouse himself refused, when invited, to take part in the action (Hobhouse, III, App. I, 342; Hobhouse to Wilmot Horton, 23 Nov., 1824; Fox, XVI, 180–1). It was performed by Colonel Doyle, Lady Byron's official representative, and by Wilmot Horton, her other adviser, whom we have already (p. 93) found joining in the blackmail against Augusta.

That Wilmot Horton appears to have thrown 'the responsibility of the destruction' on Lady Byron may be gathered from a letter by Augusta on 6 June, 1825, to Lady Byron, who had been agitated by what he had said as to her part in the matter, assuring her that it was she, Augusta, who had been persuaded by Hobhouse to give her authority, and adding, 'Wilmot must be mad!' (Mayne, *Lady Byron*, XX, 305); and yet Augusta is also reported to have said that she agreed to the burning 'for Lady Byron's sake' (Lovelace, VI, 123). The two women had, it seems, been in close touch. *The Quarterly* tells us: 'We have seen a mass of correspondence on this subject, headed by a letter of May, 1824, from Lady Byron to Mrs. Leigh, beginning, as usual, "My dearest Augusta", and proposing that they should take joint action in the matter, as they did' (*Quarterly*, Jan., 1870; Vol. 128; *230*): as we have seen, Augusta was at this period dominated by Lady Byron. Within twenty-four hours of hearing of her husband's death, Lady Byron had offered the two thousand guineas needed to redeem the papers from Byron's publisher, John Murray, who had bought them (*Quarterly*, citing Moore's *Memoirs*; July, 1883, Vol. 156; *121-4*; Moore's *Memoirs etc.*, 14, 15 May, 1824; IV, 187; Murray's Statement, *Academy*, 9 Oct., 1869; Vol. I, 8; Jeaffreson quoting Murray, XXVI, 427). The offer to buy them for 'Lord Byron's family' came through the banker, Douglas Kinnaird: the term, which is, probably intentionally, ambiguous, meant, according to Hobhouse, Augusta (Hobhouse, III, App. I, 333); but *she* did not put up the money. Both Moore's *Memoirs* and Murray, the son of Byron's publisher, implicate Lady Byron in the offer, Murray stating uncompromisingly that Lady Byron 'had actually offered' his father the two thousand guineas in question (Moore's *Memoirs* and Murray's Statement, as above). Hobhouse's own account shows that he was working in direct collusion with Lady Byron, since it reports him as saying to Moore, directly after the papers had been burned: 'I felt that by changing your mind as to the destruction of the manuscript you had compromised me with Mrs. Leigh and Lady Byron, as well as with Murray' (Hobhouse, III; App. I, 345). That is plain enough. Moore indeed notes that he and Hobhouse—which probably means *he*—had agreed that it would be 'treachery' to Byron to let his wife *have* them (Moore's *Memoirs etc.*, 15 May, 1824; IV, 187-8); but she did not want them herself; she merely wanted them—I dare not say 'destroyed', since I have no first-hand proof of that—but certainly suppressed. So did Hobhouse, and, though we shall never know who first suggested or who finally forced the *burning*, since each in turn denied it—though we do know who *did* it, Doyle and Wilmot Horton—we may conclude that Hobhouse and Lady Byron were together responsible for getting Augusta's permission for it, and that Wilmot Horton had reason for what he said.

On the evening of the burning, 17 May, Wilmot Horton wrote a letter, marked '6 p.m.', opening: 'I send an express over to Lady Byron to announce the destruction of the *Memoirs*'; a letter which leads *The Quarterly* to observe that it looks as though he had been acting directly for Lady Byron (*Quarterly*, July, 1883; Vol. 156; *122*). That Lady Byron disclaimed responsibility (Fox, XVI, 183, quoting

Athenaeum, 24 May, 1884) means nothing, since she was an adept at indirect action. It may indeed be true that, as Colonel Doyle insists, the point at issue in Lady Byron's mind had been simply suppression or partial publication (to Wilmot Horton, 18 May, 1825; Lovelace, App. A, 328); and if so, the chance of burning came as a piece of good luck which neither she nor her advisers had ever expected that Byron's party would sanction; but such a supposition is contradicted by Hobhouse's remark, and it was in actual fact her two advisers, and not Hobhouse, ardent as he was, who took advantage of it.

The same day, Monday, 17 May, 1824, Lady Byron was ready for the next step. Hobhouse's diary for that date records:

'I should mention that this day I received a curious message from Lady Byron through Captain George (Lord) Byron. It was that she wished me to give out that I should write Lord Byron's Memoirs in conjunction with the assistance of the family, including Lady Byron, as that would stop all spurious efforts and would be particularly agreeable to her. I returned for answer that I had no spirits now nor inclination for undertaking or thinking of any such task.'

(Hobhouse, III, App. I, 347)

That can well be left to speak, vociferously, for itself. We shall have more to say of the burning of the *Memoirs* in due course (pp. 152–6 below).

III

Lady Byron may, indeed, have had excuses for her actions, and these we shall discuss later on, but, after watching her frantic endeavours to suppress Byron's defence, we can no longer regard her as an honest witness. We have one peculiarly clear instance of her unreliability. This we have already noticed, but its importance is such that we must refer to it again. In her *Remarks on Moore's Life of Byron*, published in the year 1830 (p. xiii), she not only insists, against Mrs. Fletcher's evidence (p. 70), that she had been a free agent in the Separation, but also asserts:

'Conformably with this resolution, my father wrote to him on the 2nd of February to propose an amicable separation. Lord Byron at first rejected this proposal, but when it was distinctly notified to him that if he persisted in his refusal, recourse must be had to legal measures, he agreed to sign a deed of separation.'

(LJ, III, 290)

Now we have direct evidence, from a letter of her own, that she pleaded with Byron as a man of honour not to force her into court, and we also have Lord Lovelace's statement that both Byron and Hanson held out to the last, Byron being finally persuaded by Hobhouse (pp. 76–7; and see p. 147). The *Remarks* are guilty of a huge misrepresentation; and, this recognized, we shall not regard any of Lady Byron's personal records of her marriage difficulties and Byron's behaviour, on which so much Byronic biography has been hitherto based, as evidence. This is not, of course, to say that it never contains any traces of the truth; but the truth is probably falsified beyond recognition.

In these *Remarks* she printed a letter from Dr. Lushington, dated 31 January, 1830, wherein it was clearly stated that what determined Lady Byron's advisers to insist on a separation was the *information given them on Lady Byron's own visit to London on 22 February 1816 concerning something which she had not previously told her parents*. This had not been publicly revealed before, and constituted an important advance in Lady Byron's campaign against her husband's posthumous reputation. We know that the information in question had nothing whatever to do with incest; but it is probable that by the year 1830 Lady Byron hoped, and even assumed, that people would think that it did; and some have done so.

Her concentration on the incest shows a steady development. In August, 1815, she could write concerning certain items in Byron's will, 'I must tell you how lovingly Byron has been talking of "dear Goose" till he had half a mind to cry and so had I . . . And, dearest Augusta, believe that I know you too well to suppose what a certain person might suppose, or anything of the kind' (*Athenaeum*, 18 Aug., 1883; 207; Jeaffreson, App. II, 474). The 'certain person' was Caroline Lamb, who had been spreading rumours of incest. We have Lady Byron's word for it that on Augusta's second visit to Piccadilly, from November 1815 until the end, Byron's 'inclinations were most averse from her and absorbed in another direction' (to Mrs. Villiers, 12 May, 1816; Lovelace, IX, 203). We are not surprised to hear that Lady Byron's first statement, composed for her parents in January 1816 after leaving London, never mentioned incest (Lovelace, I, 21; note). The second, made before Dr. Lushington and others in March 1816, asserted that it played no important part in her decision, though she wished to record the suspicion as a possible safeguard for future use (p. 89 above). A third fragmentary statement—Lady Byron was addicted to statements—was more or less completed in March 1817. This, says Lady Lovelace, was 'mainly occupied with the story of Byron's conduct to Augusta and his constant avowals about her to Lady Byron' (Lovelace, I, 21; note); a claim obviously incompatible with the various items of correspondence which we have already studied. By then she claimed to have had a confession from Augusta (Lovelace, III, 65).

After 1830 the relationship between Augusta and Lady Byron was broken off. There was a bitter quarrel (Jeaffreson, XXVII, 455–6). Here is a letter from Augusta to Lady Byron, dated 19 January, 1830, showing the transition:

'You say from my representations and the conclusions I draw it is evident my mind is not in a state "to admit the truth". I answer, if my representations are incorrect (which I declare most solemnly I am not aware of) point out where I am mistaken, and I shall be happy to rectify them. If my conclusions are unfounded, show me where I am wrong and I shall be delighted to withdraw them. Surely this does not savour of a mind unwilling to admit the truth or undesirous to obtain it, when all I ask is to know it, and to be governed by it entirely. When you tell me that "you decline any further discussion of facts which are clearly as well known to me as yourself", you *more* than convey an insinuation that I have wilfully misrepresented motives. I *deny* having done so and I repeat that I have spoken to you openly and fairly without one word of intentional subterfuge or evasion.

'My heart is broken in every way! But with my last breath I shall acquit myself of all intentional injustice to you or want of acknowledgment of your kindness to me.'

(*Athenaeum*, 18 Aug., 1883, 210; Jeaffreson, App. II, 489)

Just like Byron, Augusta asks for, but does not receive, plain speaking. The two women are, it seems, still at cross-purposes. This is followed by a letter of yet greater bitterness on 24 February (*Athenaeum*, 18 Aug., 1883; 210; Jeaffreson, App. II, 491). Augusta from then on appeared to be no longer afraid—observe how the old confusions of her epistolary style are now gone—and could be outspoken in blaming Lady Byron for leaving her husband (Lovelace, I, 29; IV, 99–100).

Many years later, having heard that Lady Byron had said that her influence had 'prevented Byron from coming to just and kindly views about his wife', Augusta seems to have wished to establish the contrary before her death; and it was arranged that the two women, who had not seen each other or corresponded since 1830 (Fox, XVI, 177), should meet (Mayne, II; I, 29). Lady Byron consulted the Rev. F. W. Robertson of Brighton in contemplation of this meeting. On 8 January 1851 she wrote to him with reference to Augusta's soul:

'A hope has risen in my mind that through your ministry good might yet be done to that Survivor for whom I am so deeply interested. It may seem very remote—next to impossible, but if it *could*!

'You shall know then—if you recollect in our last conversation I said there was one whom I had not seen for years, but hoped before death to see again—That was the person whose *guilt* made a great part (*not* the whole) of my wretchedness—to whom, since that one impulse which I acknowledged to you, I have never had any feeling but one of—I can't get a right word . . .'
(Quoted from the Lovelace papers, Fox, XVI, 199)

During April, the two women met at Reigate, with the Rev. F. W. Robertson present. We can, I think, assume that Lady Byron's central desire was for evidence (*Quarterly*, Jan., 1910; Vol. 212, *30*).

The meeting was painful and ended, says Ethel Colburn Mayne, in bitterness. On 12 April, 1851, Lady Byron wrote to Augusta:

'As I have received the communication which you have so long and anxiously desired to make—and upon which I offered no comment except "Is that all?"—I have done all in my power to contribute to your peace of mind. But I remain under the afflicting persuasion that it is not attained by such means as you have taken. Farewell.'
(*Athenaeum*, 18 Aug., 1883; 211;
Jeaffreson, App. II, 493; Mayne, II; I, 29)

Augusta replied sharply:

'I had not, and never implied that I had, anything to reveal to you with which you were not previously acquainted on any other subject. Nor can I at all express to you the regret I have felt ever since those words escaped you, showing that you imagined I had "encouraged a bitterness in feeling in Lord Byron towards you". I can as solemnly declare to you as if I were on my oath, or on my deathbed, that I never did so in any one instance, but that I invariably did the contrary.'

(*Athenaeum*, 18 Aug., 1883, 211;

Jeaffreson, App. II, 493; Mayne, II; 1, 30)

They are still at the old cross-purposes. Lady Byron presumably wants a confession of incest; Augusta, apparently still not seeing the point, assumes that she is merely being accused of some kind of disloyalty. She repeated her denial in a letter to the Rev. F. W. Robertson (Fox, XVI, 179). Despite her claims to a confession in 1816, Lady Byron had advanced no further.[1]

On 12 October, 1851, Augusta died, according to Lord Lovelace leaving behind her a selection of papers intended to rebut the charge of incest (Lovelace, VII, 146; see p. 97). Before dying, she was comforted by a message from Lady Byron containing the phrase 'Dearest Augusta' (Fox, XVI, 177). Her death was followed on 27 November, 1852, by that of Lady Byron's daughter, Augusta Ada, Countess of Lovelace.

About the year 1854 Lady Byron started on what was to be a comprehensive narrative to supplement and replace her earlier statements, 'but' writes Lady Lovelace, 'though more than one abortive version of this later narrative exists, none was ever completed' (Lovelace, I, 21; note). Lord Lovelace quotes part of the preface to this narrative (Lovelace, VI, 140–1).

She had earlier, in 1849, consigned to Mrs. Frances Carr a box containing some relevant papers, not to be opened for thirty years, when its contents were to be used according to the judgment of the trustees. Her directions were signed in 1850 (Lovelace, VII, 158–9). This box presumably contained some, but it seems not all (Fox, XII, 95), of the papers used in *Astarte*. But it seems that after this, when at work on her uncompleted autobiography, she consulted with many friends concerning the advisability of leaving a conclusive statement for publication after her death with, presumably, no time-lag (Lovelace, VI, 141). One of these was Mrs. Harriet Beecher Stowe, author of *Uncle Tom's Cabin*, who visited her in the year

---

[1] In *The Byron Mystery* Sir John Fox attempts to argue that Lady Byron could not have been thinking of incest (Fox, XVI, 177); but this, from this writer, whom we shall discuss later, is surely a piece of special pleading.

For other accounts of the meeting, see Jeaffreson, XXVII, 455–8; Edgcumbe, III, 324–5; and Mayne, *Life of Lady Byron*, XXVII, 403–13.

1856, and after Lady Byron's death published an article *The True Story of Lady Byron's Life* in *Macmillan's Magazine* of September 1869, based on what Lady Byron had told her. This she expanded later to a volume, *Lady Byron Vindicated, a History of the Byron Controversy*, in 1870.

Mrs. Stowe's revelations aroused considerable controversy and a great deal of criticism. It is impossible to say how accurately she reports Lady Byron's conversations, but it must be admitted that the contents correspond with what we know of her views and purposes.

Lady Byron is reported as saying that during the marriage Byron openly confessed to incest and threatened its continuance (II, 159–60); that he could have had court proceedings had he wished (I, 121; II, 206); and even, in the book, though not in the earlier article—this counting slightly in Lady Byron's favour—that incest was the cause of the Separation (II, 233). Of these three assertions, the first, though in line with Lady Byron's 1817 statement, is contradicted by Lord Lovelace's assurance that she never admitted to herself that she believed the charge during her marriage (Lovelace, VIII, 179); and it utterly contradicts the tentative tone of her own March 1816 statement, as well as her letter to Colonel Doyle of 29 January, 1820 (p.104). The second, as we have seen (pp. 76–7, 110), is a grand falsification. The third is a lie (see Lovelace, VII, 159; also p. 88 above).

What Lady Byron said we cannot precisely know, but it seems that the impression she left was roughly the kind of impression she would have wished to leave. We have the direct evidence of one who knew her well, John Robertson, that, before talking to Mrs. Stowe, she had been for some time spreading the scandal of both incest and another crime among a number of friends, and that this and other communications were freely given 'as facts to be used for the defence of her conduct, character, and memory'; and the Rev. Francis Trench, who knew of her stories, clearly received the impression, just as did Mrs. Stowe, that incest had been the cause of the Separation (John Robertson, and the Rev. Francis Trench in *The Quarterly*, Oct., 1869; Vol. 127; 426–8; see my pp. 207, 234). According to *Blackwood's* there was no doubt that Lady Byron did assert this, and that she had, 'unquestionably', told the same story to other people, though exactly when she had started to do so was not clear (*Blackwood's*, Jan., 1870; Vol. 107; 132).

Anyway, Lady Byron and Mrs. Stowe together succeeded in influencing the biographers of Byron. And it is not only a question of

Mrs. Stowe's account. Both Ethel Colburn Mayne and Maurois have followed Lady Byron's unpublished reminiscences without question: 'A great part of the documents here relied on', writes Miss Mayne, 'derive their value from Lady Byron's universally recognized truthfulness' (Mayne, *Lady Byron*, Preface, v). Meanwhile Byron's attempt at truthfulness had been thrown to the flames by her accredited representative.

The falsities of Mrs. Stowe's supposed revelation were remorselessly exposed by *The Quarterly* (p. 233 below), and elsewhere. In order to defend the good name of his grandmother, Lord Lovelace, Ada's son, brought out his *Astarte* in the year 1905, and a second edition, edited by his widow, Lady Lovelace, appeared after his death, with the addition of some new correspondence, in 1921.

The author is concerned throughout to demonstrate that incest had occurred before the marriage; he never states, or appears anxious to suggest, that it had continued. This, too, is exactly, and only, what Lady Byron had set herself assiduously to establish as soon as the Separation had been obtained.

Lord Lovelace, with remarkable *naïveté*, states emphatically that incest was *not*, and then suggests we might as well consider that it was, the cause of the Separation (p. 237 below). He is himself no ungenerous critic of the sin. Indeed, he argues that there was, as between Byron and Augusta, and in this period, no great wrong in it (VI, 138–9 ; VII, 152), and that, even if there were, if only they had, most conveniently for Lady Byron and her supporters, gone away together after the Separation, the world would have sympathized:

'Societies secretly respect, though they excommunicate, those rebel lovers who sacrifice everything else, but observe a law of their own, and make a religion out of sin itself by living it through with constancy.'

(Lovelace, III, 62)

Yes, but what if Byron and Augusta did not *want* to commit incest? Why should they? They were free agents, and you cannot expect them to do it merely to oblige Byron's 'in-laws'. What *does* Lord Lovelace mean? What he means will be clear enough before we have finished. Meanwhile it will be enough to note that he is at pains to insist that incest is a sin far preferable to certain others that were in the air, and as good as urges us all to accept it as the lesser evil (VIII, 182; discussed on p. 237 below). But it is not merely a question of 'lesser evil'; incest concerned Byron and Augusta, whereas the other sin concerned Byron and his wife; that is the point.

Clearly, there was some good reason for this persistent attempt stretching through a whole century, from Lady Byron's March 1816 statement until the second edition of *Astarte* in 1921, to establish the charge of incest. It cannot be accounted for by any fears for the control of Ada, since it continued after Byron's, Ada's, and even Lady Byron's own death. Whilst the incest is played up in Lovelace's account, other unpleasant facts, as we shall see (p. 237), are, it would seem deliberately, suppressed or slighted. Drinkwater was right in regarding the evidence of *Astarte* as untrustworthy. The quality of its logic may be assessed by comparing Lovelace's insistence that the *Memoirs* could not have been destroyed through Lady Byron's influence, since it was to her interest to preserve 'all possible evidence' (VI, 122), with the terror shown by her and her advisers in the letters which he himself has printed for us when they first heard of their existence (pp. 103–6 above).

Lady Byron wished poignantly, almost pathetically, to be sure of the incest, and to have some evidence of it. It is as though she, and her grandson, wished to use it as some sort of justification for her actions, and perhaps, still more, as a veil to obscure some fact or facts of her married life; and in view of the disproportionate attention it has received, we may say that they have, quite brilliantly, succeeded.

It is not my purpose to argue that Lady Byron was either a bad or a foolish woman. She was neither, as may be gathered from Byron's eulogy of her, written during the separation proceedings, in his denunciation of Mrs. Clermont in *A Sketch*. But she had, it seems, been placed in an unusually difficult position, which to some extent impelled, though it scarcely excuses, her actions. Meanwhile, our enquiry has at least demonstrated that any evidence in her own favour drawn from her own accounts of her marriage composed after she left London in January 1816, or from any letters, or copies of letters, in her own handwriting, must be regarded as worthless. All her reminiscences and private papers must henceforth be read in the light of the deliberate campaign of suppression and propaganda which we have been analysing; and when that is recognized, the effect on Byronic studies will be great.

IV
WHAT BYRON SAID

IV. WHAT BYRON SAID

I

WE pass to a review of some of Byron's own statements after the Separation. Though it is not properly our theme, our discussion is forced to handle the question of incest, if only because Lady Byron and others have used it to confuse the issue: our aim will be to disentangle it from the real problem. Part of our business will be to show that *Manfred* does not, as Lord Lovelace argued, constitute a confession of incest. After dealing with the problem of incest we shall pass to the more important matters.

After the Separation Byron wrote three poems addressed to Augusta. In them she appears as a figure of maternal peace and, pre-eminently, 'purity'. In the first, *Stanzas to Augusta*, probably written before leaving for the Continent, she is a 'solitary star', 'unbroken light' and 'seraph's eye', shining through the midnight of disaster:

> *And when the cloud upon us came*
> *Which strove to blacken o' er thy ray—*
> *Then purer spread its gentle flame,*
> *And dashed the darkness all away.*

(P, III, 545)

She functions not as the cause, direct or indirect, of Byron's crash, but rather as the one redeeming power that enabled him to bear it. She is to be contrasted with all the confusions and torments of 'baffled' love; her 'soul' will 'never shake'. She is a semi-divine figure of Christian affinities (P, III, 544–6). In another set of *Stanzas to Augusta*, written after leaving England (July, 1816; P, IV, 54), her faithfulness and support are again emphasized. There is also the *Epistle to Augusta*, dating from the same period as the last, but, unlike the other two, withheld from publication during Byron's life:

> My Sister! my sweet Sister! if a name
> Dearer and purer were, it should be thine . . .
>
> (P, IV, 57)

He longs for a 'home' with her after his 'inheritance of storms'; he is in a mood to recapture the intuitions of 'happy childhood', and nature speaks to him now as it did in his youth, Lake Leman reminding him of 'our own dear Lake by the old Hall'. Nature is to be his 'sister' until he looks again on Augusta; and in this mood he repudiates ambition, love, fame, and all the turmoils of his recent life. 'The tie which bound the first', he concludes, 'endures the last.'

He is in a peculiarly Wordsworthian mood. Augusta is associated with nature and youth, and contrasted with the fiery passions of maturity. The same note is struck in the third canto of *Childe Harold*, written at this period. One stanza describes Byron's love of children, and the next, with the following lines to Drachenfels, referred to in his letter to her of 13 January, 1817 (Lovelace, XI, 281), passes on to notice his love for Augusta:

> And there was one soft breast, as hath been said,
> Which unto his was bound by stronger ties
> Than the church links withal; and—though unwed,
> That love was pure—and, far above disguise,
> Had stood the test of mortal enmities
> Still undivided, and cemented more
> By peril, dreaded most in female eyes;
> But this was firm, and from a foreign shore
> Well to that heart might his these absent greetings pour!
>
> (III, 55)

These poems do not disprove the charge of incest; but they do show that, whatever be the truth, Byron's love for his half-sister was, in his own mind, an experience of purity in strong contrast with sinful passion.

This third canto of *Childe Harold* contains fine descriptions of the mountain scenery of Switzerland; so does the prose 'Journal for Augusta'. There is no need to suppose, as some, including Words-worth himself, have suggested, that Wordsworth's influence was at work, since the love of mountainous nature had been bred in

Byron as surely as in Wordsworth, from childhood. In *The Adieu* (1807; P, I, 237–42) he regretted both the 'Hill' of Harrow and the mountains of his childhood. Two other early poems strike the same note. In *I Would I were a Careless Child* he contrasted these early Highland experiences of perfect insight with the hated world of false pleasures, rank, power, and society (P, I, 205); and in *When I Roved a Young Highlander* a girl called 'Mary', but not (P, I, 192, note) Mary Duff, the romance of his childhood, is the presiding spirit of the rugged, simple and idyllic state defined. It was an experience not of passion but of purity, in a setting of mountains, thundering torrents and Scottish mist. Prophetically, he looks forward to some later experience of mountains, without Mary. In 1816 there were again mountains, with Augusta taking her place in Byron's mind.

In the years between we have a third lady, Mary Anne Chaworth, similarly idealized and also associated with heights, the hills of Annesley, where she lived, near Newstead. To this, the central heterosexual love of Byron's life (pp. 24–8 above), we must now, at the risk of appearing to deviate from our story, devote a further enquiry.

There is an 1805 Fragment about her invoking the Hills of Annesley (P, I, 210), and in 1808, after her marriage, Byron addressed her in *Well! Thou art Happy* (P, I, 277). She was also addressed in two poems called *To a Lady*. In one, written in 1808 (P, I, 283), while giving his reasons for his intention to visit India in 1809, he sees himself as being exiled from the 'Eden' or 'paradise' of her presence. The other, also an early, poem offers a precise definition:

> For once my soul, like thine, was pure,
> And all its rising fires could smother;
> But now, thy vows no more endure,
> Bestow'd by thee upon another.

(P, I, 189)

What, exactly, *were* those rising fires? We must never in our study of Byron forget its under-current of homosexuality, and it may well have been this which made him look back so agonizedly on experiences of sinless purity; indeed, we need this, or some similar, anguish to make sense of his tormented conscience. So he goes on to contrast his troubled life, its palling pleasures and varied loves, with the 'calm domestic quiet' which Mary might have given him, together with the peace of nature, since in her presence 'Nature seemed to smile'. The thoughts are precisely those which were later aroused by Augusta.

In *Stanzas to a Lady on Leaving England* (1809; P, I, 285-8) he wrote, still thinking of Mary, that 'some unconquerable spell' kept his thoughts true to one alone. And the 'spell' endured. Throughout his life he looked back on this youthful romance and contrasted it with what followed. A bitter poem addressed to Francis Hodgson called *Epistle to a Friend* (1811; P, III, 28-30) records how he had seen Mary wedded to another, with another's child; he who had been formerly 'as fond and faultless' as that child itself is now thrown out on the world; and so he prophesies a dark and even criminal and bloody future for himself, without love or pity, as

> One rank'd in some recording page
> With the worst anarchs of the age . . .

This is a powerful and revealing poem, dated 11 October, 1811, the very day of his first poem to 'Thyrza', for Edleston (p. 30); for he could hold these two loves of innocence and purity in his mind almost as a single experience. Byron's future did, indeed, prove turbulent. So now, much later, during July, 1816, when so much of this prophecy must have seemed to him to have come true, he again turned to thoughts of Mary, and composed *The Dream* (P, IV, 33).

This is a poem deliberately comparing his first love for Mary with the subsequent sufferings of both. Their love is described as an experience of spiritual *identity*:

> She was his life,
> The ocean to the river of his thoughts
> Which terminated all . . .

To her, however, he was 'even as a brother—but no more'; that is what she *called* him. Their parting is described, and so is her apparent unhappiness as a married woman, which is treated as mysterious, since surely his own dark longings must have ceased to trouble her 'pure thoughts'. Surely he does not still act on her as 'a spectre of the past'? During the ceremony of Byron's own marriage, his mind was still on 'the Starlight of his Boyhood', on 'her who was his destiny'. And next Mary becomes seriously ill, and her mind gives way:

> Oh! she was changed
> As by the sickness of the soul; her mind
> Had wandered from its dwelling, and her eyes
> They had not their own lustre, but the look
> Which is not of the earth; she was become
> The queen of a fantastic realm, her thoughts
> Were combinations of disjointed things:
> And forms, impalpable and unperceived
> Of others' sight, familiar were to hers,
> And this the world calls frenzy.

She is Ophelia to Byron's Hamlet. But the 'wise', we are told, those, we may suggest, like Hamlet and Byron, endure a 'far deeper madness'. The poem describes Byron's subjection to slander, his retreat from England to the mountains of Europe, his feeding on 'poisons' which had 'a kind of nutriment' (compare *Childe Harold*, III; 7, 34), and his wrenching secrets from mountain and star and 'the quick Spirit of the Universe'. We end on thought of Mary's madness and the misery of both. The lines certainly read as though Byron had visited her, as he may have done (p. 26), during her illness.

On 13 January, 1817, Byron wrote to Augusta: 'Have you also got *Chillon* and the *Dream* and do you understand the latter?' (Lovelace, XI, 281).

Mary was never far from Byron's poetic thoughts. As late as 1818 we have *The Duel* (P, IV, 542–4), returning to the old theme of the slaying of Mary's grand-uncle by Byron's:

> 'Tis fifty years and three to boot
> Since hand to hand, and foot to foot,
> And heart to heart, and sword to sword,
> One of our Ancestors was gored.
> I've seen the sword that slew him; he,
> The slain, stood in a like degree
> To thee, as he, the Slayer, stood
> (Oh, had it been but other blood!)
> In Kin and Chieftainship to me.
> Thus came the Heritage to thee.

His love, he says, is now 'wedded to another'; both are 'to strangers vowed, with strangers bedded'. They had been forced apart by the ancestral curse:

> For many a bar and many a feud,
> Though never told, well understood,
> Rolled like a river wide between—
> And then there was the curse of blood,
> Which even my heart's can not remove.

Byron's passion for Mary remained to the last, strong though buried, like a volcanic fire.

Now a great deal of this is written into *Manfred*, composed at the same period as *The Dream*, between the summer of 1816 and the spring of 1817. *Manfred* is a drama of guilt and self-assertion wherein the hero is tormented by a female figure called 'Astarte'. Lord Lovelace quite unwarrantably identified Astarte with Augusta; but there is a far stronger case, as both Edgcumbe and Samuel Chew have recognized, for the identification of Astarte with Mary. Manfred suffers from sense of a blood-curse like that of *The Duel*:

> Away, away! there's blood upon the brim!
> Will it then never—never sink in the earth?

(II, i, 21)

Again,

> I say 'tis blood—my blood! the pure warm stream
> Which ran in the veins of my fathers, and in ours
> When we were in our youth, and had one heart,
> And loved each other as we should not love,
> And this was shed: but still it rises up,
> Colouring the clouds, that shut me out from Heaven . . .

(II, i, 24)

The blood that ran in Byron's veins ran also in those of his cousin, Mary; and this blood had been shed in the duel. Byron, says Richard Edgcumbe, from his boyhood believed that there was a blood-curse upon him (Edgcumbe, II, 293). As Byron put it during the year 1821: 'Our union would have healed feuds in which blood had been shed by our fathers; it would have joined lands, broad and rich; it would have joined at least *one* heart and two persons not ill-matched in years (she is two years my elder); and—and—and—what has been the result?' (*Detached Thoughts*, 65; LJ, V, 441).

Manfred describes Astarte in terms of spiritual identity with himself which directly recall *The Dream:*

> *She had the same lone thoughts and wanderings,*
> *The quest of hidden knowledge, and a mind*
> *To comprehend the Universe . . .*
>
> (II, ii, 109)

Manfred's assertion that he 'loved her and destroyed her' is less directly relevant, since Mary seems to have acted throughout entirely on her own initiative; if any one had destroyed her, it was her husband. In *The Dream* Byron thinks that he cannot be the cause of her trouble. But the question is at least raised there, and he may not always have been so sure. After all, he had been reluctant to see her when she wished to meet him, and it was directly after missing him at Hastings that she had broken down (p. 26). When the Witch of the Alps asks if he destroyed Astarte with his hand, he answers:

> *Not with my hand, but heart, which broke her heart;*
> *It gazed on mine, and withered. I have shed*
> *Blood, but not hers—and yet her blood was shed,*
> *I saw—and could not stanch it.*
>
> (II, ii, 118)

This is partly fictional, since Byron did not see her blood shed. But the resemblances are striking, and when Astarte appears, as a kind of living death, called 'one without a tomb' (II, iv, 82), she again recalls the description of Mary's madness in *The Dream:*

> *Can this be death? there's bloom upon her cheek,*
> *But now I see it is no living hue,*
> *But a strange hectic—like the unnatural red*
> *Which Autumn plants upon the perish'd leaf.*
>
> (II, iv, 98)

The word 'hectic' had already occurred in one of the poems *To a Lady*, applied there to Byron's own fevered existence after Mary's rejection of him; here it is transposed.

It does not all fit Mary; but, if we must have a candidate, she is easily the most promising. It is necessary to insist on this, since Lord Lovelace reads *Manfred* as a simple confession of incest with Augusta. This is fantastically off the point. The descriptions, as commentators

have often observed, do not for the most part serve to characterize
Augusta at all, and some are grossly inapposite; but they do fit Mary.
There is one strong pointer to Augusta:

> . . . *with him*
> *The sole companion of his wanderings*
> *And watchings—her, whom of all earthly things*
> *That lived, the only thing he seem'd to love—*
> *As he, indeed, by blood was bound to do,*
> *The lady Astarte, his—*

(III, iii, 42)

The speech is broken off. Is the missing word 'sister'? Or 'cousin'?
And why is it omitted? I think we can say that there may be a
reference here to Augusta. But, if so, where are we? Is Astarte both
Mary and Augusta? And, that granted, who else may be contained?
Even here, the lines are not wholly suitable, since Augusta was
scarcely quite the 'companion of his wanderings and watchings' in this
sense, Mary Chaworth being a more likely candidate. But the lines
really define the *whole complex* of lonely idealism, love-dreams, and
nature-contact which we have been surveying. And it is finally in
this more general and inclusive sense, not unlike the sense in
which Moore read the *Thyrza* poems (p. 35), that we must read
Manfred.

Then, indeed, it will be clear enough. *Manfred* is conceived as a
major work, of objective, not merely autobiographical, significance. Personal experiences may be used, but its meaning cannot
be limited by any of them.

Such phrases as 'loved each other as we should not love' (II, i, 27),
'some half-maddening sin' (II, i, 31), and 'the deadliest sin to love
as we have loved' (II, iv, 123), may be related to heterosexual
experience of a normally immoral kind; to Byron's love of Augusta,
if indeed, despite the evidence to the contrary, it ever overstepped
the limits of conscience; to homosexual relationships; or to what
may have been an illicit relationship with his own wife, which we
shall discuss later. Any, or all, of these may be contained.

As for the suggestions of bloodshed, apart altogether from Mary
Chaworth, we find evidences of guilt and horror throughout Byron;
variously in the tales, in his 1813–14 Journal—'I wish the dead would
rest' (23 Nov. 1813; LJ, II, 335)—and his letters and conversation.
There was the girl he rescued from execution in Athens, whom he

126

may himself have brought to condemnation by his own actions, though this is uncertain (pp. 13–14); as for his emotions on that occasion, 'It is *icy*', he said, 'even to recollect them' (Journal, 1 Dec., 1813; LJ, II, 361). He related *The Giaour* to this incident (p. 13).

We can deduce no specific actions from Byron's many innuendoes, since he regularly enjoyed mystifying people with suggestions of his own wickedness, and sometimes even of murder (p. 41). But he had, none the less, genuine reason for anxiety. When Manfred regards himself as responsible for Astarte's destruction, we may observe at least a half-truth, for those with whom Byron came in close contact were regularly unfortunate. Margaret Parker died young; and on his return from travel in 1811 he soon found himself bereaved of his mother, John Edleston, and others of his closest friends. 'Some curse', he wrote to Scrope Davies, 'hangs over me and mine' (7 Aug., 1811; LJ, I, 324). If they lived, things were little better. Caroline Lamb became an hysterical fury; Mary Chaworth Musters went mad; Augusta, though Byron himself does not normally associate her with tragedy, had known her name sullied, justly or unjustly, by scandal; and his wife had, in his own eyes at least, been transformed into a demi-fiend of implacable cruelty. On the death of his daughter Allegra he observed that disaster overtook 'every thing and every body' for whom he felt any real attachment; and, thinking presumably of his Newfoundland Boatswain, that he could not love even a dog without its dying (Hoppner, 2 July, 1819; LJ, IV, 325). If they did not die, they suffered. Was there indeed a curse on his love? Did indeed his 'injuries' necessarily fall on those who 'loved' him and whom he 'best loved'? Was his 'embrace' necessarily 'fatal' (*Manfred*, II, i, 84–7)? All this is written into the crucial piece of dialogue:

MANFRED: *I lov'd her, and destroy'd her!*
WITCH: *With thy hand?*
MANFRED: *Not with my hand, but heart, which broke her heart;*
    It gazed on mine, and wither'd.

                           (*Manfred*, II, ii, 117)

That tells the story of more than one romance.

Astarte, being mythologically a deity of both purity and license, is precisely suited to symbolize the part of suffering accuser striking guilt into the hero after his fall from innocence. He is now 'a blighted trunk upon a cursed root', and condemned to be so 'eternally' after 'having been otherwise' (I, ii, 68–71). Astarte is both what might have been and what is:

> *I know not what I ask, nor what I seek;*
> *I feel but what thou art, and what I am.*
>
> (II, iv, 131)

Astarte is less a person than an expression of Byron's love-life as a whole, and in particular his sense of having fallen from the high purity of his loves for Mary and Edleston. And, of course, there is much in *Manfred* of great importance that has nothing to do with love at all (CV, Index A, XI; p. 270 below). The drama is crammed with significances of all kinds; there can be few works in any literature so amazingly packed, and the total artistic awareness presented is at once so lucid and so vast that it remains discontinuous with ordinary thinking and any ordinary biography. Of the third canto of *Childe Harold*, written from a similar conception and belonging to the same period as *Manfred*, he told Moore on 28 January, 1817: 'I was half mad during the time of its composition, between metaphysics, mountains, lakes, love inextinguishable, thoughts unutterable, and the nightmare of my own delinquencies' (LJ, IV, 49). The 'thoughts unutterable' throw back to a phrase in *The Dream: Manfred* is a work of that 'deeper' madness which *The Dream* tells us is endured by the wise. The mind is too full of truth, that is the trouble; and we may suppose that it was some such 'deeper madness' as this which made Lady Byron get her husband surreptitiously examined by a doctor.

We have, I think, demonstrated the kind of approach which a work such as *Manfred* demands. Lovelace's simple reading of it as a confession of incest is puerile. That is not to say that thoughts of Augusta are not contained, though Mary Anne certainly appears to figure more prominently. These conclusions will have a direct bearing on our present enquiry.

II

We shall next examine Byron's non-poetic statements after leaving England. These we shall group in two sections: the first concerns Augusta and the question of incest; the second will deal with Byron's more general statements regarding the Separation.

With the exception of one problematical letter which we shall discuss after the rest have been dealt with, there is little to suggest that incest played any part in Byron's tormented conscience. Though he was vividly aware of 'passions and pure thoughts mixed and contending without end or order' (*Manfred*, III, i, 165) and also of the 'uneradicable taint of sin' (*Childe Harold*, IV, 126), Augusta formed no part, it seems, of his sense of guilt, being regularly associated with the 'pure thoughts' as against the 'passions'. In 1823 he spoke 'constantly' to Lady Blessington of Augusta, calling her 'the most faultless person he ever knew' and his 'only source of consolation' during the crisis; and said once that he owed to her what little good he could boast, and wished she might have influenced his destiny earlier (Blessington, 23, 349). Lady Byron appears to have recognized the part played by Augusta as a purifying and restraining influence on Byron's life (p. 207).

In *Astarte* Lord Lovelace asserts that certain of Byron's letters to Augusta held by his family, originally having been sent on to Lady Byron according to the plan which we have described, are clear evidence of incest. 'When he had gone abroad', he writes, 'Byron wrote to Augusta with passionate affection—love-letters which were afterwards shown to Lady Byron, whose advice was asked how they could be stopped, when Augusta had put herself absolutely, though temporarily, into Lady Byron's hands' (Lovelace, III, 67). He selects passages which he says spring from the world of *Manfred*, and among them this: 'When I was "gentle and juvenile—curly and gay", and was myself in love with a certain silly person—and who was she—can *you* guess?' (Lovelace, III, 78). In the original edition short extracts were offered torn from their contexts, but in view of the opposition aroused by the book, Lady Lovelace added a number of letters in full in the enlarged edition of 1921.

There is nothing in these letters to disturb us. How many families might be found guilty of bold expressions of affection were their private correspondence set out for a suspicious analysis? Indeed, once such a theory has been put forward, the test is severe. Here, if anywhere, we should find uncompromising evidence. Nothing said by Byron to Lady Melbourne or anyone else is wholly trustworthy, but his private correspondence with Augusta should, if the theory be true, show clear marks of it.

According to Samuel Chew (Chew, xv, 336) the only reference to incest which can be found in this correspondence is Byron's mention of Lucrezia Borgia in his letter to Augusta of 15 October,

1816, with which we might compare his letter of the same date to Murray (Lovelace, XI, 275; LJ, III, 376). But there is nothing here of consequence beyond a joking reference to Lucrezia's use of a cross for signature, the symbol being one that was also used by Byron in his letters to Augusta.

Let us see to what kind of relationship the letters bear witness. Augusta can function as a maternal figure, anxious regarding Byron's morals. Of Clare Clairmont (p. 22), who had originally forced herself on Byron with anonymous letters, eventually gained an interview, finally seduced him just before he left England, and had now followed him to the Continent, he wrote to Augusta on 8 September 1816, as follows:

'As to all these mistresses—Lord help me—I have had but one. Now don't scold—but what could I do? A foolish girl, in spite of all I could say or do, would come after me, or rather went before for I found her here, and I have had all the plague possible to persuade her to go back again, but at last she went. Now dearest, I do most truly tell thee that I could not help this, that I did all I could to prevent it, and have at last put an end to it. I was not in love nor have any love left for any, but I could not exactly play the Stoic with a woman who had scrambled eight hundred miles to unphilosophize me.'

(LJ, III, 347; Lovelace, XI, 267)

Augusta, who regularly functions as Byron's moral supporter and counsellor, seems to have disapproved of his romantic attachments to boys, or youths: 'As to "pages"—there be none such—nor any body else' (14 Sept., 1816; Lovelace, XI, 268). These are remarks as to a parent or guardian. There is little lover-like about them: 'I am very well, quite recovered, and as is always the case after all illness—particularly fever—got large, ruddy and robustious to a degree which would please you—and shock me' (10 May, 1817; Lovelace, XI, 283). To come upon these letters at the end of Lovelace's *Astarte*, says Chew, is, 'after the sickly motive-finding, conscience-probing epistles of Lady Byron and her set', like coming 'from a psychiatric clinic out into wide free air' (Chew, XV, 336). That everyone must feel.

Byron loved children, and was fond of Augusta's. He is pleased when Georgiana, Augusta's daughter, sends him 'a very nice letter', and if he doesn't hear from her, asks for her to write (8 Sept., 1816;

5 Oct., 1821; Lovelace, XI, 266, 308). He arranges to provide for Augusta's family, once saying that his own cannot excite the same 'unmixed' feeling because of the association with Lady Byron (4 March, 1822; Lovelace, XI, 309). But Medora, supposed by some to be his child by Augusta, does not appear to have aroused his particular interest, whereas his enduring love for his child by Lady Byron, Ada, whom he had only seen for a few weeks, is striking in both his letters and reported conversations (CV, II, 80–1). 'My whole hope and prospect of a quiet evening (if I reach it)', he wrote to Augusta, 'are wrapt up in that little creature—Ada—and you must forgive my anxiety in all which regards her even to minuteness' (1 Oct., 1816; Lovelace, XI, 274).

It is, of course, true that there are strong expressions of affection towards Augusta. She was his last link, and he loved her deeply. But his phraseology does not go beyond the bounds of normal affection. Here is perhaps our strongest example, dated 27 August, 1816:

'Do not be uneasy—and do not "hate yourself". If you hate either let it be *me*—but do not—it would kill me; we are the last persons in the world—who ought—or could cease to love one another.'

(Lovelace, XI, 265)

Observe the word 'ought'. On matters of passion Byron could be a severe moralist and stern critic of himself, but this love is regarded as righteous. Here is another strongish piece, from a letter asking Augusta to come out with 'one or two of the children' for a tour. It is dated 17 September, 1816:

'The great obstacle would be that you are so admirably yoked—and necessary as a housekeeper—and a letter writer—and a place-hunter to that very helpless gentleman your Cousin, that I suppose the usual self-love of an elderly person would interfere between you and any scheme of recreation or relaxation, for however short a period.

'What a fool was I to marry—and *you* not very wise—my dear—we might have lived so single and so happy—as old maids and bachelors; I shall never find any one like you—nor you (vain as it may seem) like me. We are just formed to pass our lives together, and therefore we—at least I—am by a crowd of circumstances removed from the only being who could ever have loved me, or whom I can unmixedly feel attached to.

'Had you been a Nun—and I a Monk—that we might have talked through a grate instead of across the sea—no matter—my voice and my heart are

Ever thine—

B.'

(Lovelace, XI, 272)

Note the words 'old maids and bachelors'; the expressed desire is clearly to live free of sexual engagements. It can, of course, be argued that this is no evidence against a previous commitment, or that Byron would naturally not talk of incest directly. But then these letters are no use for Lord Lovelace's purpose: all we are arguing is that the letters do not prove the incest.

Whatever there had been between Byron and Augusta, it was nothing that Byron thought anyone could worry about now. During 1820, says Lovelace, Byron wrote frequently to Lady Byron asking for her kindness to Augusta, and she agreed on 10 December to befriend her and her children. Byron's answer of 28 December is interesting. With a typically quixotic gesture he burns her note so that she may be under no 'constraint' but 'personal feeling'. While thanking her, he regrets that she had not so met his wishes earlier: 'It is a comfort to me *now*—beyond all comforts—that A and her children will be thought of after I am nothing; but five years ago it would have been something more. Why did you *then keep silence?*' (Lovelace, v, 109–12). This letter contains an interestingly explicit passage:

'As to Augusta—she knows as little of my request as of your answer. Whatever She is or may have been, *you* have never had reason to complain of her—on the contrary—you are not aware of the obligations under which you have been to her. Her life and mine—and yours and mine—were two things perfectly distinct from each other —when one ceased the other began—and now both are closed.'

(Lovelace, v, 111)

Again, 'She and two others were the only things I ever really loved —I may say it now—for we are young no longer' (v, 112–13). Who are the 'two others'? We may suppose them to be Mary Chaworth and Edleston; that is, in Byron's scale of values, the other two 'pure' loves.

It must be remembered that a divergence, or tug, of emotions between a family affection and the calls of marriage is not unusual, without actual incest. A similar controversy is awake today concerning Wordsworth. The point is, whatever there had been, Byron was not worried about it, could not conceive that Lady Byron need be, and regarded it all either as of minor importance or as a thing of the past; exactly as did Lady Byron originally (pp. 89, 91–2), though for reasons of her own she was afterwards anxious to get her evidence.

Meanwhile, he was completely baffled by Augusta's letters. He knew nothing of Lady Byron's machinations, nor that his own letters were being handed on for her perusal. When Augusta was disturbed about some asterisks in the lines addressed to her, feeling that 'as everything was misrepresented, these might be perverted too' (quoted by Mrs. Villiers to Lady Byron, 19 June, 1816; Lovelace, IX, 219), he replied, on 27 August, 1816: 'I do not understand all your mysteries about "the verses" and the Asterisks; but if the name is not put asterisks always are, and I see nothing remarkable in this'; and again, earlier in the same letter, 'Really this is starting at shadows. You distress me with—no—it is not *you*' (Lovelace, XI, 265). He was right; it was not; it was a new Augusta half-mesmerised by Lady Byron. Remember that this is a private correspondence; is it not remarkable, if incest were, or ever had been, a serious problem, that Byron should write in this baffled strain to his accomplice in the sin concerned? It happens again. On 28 October, 1816, he is writing: 'I really do not and cannot understand all the mysteries and alarms in your letters and more particularly in the last.' He intends to meet her, and asks why he should not? 'To talk thus—Never mind—either this must end—or I must end—but I repeat it again and again—*that woman* has destroyed me' (Lovelace, XI, 277–8). He cannot understand why the conflict with his wife should be perpetuated: 'It is now a year and I have repeatedly offered to make it up, with what success you know' (25 Feb., 1817; XI, 283). Now he won't: 'But all this is no reason for further misery and quarrel' (10 May 1817; Lovelace XI, 284). He is thoroughly baffled and deeply irritated by Augusta's enigmatic epistles, and indeed he here takes his stand with us all as we plough through the foggy and unrevealing letters she wrote at this period—though it was not at all her normal style—to Lady Byron:

'I have received all your letters I believe, which are full of woes, as usual, megrims and mysteries; but my sympathies remain in suspense, for, for the life of me, I can't make out whether your disorder is a broken heart or the earache—or whether it is *you* that have been ill or the children—or what your melancholy and mysterious apprehensions tend to, or refer to, whether to Caroline Lamb's novels—Mrs. Clermont's evidence—Lady Byron's magnanimity—or any other piece of imposture; I know nothing of what you are in the doldrums about at present. I should think all that could affect you must have been over long ago; and as for me—leave me to take care of myself.'

(3 June, 1817; Lovelace, XI, 285)

We can see how Lady Byron's scheme by which his intimate correspondence to the woman he trusted was being by her handed on to his worst enemy had placed him in an impossibly false position. So he now flounders into extreme asseverations that some, who think in such terms, may regard, though with no good reason, as incestuous: 'I always loved you better than any earthly existence, and I always shall unless I go mad'. He won't, of course, dun her husband for sums owed him, but will instead help him: '*Who does* and *who can* accuse *you* of "interested views"? I think people must have gone into Bedlam, such things appear to me so very incomprehensible. Pray explain——' (19 Aug., 1820; Lovelace, XI, 300). 'Hobhouse', he wrote on 27 Jan., 1823, 'says your coming out would be the best thing which you could do for yourself and me too' (Lovelace, XI, 312). Hobhouse, we may remember, was the last person in the world to encourage Byron in any unorthodox passion.

Once indeed Byron says that he agreed to the Separation to avoid the risk of scandal to Augusta. This may seem to contradict Hobhouse and support Lady Byron's 1830 statement (p. 76). But the facts have been presented (pp. 75-8), and they bear witness to the reverse. Byron's party was prepared for public proceedings, and the most Byron can mean is that, when Lady Byron threw herself on his mercy and asked to be excused, Byron was in part motivated by the knowledge that a quiet agreement might save Augusta from scandalous, if illegal, insinuations. The letter at least serves to show the power wielded by Lady Byron's blackmail. Here is the passage in question, from a postscript to Augusta on 19 June, 1817:

'I repeat to you again and again—that it would be much better at once to explain your mysteries—than to go on with this absurd obscure hinting mode of writing. What do you mean? what is there known? or can be known? which *you and I* do not know much better? and what concealment can you have from me? *I* never shrank—and it was on your account principally that I gave way at all—for I thought they would endeavour to drag you into it—although they had no business with anything previous to my marriage with that infernal fiend, whose destruction I shall yet see.'

(Lovelace, XI, 288)

Byron was baffled by a vague sense of things happening at home which he could not understand. The phrase 'which you and I do not know much better' must surely mean, 'Which you and I, with our better knowledge, do not know in such a way as to leave us fearless and with free consciences'.

I do not argue that there had been no love-interchange between Byron and Augusta, but merely that we do not know the exact nature of it, many varieties of amatory interchange being, of course, possible which stop short of what is normally meant by 'incest'; that we have Byron's firm statement to Lady Melbourne that it was a non-sensuous, by which he may have meant no more than a non-coitional, love (p. 40); that Lady Byron had been willing at first to pass it over; that it had nothing to do with the Separation; and that, after leaving England, Byron, with all his knowledge of the world, ingrained sensibility to guilt, and deep love and consideration for Augusta, was nevertheless frank and open about it, of a clear conscience and quite unaware of what his sister's letters were driving at. The one party are lost in a maze of blackmail, mystifications and half-truths; the other desires and offers nothing but plain-speaking. In this correspondence we watch the contrast played out.

The charge of incest would be considerably strengthened were we to have at least *one* intimate letter from either Byron or Augusta to the other admitting guilt. No letters to other people, such as Byron's to Lady Melbourne or Augusta's to Lady Byron, would be comparable as evidence, since they might have ulterior motives for what they say. Now there is just one letter which contributes the necessary link; it was the heart of Lord Lovelace's thesis in the original edition of *Astarte*; it would, if accepted, go some way to establish the case. It was, as it were, *needed* by the opposition. I refer to the famous letter of 17 May 1819, which Drinkwater

(1, 71) calls 'the classic paper of the story'. Here is the incriminating document.

'My dearest Love—

'I have been negligent in not writing, but what can I say? Three years' absence and the total change of scene and habit make such a difference that we have nothing in common but our affections and our relationship.

'But I have never ceased nor can cease to feel for a moment that perfect and boundless attachment which bound and binds me to you—which renders me utterly incapable of *real* love for any other human being—for what could they be to me after *you*? My own * * * *, we may have been very wrong—but I repent of nothing except that cursed marriage—and your refusing to continue to love me as you had loved me. I can neither forget nor *quite forgive* you for that precious piece of reformation—but I can never be other than I have been—and whenever I love anything it is because it reminds me in some way or other of yourself—for instance I not long ago attached myself to a Venetian for no earthly reason (although a pretty woman) but because she was called * * * * and she often remarked (without knowing the reason) how fond I was of the name. It is heart-breaking to think of our long Separation—and I am sure more than punishment enough for all our sins. Dante is more humane in his "Hell" for he places his unfortunate lovers (Francesca of Rimini and Paolo whose case fell a good deal short of *ours* though sufficiently naughty) in company—and though they suffer, it is at least together. If ever I return to England, it will be to see you—and recollect that in all time—and place—and feelings —I have never ceased to be the same to you in heart—Circumstances may have ruffled my manner and hardened my spirit—you may have seen me harsh and exasperated with all things around me; grieved and tortured with *your new resolution*—and the soon after persecution of that infamous fiend who drove me from my Country and conspired against my life—by endeavouring to deprive me of all that could render it precious—but remember that even then *you* were the sole object that cost me a tear! and *what tears!* do you remember *our* parting? I have not spirits now to write to you upon other subjects—I am well in health and have no cause of grief but the reflection that we are not together. When you write to me speak to me of yourself—and say that you love me—never mind commonplace people and topics—which can be in no degree interesting to me who see nothing in England but the country which holds *you* or around it but the sea which divides us—They say absence destroys weak passions and confirms strong ones—Alas! *mine* for you is the union of all passions and of all affections—Has strengthened itsel but will destroy me—I do not speak of *physical* destruction for I have endured and can endure much—but of the annihilation of all thoughts, feelings or hopes which have not more or less a reference to you and to *our recollections*——

Ever dearest
(Signature erased)'

This letter, printed, with annotations, by Lord Lovelace (IV, 81–3) was, it is stated, sent to Augusta Leigh from Venice and next handed on by her, in mutilated form, to Lady Byron. The name of the addressee at the top, says Lovelace, has been 'effaced by Mrs. Leigh', though 'care of John Murray' is preserved; the signature is also gone. Lovelace's asterisks represent a 'short name of three or four letters obliterated'. We are to suppose that Augusta handed it on after making the obliterations. We gather from the correspondence printed with it that Lady Byron took a copy and returned the original to Augusta. Sir John Fox says (XVI, 176) that Lovelace's text is printed from the copy made by Lady Byron. How Lord Lovelace could tell the original number of letters in the obliterated names from a copied script is not clear.

In *Byron: A Self-Portrait* Peter Quennell prints this letter, noting that it has been 'assumed' to be addressed to Augusta (SP, II, 451, note). There is, as we shall see, some reason to suppose that it was. The reference to Paolo and Francesca, who were brother and sister 'in law', whereas Byron and Augusta were linked by blood, fits perfectly; and the phrase 'the union of all passions' recalls a similar thought in one of Byron's letters to Lady Melbourne already quoted (p. 40). However, we must first observe certain objections raised by Richard Edgcumbe.

In *Byron: the Last Phase* (1909) Edgcumbe advanced the theory that Medora Leigh, whom some have supposed to be Byron's child by Augusta, was really the child of Byron and Mary Chaworth Musters, but that, to save her reputation, Byron and Augusta were deliberately trying to preserve Lady Byron's belief in the fiction of incest. He argues (III, 368–75) that this letter was intended for Mary and sent to Augusta for delivery, but that, in view of Mary's recent recovery from insanity and reconciliation with her husband, she thought delivery unwise and used it to send on to Lady Byron in order to drive home the deception. Governed by his theory, he refers 'our relationship' to Medora, but the phrase fits Mary in any case, since she was Byron's cousin. Though his main theory is, as we have seen (p. 27), extravagant, many of his arguments concerning this particular letter are worth pondering. He rightly urges that the suggestion of a long silence does not make sense if addressed to Augusta, who in so many matters acted as Byron's agent and with whom he was in regular correspondence. Certainly its tone, together with the opening 'My dearest love' instead of 'My dearest Augusta', is unlike the other letters written by Byron to his sister. That a letter to Mary Chaworth Musters should have been sent to Augusta to hand on is not necessarily strange; on 21 September, 1818, he sent her a letter for delivery to Lady Francis Webster (Lovelace, XI, 288), and Edgcumbe asserts that that was Byron's custom with other letters to Mary; though what letters he does not tell us (III, 368).

Byron says, as though telling his correspondent for the first time about it, that he has lately been attached to a Venetian *of the same name*. Edgcumbe takes the omitted name to be 'Mary' and assumes the Venetian to be Marianna Segati, who was Byron's mistress from November 1816 to February 1818. Augusta's full name was 'Augusta Mary'; but if Marianna Segati be meant and the letter is indeed to Augusta, the reference is strange when we consider that Byron had described her fully to his sister as far back as 18 December, 1816, besides mentioning her later (e.g., on 13 Jan., 1817; Lovelace, XI, 279, 281). Also the name's first occurrence in the text, if meant for Augusta, is quite unlike Byron's manner of address, since to him she was, so far as we know, always either 'Augusta' or 'Goose'. If the first asterisks stand for 'Augusta', 'Goose' or 'Gus' and the second for 'Mary', the problem is not substantially altered.

The name intended may not have been 'Mary', and the reference may not be to Marianna. But we do at least know that the name 'Mary' affected Byron deeply, mainly by reason of his early love for Mary Chaworth: her singing to him a Welsh song called 'Mary Anne' had, according to Moore, been an important part of that early, magical, romance (Moore, III, 27). And there were other Marys. In his 1813–14 Journal he refers to the romance of his childhood with Mary Duff, another 'distant cousin' (LJ, II, 325, note), whose memory remained powerful (Journal, 26 Nov., 1813; Hay, 26 Jan., 1815; LJ, II, 347–8; III, 173). There is the Mary commemorated, as we have seen, in *When I Rov'd a Young Highlander*, where her name occurs continually. There was yet another 'Mary' to whom Byron addressed certain early verses *To Mary, on Receiving her Picture* (P, I, 32; LJ, I, 104, note; Pigot, 13 Jan., 1807; LJ, I, 112). There was the vivid poem *To Mary*, which may, or may not, have been addressed to Mary Chaworth, and which so shocked the Rev. John Becher that Byron destroyed the whole set of *Fugitive Pieces* (printed in the facsimile of *Fugitive Pieces*, ed. Marcel Kessel, Columbia University Press, 1933).

During the years 1813 and 1814, when Byron was suffering from some mysterious anxiety or passion, we have some interesting thoughts on *names*. On 27 November, 1813, when thinking of joining the revolution in Holland, Byron noted in his Journal:

'I believe, with Clym o' the Clow or Robin Hood, "By our Mary (dear name!) thou art both Mother and May, I think it never was a man's lot to die before his day."'

(LJ, II, 349)

The reference is to the *Ballad of Robin Hood* (LJ, II, 349, note). 'Dear name' is Byron's insertion. A little earlier, on 14 November, 1813, he had jotted down, with reference to *The Bride of Abydos*:

'I believe the composition of it kept me alive—for it was written to drive my thoughts from the recollection of

> *Dear sacred name, rest ever unreveal'd.*

At least, even here, my hand would tremble to write it.'

(LJ, II, 314)

Now, as Samuel Chew has observed (*The Dramas of Lord Byron*, 74, note), Byron's 'sacred' is a misquotation of the line from Pope's *Eloisa to Abelard* which runs, 'Dear, fatal name . . .' Remembering Byron's Catholic sympathies we have accordingly some reason for supposing the name to be 'Mary'. If so, we might conceivably suspect its presence behind the famous lyric, sent to Moore on 4 May, 1814 (LJ, III, 80):

> *I speak not, I trace not, I breathe not thy name,*
> *There is grief in the sound, there is guilt in the fame.*

(P, III, 413)

In passing we may hazard the suggestion that one of the lines, 'Oh, proud to the mighty, but humble to thee', sounds more like a reference to some, not necessarily contemporary, and perhaps purely fanciful, homosexual engagement. About the same time Byron wrote the opening lines to *Lara*, which were, however, not published until 1887.[1] Here is a passage:

> *When thou art gone—the loved, the lost—the one*
> *Whose smile hath gladdened, though perchance undone—*
> *Whose name too dearly cherished to impart*
> *Dies on the lip, but trembles in the heart,*
> *Whose sudden impulse can almost convulse,*
> *And lightens through the ungovernable pulse—*
> *Till the heart leaps so keenly at the word*
> *We fear that throb can hardly beat unheard. . .*

And, later:

> *Oh! best—and dearest! Thou whose thrilling name*
> *My heart adores too deeply to proclaim . . .*

The name need not be 'Mary', but in arguing that it is, and comparing it with some lines from *The Dream*, Edgcumbe makes out a fair case (Edgcumbe, II, 268–9, and note). Samuel Chew considers that certain lines added to *The Giaour* in the summer of 1813 refer to Mary (Chew, *Dramas*, 73–4, note; the lines are, presumably, lines 1131–1256; P, III, 137, note; and see P, III, 136, note, on lines 1127–30).

Mary Chaworth Musters was often in Byron's thoughts. We have already quoted from the powerful lyric, *The Duel*, written in 1818 (p. 123), and we have clear evidence that her name could move him as late as 1820, when he wrote in *Don Juan*:

> *I have a passion for the name of 'Mary',*
> *For once it was a magic sound to me;*
> *And still it half calls up the realms of Fairy,*
> *Where I beheld what never was to be;*
> *All feelings changed, but this was last to vary,*
> *A spell from which even yet I am not quite free:*

---

[1] Hartley Coleridge refers to them as the poem's 'opening lines' and notes, correctly, their publication in *Murray's Magazine* of January, 1887 (P, III, 319); but his text omits to print them.

But I grow sad—and let a tale grow cold
Which must not be pathetically told.

(*Don Juan*, v, 4)

'What never was to be' refers to Byron's youthful wish to make Mary Chaworth his wife. Byron's bitter note in his 1821 *Detached Thoughts* tells the same story (pp. 27, 124).

We can be certain that the name 'Mary' affected Byron deeply because of his early love, and this is just what is wanted to make sense of the 'incriminating' letter. Even if Byron can be supposed sometimes to have thought of Augusta as 'Mary', she could hardly have been expected to believe that the name was associated in his mind primarily with her. Besides, if 'Mary' is the name, Byron was presumably referring to Marianna Segati, and Mary's full name was Mary Anne. Since Lord Lovelace had only Lady Byron's copy to go on, the omitted word may have been longer than he thought; it might have been 'Mary Anne'; and that may have been why he was careful to assert that it was a name of three or four letters only. Doubt would seem to be still farther removed.

But if the letter was addressed to Mary, to what can it refer? Was Edgcumbe right in supposing that Byron and Mary had been carrying on a surreptitious liaison? We have already (pp. 25-7) reviewed the evidence against such a supposition; but it may be misleading. It is not beyond the bounds of possibility that Byron did meet Mary during, or after, the year 1814. If there had been any love-interchange, it would necessarily have been surreptitious.

Edgcumbe's firm statement that just before Byron left England he 'went into the country to take leave of Mary Chaworth' may be true; but it is left in his usual manner unsupported (Edgcumbe, II, 283), and unsupported statements in such a matter are hard to accept, especially when, as here, the evidence against it is strong. We do, however, know that Byron was at one time, in 1814, living near her in London during her illness (p. 26); we should note for what, if any thing, it is worth, that Beau Brummell in 1835 said that Mr. Musters had once told him that Byron was the cause of his having deserted his wife (Richard Edgcumbe in *T.L.S.*, 22 Sept., 1921; *612*); and we know that Lady Byron saw her in London, some time about August, 1815, since she then wrote to Augusta of her husband's greatest love in true matrimonial style:

'I never told you of it, nor of my meeting with Mrs. Musters there.

She asked after B! Such a wicked-looking cat I never saw. Somebody else looked quite virtuous by the side of her. O that I were out of this horrid town, which makes me mad!'

(*Athenaeum*, 18 Aug., 1883; 207; Jeaffreson, App. II, 474)

The 'somebody else' is Caroline Lamb. Edgcumbe asserts that in November, 1819, Augusta 'stood sponsor for Mary's youngest daughter' (Edgcumbe, II, 250; also in *T.L.S.*, 22 Sept., 1921; *613*).

Samuel Chew considers that the problem of incest hinges mainly upon 'the identification of the woman to whom Byron addressed the famous letter of May 17, 1819', and agrees with Edgcumbe, whose full theory he does not accept, that 'the internal evidence supports the view that that woman was Mrs. Chaworth Musters' (Chew, XV, 338-9). This 'internal evidence' the advocates of incest tend to suppress or ignore. In her *Life of Lady Byron* (XIX, 282) Ethel Colburn Mayne quotes part of the text omitting the crucial reference to a Venetian lady, breaking off at 'of yourself', and continuing 'It is heart-breaking . . .'; and in her study of Byron she disposes of Edgcumbe's theory with no reference to names (Mayne, II; App. III, 333-4). During the Countess of Lovelace's attack on Edgcumbe's general theory, though it is in the main successful, the argument from names is not touched (Lovelace, Notes by the Editor, 314-17); and Sir John Fox goes no further than urging that, since the letter is printed from Lady Byron's copy, we can say nothing regarding the *length* of the obliterated names (Fox, XIV, 138; and see XVI, 167, 176, 189). Such silences merely serve to underline the nature of the difficulties which they ignore.

The evidence so far reviewed might be over-powering if it stood alone; but it does not. According to the letters as printed and grouped by Lord Lovelace, Augusta sent it on to Lady Byron, and the two corresponded at high pressure as to how Augusta, who writes, as usual, in a turmoil of anxiety and confusion, should answer it. One of Augusta's letters is dated Monday 28 June, and in it she says that she intends to post her reply *towards the end of the week* (Lovelace, IV, 88). Now there has recently, in 1950, been published a letter from Byron to Augusta dated, from Ravenna, 26 July, 1819, which must be taken as a reply to her reply. The letter, of which the original is in the Pierpoint Morgan Library, New York, is printed by Peter Quennell (SP, II, 464). It starts:

'My dearest Augusta—I am at too great a distance to scold you, but

I *will* ask you whether *your* letter of the *1st* July *is an answer* to the letter I wrote you before I quitted Venice? What? is it come to *this?* Have you no memory? or no heart? You *had* both—and I *have* both—at least for *you.*

'I write this presuming that you received *that* letter. Is it that you fear? Do not be afraid of the past; the world has its own affairs without thinking of *ours*, and you may write safely.'

(SP, II, 464)

The dates fit, and Byron's uncertainty as to whether Augusta is answering this particular letter corresponds with what appears (Lovelace, IV, 87) to have been the nature of Augusta's reply.

Nevertheless, a doubt lingers: both Drinkwater (I, 74) and Vulliamy (XVII, 258) approach the letter with caution, if not suspicion. If it is, and proves, all that Lord Lovelace claims, can we really believe that Augusta would have sent it on for Lady Byron to take a copy? Lovelace has printed it from the copy in Lady Byron's writing (Fox, XVI, 176). Does the original exist? If not, the letter's evidential value is nugatory, since we clearly cannot, in view of her life-long attempt to establish the incest, trust her copying of it; nor, indeed, anything in her hand-writing at all. Were the erased passages erased in the original or only in the copy? Is this really the letter to which the letters of Augusta and Lady Byron which Lovelace prints beside it, and therefore Byron's of 26 July, are referring? Why is Augusta's letter about it to Lady Byron (Lovelace, IV, 83-4) printed without a signature? And what is the history of the letter of 26 July which now so neatly helps to turn the scales of evidence?

If all is in order, we must assume, either that Byron knew a Venetian called 'Augusta', 'Goose' or 'Gus', or else that in his more secret love-passages with Augusta he had been in the habit of addressing her as 'Mary', in which case some of the 1813-1814 name-references (pp. 139-40) may apply to her. No other solution meets the hard facts of the letter itself, unless we may suppose either that some name which was not hers could yet *remind* Byron of Augusta, or that Byron now knew what was happening at home, and deliberately composed the letter to trick his wife and confuse posterity, knowing that Augusta would hand it on. Or is it possible that Byron, whose mind in *actuality* probably functioned more nearly within the poetic dimension than any of which we have record, has, on the analogy of *Manfred*, been led by some mysterious impulse to compose a letter *blending* his loves for Mary and Augusta? This would at least account for Augusta's having referred to it as the action of a 'maniac' (to Lady Byron, 25 June, 1819; Lovelace, IV, 84).

Byron had an extraordinary mind, different compartments of which could on occasion appear to function independently, if not in contradiction, of each other, even when treating of the same subject. Difficult as it is to place this letter among the others to his sister, we may have to do so. Those others are all lightly phrased, variously ironic, irascible, playful, and affectionate, but never passionate, with the emotions always, as it were, objective and distanced. They are written as to a loved friend and agent, discussing his dealings with Murray, his business concerns, his love-affairs, and above all his daughter Ada. He writes of his love-affairs with Clare Clairmont, Marianna Segati, Margarita Cogni, and Teresa as to a masculine friend. Here is a typical phrase written before the incriminating letter: 'Of Rome I say nothing—you can read the Guide-book—which is very accurate' (10 May, 1817; Lovelace, XI, 284). Here is a later example: 'Will you for the hundredth time apply to Lady Byron about the *funds*; they are now *high*, and I could sell out to a great advantage' (22 June, 1821; Lovelace, XI, 305). This, written on 18 November, 1820, is characteristic:

'
How do you get on with your affairs?—and how does everybody get on?—How is your rabbit-warren of a family? I gave you an account of mine by last letter—The child Allegra is well—but the Monkey has got a cough—and the tame Crow has lately suffered from the head-ache—Fletcher has been bled for a stitch—and looks flourishing again—Pray write—excuse this short scrawl—Yours ever, B.'

(Lovelace, XI, 301)

Could this have been written to the recipient of the 'incriminating' letter? Perhaps. After all, Byron's prose and poetry differ regularly in emotional tone, even when the same object is being treated; and his love-letters to Teresa as given in the Marchioness Origo's *The Last Attachment* bear little resemblance to his normal epistolary style. But, even remembering the uncanny variety and variations of his mind, it is only with a certain effort that we can align these crisp and practical notes with that impassioned and guilt-stricken epistle.

We may be thankful that the problem of incest is no more than

GEORGE COLMAN THE YOUNGER
from a portrait engraved by
W. Greatcatch

tangential to our present discussion. Let us now turn to Byron's general statements regarding the Separation.

III

After leaving England Byron alternated between attempts at reconciliation with his wife and outbursts of vituperation. Madame de Staël advised him to re-open negotiations, but the attempt failed, and it was not till then that his real bitterness began (Moore, XXVII, 321); such bitterness as was written into the *Lines on Hearing that Lady Byron was Ill* (P, IV, 63). But there was always another side to it, and on hearing of her illness he burned a prose romance based on his marriage (Moore, XXVII, 322), and was deeply sympathetic on the occasion of her mother's death (Medwin, 109; Moore, XLVIII, 550, note). Perhaps the best summing up of his general attitude is that given by his letter to Lady Byron of 17 November 1821 (or possibly 1822), which was, however, never actually sent, owing to his 'despair of its doing any good' (Lady Blessington, 6 May, 1823; LJ, VI, 204). Part of it runs:

'I say all this, because I own to you, that, notwithstanding every thing, I considered our re-union as not impossible for more than a year after the Separation;—but then I gave up the hope entirely and for ever. But this very impossibility of reunion seems to me at least a reason why, on all the few points of discussion which can arise between us, we should preserve the courtesies of life, and as much of its kindness as people who are never to meet may preserve perhaps more easily than nearer connections. For my own part, I am violent, but not malignant; for only fresh provocations can awaken my resentments. To you, who are colder and more concentrated, I would just hint, that you may sometimes mistake the depth of a cold anger for dignity, and a worse feeling for duty. I assure you that I bear you *now* (whatever I may have done) no resentment whatever. Remember, that *if you have injured me* in aught, this forgiveness is something; and that, if I have *injured you*, it is something more still, if it be true, as the moralists say, that the most offending are the least forgiving.'

(LJ, V, 480)

Other important letters to Lady Byron, dated 20 July and 31 December, 1819, are printed by Lovelace (XI, 291, 298). Byron's respect for his wife did, indeed, persist. Though he could be fierce in anger, or parody the whole affair in *Don Juan* (I, 26–32), he remained still, in his own mind, Annabella's husband.

He regularly asserted, as had Hobhouse, that he had been perfectly willing to take the matter to court. Here is a letter to Augusta written on 19 June 1817 when he thought that his rights over Ada were being threatened (for further details and references to the dispute, see Byron to Augusta, 13 Jan. and 10 May, 1817; Lovelace, XI, 281, 284; also Fox, XV, 149–50):

'I fear that not any good can be done by your speaking to Lady Byron—but I think it my duty to give fair warning—because *they* have *broken* their *word*. They are not aware that if I please I can dissolve the separation, which is not a legal act, nor further binding than the will of the parties. I shall therefore not only take all proper and legal steps, but the former correspondence shall be published, and the whole business from the beginning investigated in all the courts of which it is susceptible, unless the reasonable assurance which I have required with regard to my daughter be accorded—and now—come what may—as I have said, so will I do—and have already given the proper instructions to the proper persons—to prepare for the steps above mentioned . . . Recollect that I have done all in my power to avoid this extremity.'

(Lovelace, XI, 287)

There is no point in such a letter unless Byron, for the moment anyway, meant to risk proceedings. Notice (i) that he appears to believe that a complete exposure would justify him, and (ii) that he realizes that such an 'extremity' would be a very serious matter. However, what Byron was opposing—the taking of Ada on the Continent—did not, in fact, happen.

A little later, in August 1817, Byron prepared, and gave to M.G. ('Monk') Lewis at La Mira, Venice, a statement, not, it is true, for general publication, but for circulation among his friends in England, which ran as follows:

'It has been intimated to me that the persons understood to be the legal advisers of Lady Byron have declared "their lips to be sealed up" on the cause of the separation between her and myself. If their lips are sealed up, they are not sealed up by me, and the greatest favour *they* can confer upon me will be to open them. From the first hour in which I was apprized of the intentions of the Noel family to the last communication between Lady Byron and myself in the character of wife and husband (a period of some months), I called repeatedly and in vain for a statement of their or her charges, and it was chiefly in consequence of Lady Byron's claiming (in a letter still existing) a promise on my part to consent to a separation if such was *really* her wish, that I consented at all; this claim and the exasperating and inexplicable manner in which their object was pursued, which rendered it next to an impossibility that two persons so divided could ever be reunited, induced me reluctantly then, and repentantly still, to sign the deed which I shall be happy—most happy—to cancel, and go before any tribunal which may discuss the matter in the most public manner.

'Mr. Hobhouse made this proposition on my part, viz.: to abrogate all prior intentions and go into Court, the very day before the separation was signed, and it was declined by the other party, as also the publication of the correspondence during the previous discussion. Those propositions I beg here to repeat and to call upon her and hers to say their worst, pledging myself to meet their allegations—whatever they may be—and only too happy to be informed at last of their real nature.

'P.S.—I have been and am now utterly ignorant of what description her allegations, charges, or whatever name they may have assumed, are; and am as little aware for what purpose they have been kept back—unless it was to sanction the most infamous calumnies by silence.'

(LJ, III, 329)

Hobhouse, who was with Byron at the time, according to Augusta, tried hard but ineffectually to persuade him not to give it to Lewis (Mayne, II; IV, 107). However, it was not actually circulated, nor published at all until it appeared in *The Academy* of 9 October, 1869 (I, 1), after having been found among Lewis' papers on his death.

There is another, longer, statement of first importance dated 15 March, 1820, which Byron composed after reading an attack on him in *Blackwood's Magazine*. This is the apologia which I call, here and elsewhere, Byron's '*Blackwood's* Defence'. The relevant passage, which repeats and expands the substance of the La Mira statement, and deserves the closest study by anyone interested in our present argument, I have already quoted elsewhere (CV, I, 34–7; LJ, IV,

478–9). This defence was sent to Murray, with directions that he should keep it by him in case of need (23 April, 1820; LJ, v, 17). Byron calls it an answer to John Wilson, of *Blackwood's*, whom he supposed to have written the attack, though he had not. Probably it was shown to Wilson and others of those whom Byron on such occasions sometimes called 'the elect'; and indeed it appears to have changed substantially the attitude of *Blackwood's* to the whole matter of the Separation. But it was not actually published until after Byron's death, in the year 1830.

Sir John Fox (xvi, 156) and others hostile to Byron naturally enough emphasize that Byron did not actually publish these two statements; and yet there can be no doubt that he meant them. He was, as it were, itching to publish them, whilst simultaneously held back by other considerations. There would be no point in letting his most influential friends see them had he not thought that his case was strong. He did not, naturally, enjoy the prospect of an open conflict, if only because, as Lady Byron knew, he did not wish Augusta to be brought into it; and this is why, as we have seen, the opposing party were so anxious for evidence against her; and there were, no doubt, other reasons of weight. But that he was, in certain moods at least, ready to go to an extreme, is obvious. He could perfectly well have left matters where they stood.

His reported conversations all correspond with these written pieces, and with Hobhouse's story of the Separation. To Medwin in the year 1821 he gave a full account, maintaining that Lady Byron had been influenced by her parents and Mrs. Clermont (Medwin, 40–5). In his conversations with Lady Blessington in 1823 he recurred continually to Lady Byron (Blessington 110); he never spoke against her and continued to give her credit for many fine qualities (117); she was, indeed, always in his thoughts and he seemed genuinely to desire a reconciliation (162). He remained, however, 'totally unconscious' of her real reasons for demanding a separation (22). His letters remained unanswered, she still offered no explanation, there appeared to be no hope of their child being a bond to their affection, and he began to feel it a weakness to think so often of her and so kindly (83–4). He would have liked to return to England before going to Greece to forgive and be forgiven, but did not, for fear of closed doors, gross misrepresentation, and a lying press (400–1). Perhaps his most important remarks concern his own wayward passions. Had he possessed sufficient command over his own 'wayward humour' he might have held her (109); his own 'besetting sin' was 'a want of that self-respect' which she had 'in excess'; she herself, he said, had 'a degree of self-control that I never saw equalled'; and this self-control used to 'infuriate' him and make him break out 'on slight provocations' into 'one of my ungovernable fits of rage'. Now, however, he had learned to appreciate her, 'as I look upon self-command as a positive virtue, though it is one I have not courage to adopt' (315–16). When Lady Blessington took his wife's part, urging that the woman always suffers most and reminding Byron of his Venetian *liaisons*, he answered that perhaps she was indeed more to be pitied than himself (89).

At Cephalonia in 1823 he told Kennedy that he was still ready for reconciliation and reunion; that he still did not know the cause of his wife's sudden aversion; that Hobhouse had all but gone 'on his knees' to her, and that 'at length I wished to institute an action against her, that it might be seen what were her motives'. He insisted that he had done all that was possible and would never himself close the door to reunion (Kennedy, 264–7). At Missolonghi, in 1824, he discussed it all again with Parry, making the vivid remark, 'The causes, my dear sir, were too simple to be easily found out' (Moore, xxv, 296). His attitude from first to last remained consistent. From the time of his conversation with Francis Hodgson in February 1816 (Hodgson to Lady Byron, February, 1816; LJ, III, 307) to the very end, he asserted that he did not know what were the charges against him. On the whole, we can say that it appears hard to deny the truth of his remark made to Parry: 'My conduct has been like the arrow's flight compared to their sinuous, serpent-like track' (Parry, IX, 204).

Finally, we come to the ill-fated *Memoirs*. In October 1819 Byron gave the first part of them to Moore. On 10 December, he told his publisher, John Murray, of them, saying he could read them and show them to John Wilson of *Blackwood's*, whom he respected; and that he wished Lady Byron to read them and mark any errors, as a matter of fair dealing (LJ, IV, 385). On 31 December he wrote to Lady Byron herself:

'I saw Moore three months ago and gave to his care a long Memoir, written up to the summer of 1816, of my life, which I had been writing since I left England. It will not be published till after my death, and in fact it is a "Memoir" and not "confessions". I have omitted the most important and decisive events and passions of my existence not to compromise others. But it is not so with the part you occupy, which is long and minute, and I could wish you to see, read and mark any part or parts that do not appear to coincide with the truth. The truth I have always stated—but there are two ways of looking at it—and your way may not be mine. I have never revised the papers since they were written. You may read them and mark what you please. I wish you (to) know what I think and say of you and yours. You will find nothing to flatter you, nothing to lead you to the most remote supposition that we could ever have been, or be, happy together. But I do not choose to give to another generation statements which we cannot arise from the dust to prove or disprove, without letting you see fairly and fully what I look upon you to have been, and what I depict you as being. If, seeing this, you can detect what is false, or answer what is charged, do so— *your mark* shall not be erased.

'You will perhaps say *why* write my life? Alas!—I say so too, but they who have traduced it and blasted it and branded me, should know—that it is they, and not I—are the cause. It is no great pleasure to have lived, and less to live over again the details of existence, but the last becomes sometimes a necessity and even a duty.

'If you choose to see this you may, if you do not—you have at least had the option.'

(Lovelace, XI, 299; SP, II, 494)

This letter set Lady Byron and her advisers in a turmoil of anxiety. After a considerable delay caused by the discussions and planning which we have already analysed (pp. 102-6), the following reply was devised, written by Lady Byron on 10 March, 1820:

'I received your letter of January 1st offering to my perusal a Memoir of part of your life. I decline to inspect it. I consider the publication or circulation of such a composition at any time as prejudicial to Ada's future happiness. For my own sake I have no reason to shrink from publicity, but notwithstanding the injuries which I have suffered, I should lament some of the *consequences*.

A. I. Byron'
(LJ, v, 1, note; Lovelace, v, 108)

Byron replied, on 3 April, 1820, from Ravenna:

'I received yesterday your answer dated March 10th. My offer was an honest one, and surely could be only construed as such even by the most malignant Casuistry. I *could* answer you, but it is too late, and it is not worth while——

'To the mysterious menace of the last sentence—whatever its import may be—and I really cannot pretend to unriddle it—I could hardly be very sensible even if I understood it as, before it could take place, I shall be where "nothing can touch him further". I advise you however to anticipate the period of your intention—for be assured no power of yours can avail beyond the present, and if it could I would answer with the Florentine

> *Et io, che posto son con loro in croce*
> .   .   .   .   .   .   *e certo*
> *La fiera Moglie, più ch'altro, mi nuoce.*
>
> Byron'

(LJ, v, 1; *Macbeth*, III, ii; *Inferno*, XVI, 43)

And here the correspondence closes. That Byron regarded his wife's refusal to see the papers as a matter of considerable importance may be gathered from his letter to Murray of 10 August, 1821, stating that Lady Byron's reply had been placed in the hands of Thomas Moore (LJ, v, 343).

Moore was allowed to show the *Memoirs* to selected persons. They were, indeed, quite widely read, and Moore, being afraid that the first copy would get worn out (Moore's *Memoirs, etc.*, 7 May, 11 Aug., 1820; III, 116, 137; LJ, v, 105, note), suggested having a copy made. Byron agreed, wishing it to be lodged for safety in 'honourable hands', and said that he was willing that any 'proper person' should see them (13 July, 1820; LJ, v, 48–9). Afterwards, he added more material on his life abroad subsequent to the Separation, and suggested that Moore, who was in financial difficulties, should raise money on the papers for posthumous publication with Longman or Murray (Moore's *Memoirs, etc.*, 22 Dec., 1820; III, 182). Moore was to have 'discretionary power' over the new material, since it 'contains, perhaps, a thing or two which is too sincere for the public'; but 'tastes may change'; and in any case he would not himself consent to alter anything in the first part (Moore, 9 Dec., 1820; 2 Jan., 1821; LJ, v, 131, 212). However, Moore says that he was subsequently given the power of omitting objectionable passages over the whole manuscript (Moore, XL, 465, note). When, on the death of Lady Noel in January 1822, Byron had thoughts of a reconciliation with his wife, he had doubts as to his wisdom in parting with the rights (Mayne, II, App. II, 321), and on 6 May 1822 Murray, who had paid Moore two thousand guineas for them, executed a deed giving either Byron or Moore the power to redeem them during Byron's life (Murray to Wilmot Horton, 19 May, 1824; quoted *Quarterly*, June, 1853; Vol. 93; *312*). But on 10 June Byron *was still assuming their publication after his death* (Isaac D'Israeli, LJ, VI, 88), and took no further steps. This was the position when he died.

The news was received in London on 14 May, 1824. Hobhouse visited Augusta, urging on the latter, as Byron's relative, the necessity of destroying the papers. She had never read them, but finally agreed to give her authority (Mayne, II; App. II, 326). Hobhouse, Moore, Sir Francis Burdett, Douglas Kinnaird, Samuel Rogers, Lord Lansdown, Henry Luttrell, Colonel Doyle and Wilmot Horton were all variously involved in the conflict of opinions. Hobhouse appears to have been firm for destruction, and Moore against it.

On Monday, 17 May, only three days after the news of Byron's death had been received, there was a meeting in Murray's room in Albemarle Street. Lady Byron was represented by Colonel Doyle and Augusta by Wilmot Horton, who had also for long been the adviser and friend of Lady Byron. Moore still protested, thinking he had some rights in the matter, though it was later discovered that they were, now that Byron was dead, the property of Murray. From the start Murray was, if necessary at the cost of losing the two thousand guineas, in favour of destruction. Colonel Doyle and Wilmot Horton tore up both the original and the copy which had been made, and gave them to the flames, Colonel Doyle saying, 'On the part of Mrs. Leigh I put them into the fire' (Hobhouse, III, App. I, 338–45). It was only after this that they all realized that the sole rights were Murray's.

The responsibility appears, apart from Moore's reluctance, to have been shared. Moore tells us that he strongly disapproved of treating these papers as a 'pest-bag' without even a 'perusal' of their contents, thereby setting for all time a 'stigma' on a work which contained much that was 'creditable' to the author; but he was willing to allow Mrs. Leigh to decide (Moore's *Memoirs, etc.*, 15, 16 May, 1824; IV,

188–91). He seems to have gone on protesting until it was clear that he had no rights in the matter (Mayne, II, App. II, 324). Hobhouse was vigorous for destruction and worked hard on Augusta to give her authority (Augusta's Statement, as above, p. 106; and see her letter of 6 June, 1825; p. 107); even though, according to his own account, he was not unwilling to let them go to a bank if others consented (Hobhouse, III, App. I, 341–2), and in a letter to Wilmot Horton of 23 November, 1824, said that he refused to put them on the fire with his own hands, though he admits that he strongly approved of the action (Fox, XVI, 180–1). According to Moore, Wilmot Horton was not averse to the publication of extracts (Moore's Memoirs, etc., 16 May, 1824, IV, 190), and according to Augusta he suggested putting them in a bank (Augusta's Statement, as above; and see Mayne, II, App. II, 323). Disentanglement is hard, since no one afterwards was willing to admit responsibility, each in turn putting it on to someone else; but when Moore said that Wilmot Horton and Colonel Doyle, both 'friends of Lady Byron and of Lord Byron's family', saw no objection to a 'perusal', Hobhouse himself tells us that he remarked 'that he could hardly bring himself to believe that' (Hobhouse, III; App. I, 339), insinuating that they were not sincere. We know that Lady Byron was from the start fearful of the Memoirs and wished to suppress them, and there is the solid fact that her two advisers, and one of them, Colonel Doyle, her accredited representative, did the actual burning (Hobhouse, III; App I, 342). We can say that Hobhouse, Colonel Doyle, Wilmot Horton and John Murray were jointly responsible; and that Augusta, who had neither read them nor barely knew of their existence, who did not at first wish to interfere, and indeed 'shrank from the responsibility' (her own Statement, as above, p. 106), was used by the others. And behind it all, if my reading already set out (pp. 107–9) be correct, was Lady Byron, whose interests and desires were being directly implemented. We know how horrified she had been at the first news of the Memoirs and that, on hearing of Byron's death, she appears to have offered a sum for their redemption, though it was eventually paid by Moore; and that, as soon as the burning was accomplished, she suggested to Hobhouse that they should replace them with a version of their own (pp. 108–9).

Afterwards Hobhouse attempted to quiet Moore's conscience, since he had a certain *moral* right to the papers, by telling him that Byron had, *in response to his own remonstrances*, regretted having put

WHAT BYRON SAID

them out of his power, and had only left things as they were out of consideration for Moore. Moore at once got Hobhouse to promise him a statement in writing to this effect, and later reminded him of the promise, though there seems no record of his having received the statement (Moore's *Memoirs, etc.*, 18 May, 15 Dec., 1824; 26 Jan., 1826; IV, 193–4; 257–8; V, 43). Hobhouse, rather unscrupulously, *had told Augusta this too*, in order to force her decision (Augusta's Statement, as above). But John Fox, the author of *Vindication of Lady Byron*, tells us that Hobhouse and Kinnaird had 'over and over again' advised Byron 'to resume possession' of the *Memoirs* (*Vindication*, II, 95); and Hobhouse was probably merely reporting an off-hand remark made by Byron in response to his own insistences. Had Byron really wished to suppress them, he could at any time have done so by paying the money; and he knew that he was likely to die in Greece. Lovelace is right in saying: 'Their destruction he never contemplated' (Lovelace, VI, 119). Byron told Medwin that Kinnaird was always trying to persuade him to resume possession, but that he was 'quite indifferent about the world knowing all that they contain' (Medwin, 35).

Why the *Memoirs* were destroyed has never been explained. Byron told Medwin (35) that they contained 'a very full account' of his marriage and separation; but the aim was also severely self-critical, as appears from a passage of his conversations with Lady Blessington in 1823, which incidentally shows that he had no regrets at that date, so exactly Byronic in manner that one suspects it to be a dictated piece:

' "I know so well the sort of things they would write of me—the excuses, lame as myself, that they would offer for my delinquencies, while they were unnecessarily exposing them, and all this done with the avowed intention of justifying what, God help me! cannot be justified, my *unpoetical* reputation, with which the world can have nothing to do! One of my friends would dip his pen in clarified honey, and the other in vinegar, to describe my manifold transgressions, and as I do not wish my poor fame to be either *preserved* or *pickled*, I have lived on and written my Memoirs, where facts will speak for themselves, without the editorial candour of excuses, such as 'we cannot excuse *this* unhappy error, or defend *that* impropriety'—the mode", continued Byron, "in which friends exalt their own prudence and virtue by exhibiting the want of those qualities

154

in the dear departed, and by marking their disapproval of his errors. I have written my Memoirs", said Byron, "to save the necessity of them being written by a friend or friends, and have only to hope they will not add notes".'

(Blessington, 57)

He derived a Puckish pleasure from thought of the embarrassment knowledge of their existence might cause. Had they made a great sensation? And were not people greatly alarmed at the thought of 'being shown up' in them? 'He seemed,' says Lady Blessington, 'much pleased in anticipating the panic it would occasion, naming all the persons who would be most alarmed' (260). We need not quite believe this. He once admitted that it would not *all* do, 'even for the posthumous public'; and he had been at pains to avoid hurting people's feelings (Moore, 3 Sept., 1821; *Detached Thoughts*, 74; LJ, v, 356, 446). He had told the truth 'as far as regard for others' allowed (Isaac D'Israeli, 10 June, 1822; LJ, vi, 88).

The *Memoirs* formed Byron's considered defence and meant much to him. He may at times, thinking of the feelings of others, have had doubts as to their immediate posthumous publication; he had, indeed, started composing them for publication after the lapse of an hundred years (*Vindication*, ii, 93); but their destruction he certainly never contemplated. When telling Moore on 13 July, 1820, that he would like a copy made for safety, and that he was willing for any 'proper' person to see them, he added: 'I wish to give everybody concerned the opportunity to contradict or correct me' (LJ, v, 48–9). Again: 'If *you* (as is most likely) survive me, add what you please from your own knowledge, and, *above all*, *contradict* anything, if I have *mis*-stated; for my first object is the truth, even at my own expense' (Moore, 9 Dec., 1820; LJ, v, 131). The *Memoirs* were to be 'a kind of guide-post in case of death', and to 'prevent some of the lies which would otherwise be told, and destroy some which have been told already' (Edgcumbe, asserting that these are 'Byron's words', iii, 393; no ref.).

The loss to the student of Byron is formidable and irreparable, and their destruction stands at the heart of the Byronic problem. No solution is satisfactory which does not cover it. It is to be observed that though the *Memoirs* were written in his own defence, they were destroyed not simply by his enemies, but by his friends and enemies in alliance, each one of whom in turn disclaimed personal responsibility for what had been done. 'It was enough for me', wrote Murray in a letter to Wilmot Horton dated 19 May, 1824 (*Quarterly*, June, 1853; Vol. 93; *314*), 'that the friends of Lord and Lady Byron united in wishing for their destruction'. All this, too, must be taken into account.

In conclusion, we may record that Lord John Russell (p. xiii) entirely omits from Moore's diary a 'long account' of the destruction of Byron's *Memoirs*, substituting a brief note of his own (Moore's *Memoirs, etc.*, IV, 191). Moore's account was presumably too forthright, and so the one sympathetic and therefore vital witness has been silenced.

V

THE *DON LEON* POEMS

V. THE *DON LEON* POEMS

I

W E should probably have had to remain content with this *impasse*, were it not for the mysterious *Don Leon* poems. There are two: *Don Leon*, and *Leon to Annabella*. I am using a London edition brought out in 1866 with the two poems bound together.

The first is printed as 'by the late Lord Byron' with the additional statement 'and forming part of the private journal of his Lordship, supposed to have been entirely destroyed by Thos. Moore'. This purports to tell the inside story of Byron's homosexual propensities and concludes with his engaging in an abnormal sexual relationship with his own wife. The poem is in rhymed couplets, and runs—though the printed numerals go wrong—to 1465 lines; it has 63 pages of notes, by various, unnamed hands.

The second poem, *Leon to Annabella*, is in the same style, but shorter, totalling 330 lines. It is subtitled: 'An Epistle from Lord Byron to Lady Byron explaining the real cause of eternal separation and forming the most curious passage in the secret history of the noble poet'. Under this is printed:

'Lady Byron can never cohabit with her noble husband again. He has given cause for a separation which can never be revealed; but the honour due to the female sex forbids all further intercourse for ever.

—Opinion of Dr. Lushington on the question of divorce.'

There is an introduction, in prose, stating that the poem was discovered in the possession of a peasant in a cottage near Pisa where it had been left as a wrapping for some pieces of lead by a certain 'English gentleman' who used to visit the place 'for the purpose of firing at a mark with pistols'. The paper had been torn, but the finder put it together, and tells us that he is himself responsible 'for the interpolation of ten whole lines in one place, two couplets and a half in another, and several patches here and there'. No name or date is given to this introduction, which is probably quite fictional, and probably intended to be so understood.

The 'English gentleman' is, of course, supposed to be Lord Byron, who was at Pisa in 1821 and 1822. The poem continues from where *Don Leon* left off, describing Byron's distress at his wife's desertion and gradual realization that she must have revealed the secret and allowed lawyers to ruin her marriage. *Leon to Annabella* is only sparsely annotated, with footnotes.

The poems are unedited and the whole 1866 volume is carelessly set up, with misprints and notes out of place. The notes to *Don Leon* have been done at various times by different hands. No publisher is named, the title-page merely stating 'London: Printed for the Booksellers: 1866.' In his *Index Librorum Prohibitorum* (1877) 'Pisanus Fraxi', that is H. S. Ashbee, gives us reason to suppose that the publisher was W. Dugdale. Samuel Chew's *Byron in England* (x, 178, note) refers to Dugdale and also to a book catalogue which ascribes the publication to John Camden Hotten.

Other valuable bibliographical details are given by Chew (x, 173–4; 177–8). He shows that *Don Leon* must have appeared during the first half of the century, since it was referred to in *Notes and Queries* for 15 January, 1853 (1st Series, vii, 66), the writer 'I.W.' saying that it was 'printed abroad many years since', and asking for information regarding it, which was not, however, forthcoming. Chew has nothing to report beyond that; but there may have been an 1842 edition, since note 27 to line 385 contains the words 'it being now 1842'. There appears to be no copy extant until the 1866 printing.

Of *Leon to Annabella* there does exist an early but undated copy, brought out by MacJohn, Ramur & Co.; and this, according to Chew, 'is in the library of Mr. J. Pierpoint Morgan' (the 'Pierpoint Morgan Library', New York). In 1865 it was reprinted 'for the booksellers' and was reissued again in 1866, with the title 'The Great Secret Revealed'. Chew says that copies of this 1866 reprint were bound up with the 1866 *Don Leon*, but in my composite 1866 volume the title-page of *Leon to Annabella* bears the date 1865. Anyway, the two appeared bound together, perhaps for the first time, in 1866, and appear to have created some interest. On 15 June, 1867,

THE HON. AUGUSTA LEIGH
from a sketch by
Sir George Hayter

we find 'S. Jackson' writing to *Notes and Queries*, as did 'I.W.' earlier in the century, asking for information; he was answered, quite irrelevantly, by 'Filius Eccleslae' on 29 June, and wrote again, saying that he had heard that the work had been withdrawn, on 17 August (3rd Series, XI, 477, 528; XII, 137; and see pp. 232-3 below).

In *Index Librorum Prohibitorum*, H. S. Ashbee prints a note by one who claimed to be 'acquainted with the publisher', who says that W. Dugdale showed him the manuscript of *Don Leon* some time before its publication, and a reference to Lady Byron (see p. 232 below) suggests that this must have been just before her death in 1860. The manuscript at that time appeared to have been 'written some years previously', but 'was evidently not the original written by the author', having been copied by some 'illiterate person' with many errors among the Latin and Greek quotations of the notes. He records that he pointed out to Dugdale that *Don Leon* contained references to events which occurred after Byron's death.

This is true, and disposes of Byron's authorship, at least so far as *Don Leon* is concerned. In his 1933 bibliography of Byron's works, T. J. Wise writes (II, 103), 'Both poems, of course, are spurious.' On a reissue printed from the 1866 composite volume in 1934 by The Fortune Press, they were ruled as spurious, and the stock seized by the police. Chew tells us that various printings have appeared on the Continent.

No serious attention has been given to the poems. They have in general been written off as 'forgeries', and the most opprobrious epithets been fixed to them, such as: 'little filthy contraband brochures' (Mayne, II; I, 1); 'infamous piece', 'off-scourings of literature' (Chew, x, 177, 178); 'obscene squibs' (Joyce, Notes, 358).

There have been two grave omissions in the treatment accorded them. First, it has been considered sufficient to write them off as 'forgeries'; and indeed they have been often regarded as dating from the eighteen-sixties, though Chew, giving the *Notes and Queries* reference, rightly dates them earlier, putting *Leon to Annabella* about 1817 or 1818 and *Don Leon* itself as 1824–1830: Chew does not give his reasons for putting *Leon to Annabella* quite so early, and it is, as we shall see, certain that a rather later limit than his is needed for *Don Leon*. But what no one appears to have realized is this: granted that Byron's authorship is easily disposed of, there still remains the important question who did write them, and why; and, following that, whether they tell the truth.

The second grave omission concerns the closely related matter of the poetry. However deeply we may be horrified by the subject, that does not excuse us from recognizing that the quality of the writing is of the highest order. Indeed, no such brilliant manipulation of the rhymed couplet has been known since Pope.

Who, then, wrote them, and with what purpose? This, fortunately, is not difficult to answer. There appears to exist a kind of submerged tradition, or unformulated suggestion, the origin of which I have not been able to trace and which has not, so far as I know, ever appeared in print, that they were the work of the well-known dramatist, George Colman the Younger; and the most cursory inspection of Colman's plays and, still more, of his humorous poetry, should be sufficient to form a strong case. For my part, the argument from subject matter, viewpoint, style, wit and punning, and above all, parallels in phrase and vocabulary, appears so overpowering as to be, failing evidence to the contrary, conclusive; and I am content, for my present purpose, to assert simply that both poems *are* Colman's work, and to refer to them henceforward as his. My evidence is summarized in my article *Colman and Don Leon* in *The Twentieth Century*, June, 1956.

The notes to *Don Leon—Leon to Annabella* has few—consist of various strata: some, with probably most of the many quotations from Latin poetry, may be supposed to be Colman's; one, and probably more, belong to the 1842 printing; others refer to later dates, quoting *The Times* of 8 March, 1850, and 2 September, 1856 (Note 7 to line 88; Note 51 to line 824). There is much obscenity in these notes; the various authors may be suspected of various purposes, ranging from scholarship to pornography.

As for the date of the main poems, there appears to be nothing to fix *Leon to Annabella*, but a study of the events, people and notes of *Don Leon* suggests composition later than the dates given by Chew, covering 1833 (p. 189) to 1836; a reference to Charles Manners-Sutton (p. 186) points to 1835, and one passage, perhaps added later, may, if we accept the corresponding note on Gray Bennett, seem to have been written, though it is not really necessary to suppose so, after his death on 16 June, 1836 (Note 66 to line 986). Colman died on 26 October of that year. In his recent study *George Colman the Younger*, Jeremy F. Bagster-Collins tells us that Colman's mental powers were vigorous to the last. His doctor records:

It is remarkable that, although the disease of Colman was of a most painful and irritating nature, yet his mind and temper were seldom disturbed: it appeared often to me, that in the same ratio he lost physical power and suffered bodily pain, there was increased cerebral energy, intellectual activity, and wit of the most genuine character.'
(Bagster-Collins, XIII, 321)

He was reported by his friend General Augustus Phipps to be 'more witty and intellectual than ever' (Bagster-Collins, XIII, 321). It is accordingly not strange that he should have been able to compose what is, indubitably, his masterpiece, during his last years.

Colman was born in 1762, son of George Colman, theatre-manager, dramatist and friend of David Garrick, with whom he wrote *The Clandestine Marriage*. The boy was educated at West-minster, Oxford and Aberdeen. At Oxford he was at Christ Church, but was soon, as he himself tells us in a footnote to his poem *Vagaries Vindicated*, 'transplanted' from those 'warmer regions'—'warmer' containing an innuendo—to the 'cold latitude' of King's College, Aberdeen, as a result of certain 'juvenile vagaries'. At Aberdeen he saturated himself thoroughly in the classics. Not long after his return to London, he was sent abroad by his father with a tutor. In this, as he tells us in his *Random Records*, there was 'a deeper policy than appears upon the surface'; he had not yet sowed his 'wild oats', and the 'diversion' was intended to remove him from certain 'London pursuits' which were considered inadvisable (*Random Records*, II, 225). We may suppose that these Oxford 'vagaries' and London 'pursuits' were of a less orthodox kind.

Though at first intended for the law, he preferred to follow in his father's steps, took to dramatic work, and, on his father's death, became controller, at a comparatively early age, of the Haymarket Theatre.

His output of plays during the years that followed was consider-able. These varied in quality and subject matter. The best known are probably *The Heir-at-Law* and *John Bull*, both realistic and con-temporary studies, and *The Iron Chest*, adapted from William Godwin's *Caleb Williams*; but he had also a flair for colourful and exotic works of southern or oriental atmosphere, such as *Turk and Turk*, *The Mountaineers*, *Blue-Beard*, *The Africans*, *Inkle and Yarico*, *The Law of Java*, and *The Gnome King, or The Giant Mountains*. None of his plays shows a really substantial art; they are works of a

163

purely professional nature, intended to fill the theatre, and successful in their aims.

But, though so intended and often, too, most hurriedly and carelessly composed, these plays nevertheless contain thought and establish values. There is a general satire against selfish nobility, the heartless rich, the illogicality of a business society based on the admitted system of everyone trying to ruin every one else (*John Bull*, II, i), tyranny of any kind, brutal justice, and humbug of all sorts, with an especial horror of executions, the slave-trade, and imperialistic exploitation. Throughout we find a firm support of the lowly, of simple country-folk at home and savages abroad, and all in whom the vices of civilization and sophistication are not present. Love is central, shown as suffering or succeeding in relation to these various themes and values. There is a strong, Shakespearian, emphasis on emotional integrity, with an insistence on generosity and gratitude as primary virtues; and, on the other side, continual satire against false friends, money-greed, ingratitude, and time-servers.

Colman's dramatic work is to this extent both Shakespearian and Byronic. The easiest way to characterize it briefly is to say that it exists and appeals on the wave-length of *Timon of Athens*. In *John Bull* gratitude is a leading value, and the embittered recluse Orzinga in *The Law of Java* is a replica in outline of Shakespeare's hero. That Colman's powers and potentialities were recognized by Byron is clear when, in *English Bards and Scotch Reviewers* (578; P, I, 343), he appears as one of the few to receive acclamation, being urged to 'awake' and chastise the age as it deserved.

Colman's contemporary reputation was that of a successful manager and dramatist and a brilliant wit. Like Shakespeare, he showed a peculiar delight and skill in punning. His political interests were lively and he mixed with the aristocracy. But he also had many enemies, and was darkly accused of vice.

These accusations were encouraged, and perhaps partly based on, his humorous poems. *Broad Grins* appeared in 1802, *Poetical Vagaries* in 1812, and *Eccentricities for Edinburgh* in 1816; a more serious satire on flogging, *The Rodiad*, in 1810; and a reply to critics, *Vagaries Vindicated*, in 1813.[1]

The plays are deeply satiric in what may be called a 'respectable'

[1] A copy of the first edition of *Vagaries Vindicated*, inscribed by Colman to his friend, General Augustus Phipps, and with two textual corrections in his own hand, is lodged in the Brotherton Library, in the University of Leeds.

THE *DON LEON* POEMS

way; the poems are equally satiric, but less respectable. They vary
from sheer fun to strong satire; but through them runs a vein of
indecency and a strong prepossession, whether in comedy or satire,
with the posterior areas of the human body: we could say that,
poetically, he expresses an 'anal' complex. What is remarkable is
the extent to which, through his favourite medium of puns and
striking skill in rhyme, he renders his work not only acceptable, but
enjoyable. There is an amazing technical virtuosity.

His stories often, in Chaucer's manner, derive part of their humour
from events usually left unmentioned, as in the extraordinarily comic
part played by a privy in *The Knight and the Friar* in *Broad Grins*.
In *Poetical Vagaries* the story *Low Ambition* is a vastly amusing narrative of the rivalry of two actors who together perform the fore
and hind parts of a stage animal. In the same collection, if you know
Colman, you immediately suspect an innuendo, with a pun on
'tale', in the title of a poem called *Two Parsons, or The Tale of a
Shirt;* but, though the comic action leads to the two parsons going
to bed together with no clothes on, nothing actually happens, though
there may be an overtone of suggestion, which could be called
immoral. *The Rodiad* is a most indecent piece satirizing the practice
of birching at schools, with a development of flagellatory excitement
and physical detail which might have made Swinburne blush, and
a truly magnificent conclusion in which the Schoolmaster, who has
no fancy for a Heaven peopled by 'unbottomed cherubs', freely offers
instead to continue his favourite pastime in Hell, itching, in four
lines packed with a multi-directional satire, to

> *Cut up with red-hot wire adulterous Queens,*
> *Man-burning Bishops, Sodomizing Deans;*
> *Punish with endless pain a moment's crime,*
> *And whip the wicked out of space and time.*

Vagaries Vindicated is an expert, witty, and indeed brilliant defence
of the humorous tales, with a skilful use of obscene overtone and
pun and a masterly manipulation of the rhymed couplet pointing
on, as does *The Rodiad* too, to *Don Leon*. How far Colman is being
indecent and how far he is merely satirizing indecency cannot always
be assessed; this is, after all, a well-known problem. All we can say
is that, with his peculiar prepossession, he is simultaneously revealing
himself and charging others.

We cannot here do more than give two more samples of his

manner.[1] Here is the opening to *The Knight and the Friar* in *Broad Grins*, which suggests that Byron's *Don Juan* owed something to Colman's lighter style:

> In our Fifth Harry's reign, when 'twas the fashion
>   To thump the French, poor creatures! to excess—
> Tho' Britons, now-a-days, show more compassion,
>   And thump them, certainly, a great deal less—
> In Harry's reign, when flush'd Lancastrian roses
>   Of York's pale blossoms had usurp'd the right;
> As wine drives Nature out of drunkards' noses,
>   Till red, triumphantly, eclipses white;—
> In Harry's reign—but let me to my song,
> Or good King Harry's reign may seem too long.

That is light enough. But even in a comic narrative he may rise to weighty satire. His verbal resource is remarkable, and his more bitter thrusts, levelled against pomposity and pride, form an excellent introduction to *Don Leon*. So in *Two Parsons or the Tale of a Shirt* in *Poetical Vagaries* we find him writing of Bow Street officers and

> Those infinitely grander Drudges,
> The big-wigg'd circuiteering Judges.

He next proceeds to characterize

> The Vice-Suppressing, starch'd Society—
> That tribe of self-erected Prigs—whose leaven
> Consists in buckramizing souls for Heaven;
> Those stiff-rump'd Buzzards, who evince the vigour
> Of Christian virtue by Unchristian rigour;
> Those Quacks and Quixotes, who, in coalition,
> Compose the Canters' secret Inquisition;
> Dolts, in our tolerating Constitution,
> Who turn Morality to Persecution,
> And through their precious pates' fanatick twists,
> Are part Informers, Spies and Methodists.

Though this is early work and occurs in a mainly humorous poem, we find the same punch and pungency, the same easy use of well-loaded, yet never over-assertive, single words, the same bitterness

---

[1] Other examples are given in my article *Colman and Don Leon* (p. 162).

and moral valuation, as we shall find in *Don Leon*. As a master of comic narrative, Colman reminds us of Chaucer; and as a denouncer of cant, of Byron.

During his life Colman encountered many difficulties. He was separated from his wife, after the birth of a son. For some years he was in trouble for debt. But he was, in the main, recognized as the leading professional theatre-manager and dramatist of his day, and towards the end of his career, partly through his friendship with the Duke of York, won advancement for his son and honour for himself, being given an honorary Lieutenantry of the Yeomanry Guards, and made 'Examiner of Plays' by the Lord Chamberlain (Bagster-Collins, XI, 270, 282).

His term of office as censor was remarkable, if not unique. Though at his best, or worst, perhaps the most indecent poet of high quality in our literature, he has left behind him the name of the strictest censor of plays England has ever known; if a lover called his love an angel, that was blasphemy, and the mention of a 'thigh' was ruled as indecent. Perhaps he had been appointed on the principle of 'set a thief to catch a thief'; perhaps his genius for the pun and *double entendre* caused him to see layers of unintended implication to which the rest of us are blind; perhaps he would have claimed that his work had always been, in the best sense, moral, that his plays themselves had never shocked, that public performances were different from private reading, and that he was merely fitting his conscience to his office; perhaps the reasons for his actions were in part political [1]; or perhaps his incorrigible sense of humour was at work. And, though it may at first appear strange that he should have been composing such a work as *Don Leon* during his term of office, which lasted until his death, yet if only we can, for a while, assume the viewpoint from which it was written, this extraordinary piece may perhaps be seen as one of the most indecent and yet deeply moral poems in our language; when perhaps the anomaly ceases to exist.

It was natural that Colman and Byron should have been interested in each other. The young Byron, as we have seen (p. 164), respected his powers and integrity. Byron's letters contain many references to his plays; and during his wife's pregnancy in the autumn of 1815, just before the Separation, he attended a number of drinking parties

[1] Dr. Bernard Jones tells me that there is some evidence of a political purpose behind both Colman's appointment and the nature of his censorship.

of which Sheridan and Colman were leading spirits. 'Both he and Colman', he wrote to Moore on 31 October, 1815, 'were, as usual, very good' (LJ, III, 243). These brilliant parties were recalled when, in 1821, he wrote:

'I have met George Colman occasionally, and thought him extremely pleasant and convivial. Sheridan's humour, or rather wit, was always saturnine, and sometimes savage: he never laughed (at least that *I* saw, and I watched him), but Colman did. I have got very drunk with them both; but, if I had to *choose*, and could not have both at a time, I should say, "Let me begin the evening with Sheridan, and finish it with Colman." Sheridan for dinner— Colman for supper. Sheridan for claret or port; but Colman for every thing, from the madeira and champaigne at dinner—the claret with a *layer* of *port* between the glasses—up to the Punch of the Night, and down to the grog or gin and water of day-break. All these I have threaded with both the same. Sheridan was a Grenadier Company of Life-Guards, but Colman a whole regiment—of *light Infantry*, to be sure, but still a *regiment.*'

(*Detached Thoughts*, 107; LJ, V, 461)

Remembering Byron's admiration for Sheridan, we can call that high praise. Indeed, with three such contributors as Sheridan, Colman and Byron, we may suppose that nothing at the Mermaid Tavern can have surpassed the brilliancy of these engagements.

What, then, was Colman's purpose in composing the two *Don Leon* poems? Since *Don Leon* itself deliberately refers to events which happened after Byron's death, he cannot obviously have expected Byron's authorship, at least of this poem, to have been accepted; but he is equally clearly claiming to tell the truth of Byron's life. He may well have been in a position to know the truth, since he was in so many ways a kindred spirit, and had met Byron during the period leading up to the marriage-disaster under conditions which might well have encouraged the boldest confidence. He must, moreover, with all that abhorrence of hypocrisy so evident in his work, have been deeply shocked by the burning of Byron's *Memoirs*, which he had in all probability seen, and by the general conspiracy of silence which covered the whole affair of the Separation. He probably had information from Byron himself during their convivial meetings; and he believed that the truth should be told, the more fervently, we may suppose, since so much of his own cherished 'complex' was involved. It was, indeed, the perfect theme for him. Then Moore's *Life of Byron* appeared, in 1830, with a discreet veiling of the crucial issue. So, though suffering intensely from his last illness and also pursuing the course of guardian of public morals as dramatic censor, he nevertheless found time to compose *Don Leon*, though when he wrote *Leon to Annabella*, which Chew regards as earlier, is less easy to determine. *Don Leon* was undertaken as the fullest expression of his own personality, as a denunciation of society, and as the defence of a great man whose name was suffering under a conspiracy of silence propping a moral system rotten to the core. That, at least, is how Colman would have seen it.

II

We now pass to a short exposition of the two poems. I ask the reader to be prepared to respond to the rich quality of the writing in all its lack of artifice, force of idiom and poetic vigour.

Since Byron is supposed to be speaking, though we know that he is not, I shall refer to the speaker variously as 'Leon' or 'Colman', according to the occasion.

Don Leon, which is in epistle form addressed to Thomas Moore, opens with a sharp attack on the judge responsible for the execution, for the penalty was at this period death, of a man condemned for homosexual practices:

> *Thou ermined judge, pull off that sable cap!*
> *What! Can'st thou lie, and take thy morning nap?*
> *Peep thro' the casement; see the gallows there:*
> *Thy work hangs on it; could not mercy spare?*
> *What had he done? Ask crippled Talleyrand,*
> *Ask Beckford, Courtenay, all the motley band*
> *Of priest and laymen, who have shared his guilt*
> *(If guilt it be), then slumber if thou wilt.*
> *What bonds had he of social safety broke?*
> *Found'st thou the dagger hid beneath his cloak?*
> *He stopped no lonely traveller on the road;*
> *He burst no lock, he plundered no abode;*
> *He never wrong'd the orphan of his own;*
> *He stifled not the ravish'd maiden's groan.*

His secret haunts were hid from every soul,
Till thou did'st send thy myrmidons to prowl,
And watch the prickings of his morbid lust,
To wring his neck and call thy doings just.

(1–18)

The relationship of William Beckford and Lord Courtenay was a well-known scandal referred to by Byron in a letter to Francis Hodgson of 25 June, 1809, where he calls Beckford 'the martyr of prejudice' (LJ, 1, 229). Observe Colman's phrase 'morbid lust'. There is throughout no attempt to ignore the conventional valuations: they are, it is true, attacked, denied and surpassed; but they are at least recognized. There follows a strong introductory paragraph:

And shall the Muse, whilst pen and paper lie
Upon the table, hear the victim's cry,
Nor boldly lay her cauterizing hand
Upon a wound that cankers half the land?
No! were the bays that flourish round my head
Destined to wither when these lines are read:
Could all the scourges canting priests invent
To prop their legendary lies, torment
My soul in death or rack my body here,
My voice I'd raise insensible to fear.
When greedy placemen drain a sinking state,
When virtue starves and villains dine off plate;
When lords and senators, untouched by shame,
For schemes of basest fraud can lend their name;
When elders, charged to guard the pauper's trust,
Feast on the funds, and leave the poor a crust;
When knaves like these escape the hangman's noose,
Who e'en to Clogher a pardon would refuse?
Who would not up and lend a hand to save
A venial culprit from a felon's grave?
Sheer indignation quickens into rhyme,
And silence now were tantamount to crime.
I know not in what friendly breast to pour
My swelling rage, save into thine, dear Moore,
For thou, methinks, some sympathy will own,
Since love, no matter in what guise 'tis shown,

170

Must ever find an echo from that lyre
Which erst hath glowed with old Anacreon's fire.

(19–46)

'Canting priests' and 'legendary lies' do not quite ring true for Byron, since his respect for traditional religion was too firmly planted for such phrases. The Bishop of Clogher had, according to our note (Note 3 to line 36), committed an indecent offence in 1822 and fled to Scotland, where he lived *incognito*, dying in 1844. As in 'priest and laymen' before (7), the poet is anxious to remind us that the sin in question is found among the priesthood. This emphasis recurs throughout.

Leon proceeds to warn Moore not to erase 'one single line' of these confessions for the sake of money or in order 'to dine at Holland House' (51–2). Moore was not, as we have seen, primarily responsible for the loss of Byron's *Memoirs*, but Colman, who returns to the subject later, follows a contemporary impression in supposing that he was. He is next told, in good Byronic style (see p. 155), to 'print my thoughts through good or ill report', thus serving the cause of 'common-sense' (54–6).

The hypocrisy of England, a land 'where every vice in full luxuriance flowers' (60), is impugned. Normal immorality is rife and shamelessly open; why persecute a 'sport obscene' which naturally hides itself from view, one

Which none so brazened e'er presume to own,
Which, left unheeded, would remain unknown,

(69)

hanging the offender and even after death pursuing him?

And base Smelfunguses insult his ghost
With sainted columns in the Morning Post.

(79)

'Smelfungus' is a reminiscence from Sterne.

There follows a strange passage, toned for contemporary belief, meeting the argument that God destroyed Sodom with the thought that He has similarly destroyed other great cities of the ancient world that are now no more than names. The Church is next blamed for trickery and greed, and charged with refusing to sanction any pleasures which fail to bring fees to her altars.

171

In sharp distinction from the modern view of it as a sexual 'perversion', homosexuality is regarded as a *natural* instinct, which leads to no bad effects outside itself. Leon at this point confesses to having known these instincts from youth:

> Then, say, was I or nature in the wrong,
> If, yet a boy, one inclination, strong
> In wayward fancies, domineered my soul,
> And bade complete defiance to control?

(129–32)

True, he had his more conventional loves with Mary Chaworth and Margaret Parker, and these, though placed in the wrong order, are correctly handled. There was also the son of one of Leon's tenants, Robert Rushton (p. 10), whom, though decency forbade caresses, he genuinely loved:

> Love, love it was, that made my eyes delight
> To have his person ever in my sight.
> Yes, Rushton, though to unobserving eyes
> My favours but as lordly gifts were prized,
> Yet something then would inwardly presage
> The predilections of my riper age.
> Why did I give the gauds to deck thy form?
> Why for a menial did my entrails warm?
> Why? but from secret longings to pursue
> Those inspirations, which, if books speak true,
> Have led e'en priest and sages to embrace
> Those charms, which female blandishments efface.
> Thus passed my boyhood . . .

(171–83)

Robert is placed too early in Byron's story; perhaps Colman has confused him with the other boy mentioned by Moore (p. 5).

Leon goes to Cambridge, and indulges for a while in 'mirth and revels' which give no satisfaction; nor would the 'muse' bring its usual solace. But now Edleston comes into the picture, strongly *countering* the vices of Cambridge:

> As manhood came, my feelings, more intense,
> Sighed for some kindred mind, where confidence,
> Tuned in just unison, might meet return,
> And whilst it warmed my breast, in his might burn.

Oft, when the evening bell to vespers rung,
When the full choir the solemn anthem sung,
And lips, o'er which no youthful down had grown,
Hymned their soft praises to Jehovah's throne,
The pathos of the strain would soothe my soul,
And call me willing from the drunkard's bowl.
Who, that has heard the chapel's evening song,
When peals divine the lengthened note prolong,
But must have felt religious thoughts arise,
And speed their way melodious to the skies?
  Among the choir a youth my notice won,
Of pleasing lineaments named Edleston.
With gifts well suited to a stripling's mood,
His friendship and his tenderness I wooed.
Oh! how I loved to press his cheek to mine;
How fondly would my arms his waist entwine!
Another feeling borrowed friendship's name,
And took its mantle to conceal my shame.
Another feeling! Oh! 'tis hard to trace
The line where love usurps tame friendship's place.
Friendship's the chrysalis, which seems to die,
But throws its coil to give love wing to fly.
Both are the same, but in another state;
This formed to soar, and that to vegetate.
  Of humble birth was he—patrician I.
And yet this youth was my idolatry.
Strong was my passion, past all inward cure,
And could it be so violent, yet pure?
'Twas like a philter poured into my veins—
And as the chemist, when some vase contains
An unknown mixture, each component tries
With proper tests, the draught to analyze,
So questioned I myself: What lights this fire?
Maids and not boys are wont to move desire;
Else 'twere illicit love. Oh! sad mishap!
But what prompts nature then to set the trap?
Why night and day does his sweet image float
Before my eyes? or wherefore do I doat
On that dear face with ardour so intense?
Why truckles reason to concupiscence?

Though law cries 'hold!' yet passion onward draws;
But nature gave us passions, man gave laws.
Whence spring these inclinations, rank and strong?
And harming no one, wherefore call them wrong?
What's virtue's touchstone? Unto others do,
As you would wish that others did to you.
Then tell me not of sex, if to one key
The chords, when struck, vibrate in harmony.
No virgin I deflower, nor, lurking, creep,
With steps adult'rous, on a husband's sleep.
I plough no field in other men's domain;
And where I delve no seed shall spring again.
Thus with myself I reasoned.

(197–253)

Byron's poetry is perhaps being remembered. The references to
'some kindred mind', 'unison' and 'harmony' (198–9, 248) recall
'our souls were equal' in *The Adieu* (p. 30). The comparison of
friendship and love (221–2) is drawn from Byron's early lyric,
L'Amitié est L'Amour sans Ailes (P, I, 220); and Byron's reminiscence
of his 'violent, though *pure*', passion (p. 28) for Edleston is recaptured (228).

Faced by this moral *cul-de-sac*, Leon turns to literature for assistance. But, instead of help, he finds merely more and more support
for his own dangerous propensities:

Then I read,
And counsel asked from volumes of the dead.
Oh! flowery path, thus hand in hand to walk
With Plato and enjoy his honeyed talk;
Beneath umbrageous planes to sit at ease,
And drink from wisdom's cup with Socrates;
Now stray with Bion through the shady grove;
Midst deeds of glory, now with Plutarch rove.
And oft I turned me to the Mantuan's page,
To hold discourse with shepherds of his age;
Or mixed with Horace in the gay delights
Of courtly revels, theatres, and sights;
And thou, whose soft seductive lines comprise
The code of love, thou hadst my sympathies;

But still, where'er I turned, in verse or prose,
Whate'er I read, some fresh dilemma rose,
And reason, that should pilot me along,
Belied her name, or else she led me wrong.
I love a youth; but Horace did the same;
If he's absolv'd, say, why am I to blame?
When young Alexis claimed a Virgil's sigh,
He told the world his choice; and may not I?
Shall every schoolman's pen his verse extol,
And, sin in me, in him a weakness call?
Then why was Socrates surnamed the sage,
Not only in his own, but every age,
If lips, whose accents strewed the path of truth,
Could print their kisses on some favoured youth?
Or why should Plato, in his Commonwealth,
Score tenets up which I must note by stealth?
Say, why, when great Epaminondas died,
Was Cephidorus buried by his side?
Or why should Plutarch with eulogiums cite
That chieftain's love for his young catamite,
And we be forced his doctrine to decry,
Or drink the bitter cup of infamy?

(253–88)

The attribution of 'kisses' to Socrates may, in view of *The Symposium*, be questioned, but it is defended in a note, probably Colman's (Note 20, to line 280).

All these were examples from pagan literature. But when Leon turns to the Christian tradition, he finds precisely the same:

But these, thought I, are samples musty grown;
Turn we from early ages to our own.
No heathen's lust is matter of surprise;
He only aped his Pagan deities;
But when a Saviour had redeemed the world,
And all false idols from Olympus hurled,
A purer code the Christian law revealed,
And what was venial once as guilt was sealed.
With zeal unwearied I resumed again
My search, and read whate'er the layman's pen

In annals grave or chronicles had writ;
But can I own with any benefit?
'Tis true, mankind had cast the pagan skin,
But all the carnal part remained within
Unchang'd, and nature, breaking through the fence,
Still vindicated her omnipotence.
    Look, how infected with this rank disease
Were those who held St. Peter's holy keys,
And pious men to whom the people bowed,
And kings, who churches to the saints endowed;
All these were Christians of the highest stamp—
How many scholars, wasting o'er their lamp,
How many jurists, versed in legal rules,
How many poets, honoured in the schools,
How many captains, famed for deeds of arms,
Have found their solace in a minion's arms!
Nay, e'en our bard, Dame Nature's darling child,
Felt the strange impulse, and his hours beguiled
In penning sonnets to a stripling's praise,
Such as would damn a poet now-a-days.

(289–318)

The conclusion is, briefly, that men of highest fame and virtue have
'ate' of this 'forbidden tree' (323); and are we to suggest that 'the
great, the wise, the pious and the good' (327) in every age were all
somehow in error?

Leon is in doubt. At one moment he accuses all these books as
'false-named beacons of mankind' leading to 'perdition' (332-3);
and the next, he is back at his questioning. The natural loves of boys
at school, he is sure, are not in essence vicious, the thought following
Byron's in *Childish Recollections*, where he speaks of the innocence
of youth 'untaught by worldly wisdom' to 'check each impulse
with prudential rein' (59-60; P, I, 87):

In vice unhackneyed, in Justine unread,
See schoolboys by some inclination fed,
Some void, that's hardly to themselves confest,
Flying for solace to a comrade's breast.
In lonely walks, their vows of friendship pass,
Warm as the shepherd's to his rustic lass.

Their friendship ripens into closer ties:
They love.

(349–56)

After all, the alternatives are worse:

> *Fond parents, speak! if truth can find her way*
> *Through fogs of prejudice to open day.*
> *Is there a father, when, instead of this,*
> *His offspring sickens with a syphilis,*
> *Who can unmoved his tender bantling see*
> *Devoured with chancres, writhing with chordee,*
> *His blooming looks grown prematurely old,*
> *His manhood wasted ere its hours are told,*
> *His means with harlots and in brothels spent,*
> *His breath infected and his body bent,*
> *And will not own that any means were good*
> *To save from taint so foul, if save he could?*
> *Reflect, and chide not errors that arise*
> *Less from design than man's infirmities.*
> *Shut, shut your eyes, ye pedagogues, nor keep*
> *Too close a watch upon your pupils' sleep.*
> *For though, in boyish ignorance, they may*
> *Stumble perchance on some illicit play,*
> *Which looks like lechery the most refined,*
> *In them 'tis not depravity of mind.*
> *Ingenuous souls, oft innocent of wrong,*
> *For some enjoyment yet untasted long:*
> *'Twas ye who roused the latent sense of shame,*
> *And called their gambols by an odious name.*

(363–85)

Again, observe the word 'infirmities'. The weakness of human nature, in its present state, is admitted, and no easy solution expected.

Edleston dies and Leon, sick of the superficial learning and superficial pleasures which make up university life, decides to leave. Actually, of course, Edleston did not die until later, and Colman is in error. But he has the important things right.

Leon yearns for more licentious countries:

> *Methought there must be yet some people found,*
> *Where Cupid's wings were free, his hands unbound;*

Where law had no erotic statutes framed,
Nor gibbets stood to fright the unreclaimed.
I'll seek the Turk—there undisputed reigns
The little god, and still his rights maintains.

(424–28)

We pass to Turkey. Leon and his friend, that is Hobhouse, visit a brothel:

I sought the brothel, where, in maiden guise,
The black-eyed boy his trade unblushing plies;
Where in lewd dance he acts the scenic show—
His supple haunches wriggling to and fro:
With looks voluptuous the thought excites,
Whilst gazing sit the hoary sybarites:
Whilst gentle lute and drowsy tambourine
Add to the langour of the monstrous scene.

(445–52)

There is no attempt whatever to idealize the more lustful aspects of the subject: in every variation, the poetry remains true, and honest. Though Leon pretends to be deeply shocked at this 'second Sodom' (464), he is not really sincere; and when Hobhouse leaves for England he is, as was Byron (p. 203), relieved. But, in correct Byronic style, there is no sentimentalizing of the vice: Leon is urged on by a 'demon' of 'Satanic force' (494). He moves to Athens, thinking of Plato's *Phaedrus*. There, bathing from the Piraeus, he is happy, and such hours he will never forget. The truth of Byron's life at this period appears to be exactly stated.

Leon meets Nicolo Giraud attending, oriental-fashion, on his father, and the boy enters Leon's service as a page. Here Colman appears to be again in error, since Nicolo, called by Moore 'the son, I believe, of a widow lady in whose house the artist Lusieri lodged' (Moore, x, 114), and by Byron 'Lusieri's wife's brother' (Hobhouse, 16 August, 1810; C, I, 13), was of French descent. Nor was he, it seems, ever exactly in Byron's service. However, Leon takes Nicolo in his train, and stores his mind with 'culture' and 'choice instruction'—it is in part an educational relationship—

Till like the maiden, who some budding rose
Waters with care and watches till it blows,

178

THE *DON LEON* POEMS

Then plucks and places it upon her breast,
I too this blossom to my bosom pressed.

(577–80)

The romance which follows in the convent, though Colman says
nothing of the school, is well described from Byron's view, with
the true Byronic emphasis on *protection*. There is in it as much of
the maternal as of the sexual. Emphasis on the pleasure derived
from watching the loved one asleep recalls those exquisite stanzas
of *Don Juan* (II, 196, 197) on the sweet experience of seeing the
other 'hush'd into depths beyond the watcher's diving'. The description includes a correct treatment of Byron's bathing with Nicolo,
probably following the *Memoirs*, which Lord John Russell tells us
had a vivid account of Byron's swimming excursions from the
Piraeus (Moore's *Memoirs, etc.*, IV, 192; and see p. 12 above), and
shows a remarkable insight into the semi-maternal nature of Byron's
romantic friendships:

> *How many hours I've sat in pensive guise,*
> *To watch the mild expression of his eyes!*
> *Or when asleep at noon, and from his mouth*
> *His breath came sweet like odours from the south,*
> *How long I've hung in rapture as he lay,*
> *And silent chased the insect tribe away.*
> *How oft at morn, when troubled by the heat,*
> *The covering fell disordered at his feet,*
> *I've gazed unsated at his naked charms,*
> *And clasped him waking to my longing arms.*
> *How oft in winter, when the sky o'ercast*
> *Capped the bleak mountains, and the ruthless blast*
> *Moaned through the trees, or lashed the surfy strand,*
> *I've drawn myself the glove upon his hand,*
> *Thrown o'er his tender limbs the rough capote,*
> *Or tied the kerchief round his snowy throat.*
> *How oft, when summer saw me fearless brave*
> *With manly breast the blue transparent wave,*
> *Another Daedalus I taught him how*
> *With spreading arms the liquid waste to plough.*
> *Then brought him gently to the sunny beach,*
> *And wiped the briny moisture from his breech.*

179

Oh! how the happy moments seemed to fly,
Spent half in love and half in poetry!
The muse each morn I wooed, each eve the boy,
And tasted sweets that never seemed to cloy.
Let those, like Oedipus, whose skill divine
Can solve enigmas strange, unriddle mine.
How can two rivers from one fountain flow,
This salt, that fresh, and in two channels go?
Why one while would a living well-spring gush
Forth from my brain, and with pure waters rush
In copious streams to fertilize the rhyme,
Which haply yet shall live to later time?
And why, anon, like some Artesian fount,
Would oozings foul e'en from my entrails mount,
Salacious, and in murky current wet
The urn beneath with interrupted jet?

(592–632)

Again, we find a harsh realism, with a Byronic sense of unease concerning sexual activity, as in the 'passions and pure thoughts mixed and contending without end or order' of *Manfred* (III, i, 165).

The Athenian lady and her three daughters (p. 11) are duly noticed, and Leon's comparative lack of interest correctly recorded, with a diagnosis casting a light on many other of Byron's heterosexual engagements:

Felt I their charms? I felt them not; for me,
They just sufficed to tune my poetry.
And though some leaf, which to the winds I cast,
Might say Theresa all her sex surpassed,
I did as doctors do, who potions make,
Which they prescribe much oftener than they take;
Or as the preacher lauds the angels, more
To make his hearers than himself adore.
Women as women, me had never charmed,
And shafts that others felt left me unharmed.

(668–77)

There may be an over-emphasis here, but there is some authority for it, Byron himself once remarking that 'woman *quoad*' woman meant nothing to him (p. 9).

We return to Nicolo Giraud:

> But thou, Giraud, whose beauty would unlock
> The gates of prejudice, and bid me mock
> The sober fears that timid minds endure,
> Whose ardent passions women only cure,
> Receive this faithful tribute to thy charms,
> Not vowed alone, but paid too in thy arms.
> For here the wish, long cherished, long denied,
> Within that monkish cell was gratified.
> And as the sage, who dwelt on Leman's lake,
> Nobly his inmost meditations spake,
> Then dared the man, who would like him confess
> His secret thoughts, to say his own were less;
> So boldly I set calumny at naught,
> And fearless utter what I fearless wrought.
> For who that's shrived can say he never slipped?
> Had conscience tongues what back would go unwhipt?
>
> (678–93)

This may, or may not, be true. Colman's knowledge was probably drawn from Byron's often cryptic conversation, and that is, on such a point, poor evidence; but we may recall the legacy to Nicolo of £7000 in his 1811 will (p. 12).

Another boy, fifteen years old, near the age which seems most to have attracted Byron, for Nicolo must have been about that, and Edleston was nearing sixteen and Loukas fifteen when Byron met them, is idyllically described. He attends the Turkish Governor:

> Beside him sat a boy of gentle mien,
> In rich attire, in age about fifteen.
> His red tarbush o'ertopped his jet black hair,
> His cheeks were comely and his skin was fair.
> His faultless form, in Grecian garments cloaked,
> Thoughts more than mere benevolence provoked.
> Not Ganymede, whose all bewitching shape
> Could in Olympus sanctify a rape;
> Not Ali, long the Moslem prophet's joy,
> Bloomed with such graces as this Grecian boy.
>
> (718–32)

He is called the Governor's 'catamite' (733). According to the

prevailing custom, there was no odium attached to such a relationship, and from this description the poet passes to a general review of
Levantine acceptances.

The poem has no considered structure. We are next brought up
against the Malthusian doctrine of the dangers of excessive propagation to the human race, with the obvious corollary that homosexuality may hold justification in terms of economics. It is, indeed,
true that morality in such matters is usually based, one way or the
other, on very practical considerations, using moral or religious
sanctions as a mask, and that such considerations may on occasion
need revision. But this lies outside our present sphere.

Other perversions, including exhibitionism, incest, and maso-
chism—God giving 'every man at birth a different stamp' (785)—
are touched on in a passage of some indecency, with a number of
references to people of note, but none to Byron himself, mainly in
order to establish a general accusation of hypocrisy:

> Oh! England, with thy hypocritic cant,
> To hear the bench declaim, the pulpit rant,
> Who would not say that chastity's pure gems
> Had shed their lustre o'er the muddy Thames?
> That self-condemned, decried, ineffable,
> Innominate, this blackest sin of hell,
> Had fled dismayed to some Transalpine shore,
> To sully Albion's pudic cliffs no more?
>
> (850–7)

There follows a bitter denunciation of 'Bow Street bloodhounds'
(860), a vile news-system revelling in sordid detail, and the idle
rich in feigned horror prophesying the downfall of some unfortunate
whom they lift no hand to save. And, after all, what do we know of
the sinner's past? Of his psychological conditioning? He may have
been too virtuously soft-hearted to engage in normal seductions,
too sensitive for brothels, preferring 'harmless vice' to a 'heartless
crime' (879). Included in this movement is a vivid couplet whose
general significance is clearer than its relevance in its particular
context:

> Or feared the scald of that infectious taint
> Which makes a man or sodomite or saint.
>
> (872–3)

But, indeed, every vice, including homosexuality, is rampant in England. What of the barrack-room?

> Drummers may flog, judge advocates impeach,
> The soldier's post is ever at the breach.

(894–5)

A typical instance of Colman's punning. Sailors, we are told, are as bad. And as for schoolmasters, it merely takes a different form:

> Flog, lechers, flog, the measured strokes adjust:
> 'Tis well your cassocks hide your rising lust.

(920–1)

Nor are things any better in parliament itself, 'where legislators sit in grave debate' (927), where

> They make our laws, and twist the hempen cord,
> That hangs the pennyless and spares the lord.

(928–9)

Though social injustice is a leading theme, emphasis is also laid on the scandals which accumulate about men of first distinction.

Among these grave senators, a renowned scholar, Richard Heber, Member of Parliament for Oxford, is indicated, who must shortly fall a victim to calumny, though it is not clear whether the charge is true or false (note 63 to line 954):

> Behold that shining forehead, scant of hair:
> Our learned schools are represented there.
> He moves his seat. His limping steps denote,
> The gout has found a passage down his throat.
> Yet judge not rashly; for his mind's a hoard,
> With Bodley's tomes and Boyle's acumen stored.
> Alas! the time shall come, when he, like me,
> Shall fall a victim to foul calumny.
> Then all his love of learning, all his worth,
> The seat he holds by talent and by birth,
> Shall count as dross; whilst basest rumours, spread
> Folks care not how, shall light upon his head.
> Then friends shall shun him, and a venal press
> Shall seal in blackest types his wretchedness,
> Whilst some false lawyer, whom he called his friend,
> To damn his name his arguments shall lend;

183

Shall take a brief to make his shame more clear,
And drop his venom in a jury's ear.
But had that tongue with earnest friendship glowed,
His words had lighted, not increased the load,
Had poured a balmy unguent on his sore,
And chased mendacious slander from his door.
So uncorked hartshorn, when its odour flies
Forth from the phial, almost blinds the eyes;
But, if the stopper is replaced with care,
The scent diffused evaporates in air.

(930–955)

'False lawyer' may contain a reference to the part played by Sir Samuel Romilly in Byron's story. 'Sore' is an admission of disease; but the following lines also drive home a truth of first importance, converging on the word 'scent'. Richard Heber died in the year 1833.

A noble youth is here, too, one destined likewise to a miserable fall, having caught the infection from living in Sicily. One of our notes (Note 65 to line 976) takes him to be the Hon. James Stanhope, who committed suicide soon after the supposed revelations made concerning his friend Richard Heber. The vice is widespread, but, no matter what your virtues, the merest suspicion of homosexuality will discount them all:

Now turn your eyes athwart the Speaker's chair:
A pious orator is seated there.
In vain the negro's cause he nightly pleads;
Tells how the gangrened back with lashes bleeds;
Delights with philanthropic zeal to rail,
And paint the horrors of the felon's jail;
Let but some knave vituperate his name,
Adieu to all his former well-earned fame!
An exile to a foreign land he'll fly,
Neglected live, and broken-hearted die.

(978–997)

According to the note (Note 66 to line 986), the reference is to Gray Bennet, who died in June, 1836; but the last, perfunctory, line does not necessarily prove that the piece was written after his death.

The satire gathers yet greater indignation:

Britons! and will no penalty suffice
Except the gibbet for a lecher's vice?
To lose his country, to behold the chain
That linked his best affections snapt in twain,
To find no refuge for his stricken head,
Wher'er he goes to know his shame is spread;
And is not this enough, without he's cast
By judge and jury? Fiends would cry 'Avast!'
Blot out the crimson leaf! the glaive [1] *forbear!*
Count o'er the wretched victims of despair.
The panic flight, the suicidal beam,
The knife, the bullet, do they trifles seem?
Thirst ye for blood? and will no punishment,
But what Old Bailey metes, your hearts content?

(988–1001)

Peel is denounced for his 'nefarious' failure (1002) to amend the law; and the attack further includes Mackintosh and Sidmouth, the latter hit off by the telling couplet:

Whilst every circuit death was riding post
With warrants, signed by Sidmouth o'er his toast.

(1024)

The statesmen of England, themselves as guilty as those whom they punish, are living in a fool's paradise:

Shore up your house; it totters to the base;
A mouldering rot corrodes it; and the trace
Of every crime you punish I descry:
The least of all perhaps is sodomy.

(1036–9)

So the dark anger is driven home.

And now Byron's, or Leon's, personal drama swings back to view. Here is, according to our notes, either Dr. Lushington, or Sir Samuel Romilly (Note 70 to line 1042). We are still in the House of Commons:

Close to the chair, where Sutton half the year
Counts Ayes and Noes to make himself a peer,
Behold yon reptile with his squinting eyes:
Him shall my curses follow till he dies.

[1] Glaive = sword, here used for the Sword of Justice.

185

'Twas he that plugged my Annabella's ears
With vile opinions, fallacies, and fears;
The richest treasure of my youth purloined,
And put asunder those whom God had joined.
Forgive these railings, much lamented bride!
Who said I wronged my Ada's mother lied.
Thee, whom remembrance, wheresoe'er I go,
Maketh a source of happiness and woe:
Since, when dejected to the past I turn,
I fancy griefs like mine thy bosom burn.
For if the vows we plighted once were true,
So needs must be our mutual sorrows too.

(1040–55)

Sutton is, presumably, Charles Manners-Sutton, Speaker in the House of Commons from 1817 to 1835, who on 10 March 1835 was created the first Viscount of Canterbury. For the rest, the accent is correct. We may recall Byron's terrible letter to Murray on Sir Samuel Romilly's death (7 June, 1819; LJ, IV, 316; and see DP, 19–22).

Leon passes to recollection of his marriage, and how once, in bed with his wife during her pregnancy, he discussed Eastern customs. These are always richly described in *Don Leon*: Colman's oriental plays would have given him the required insight and sympathy. Leon explains how in the East the woman is utterly subservient to her lord, and without freedom:

'For her, 'tis true, the carpet spreads its flowers;
For her the arbour twines its roseate bowers;
For her the vase exhales its choice perfume;
For her rich sofas cushion every room;
Bazaars supply their muslin and brocade,
And pearls of many a carat's worth are weighed.
The jet black girl, from Darfur's burning sands,
Bears fragrant Moka to her lily hands;
And slaves unnumbered all her wants supply,
All, but that vital one of liberty.'

(1084–93)

When he describes how the husband often leaves his harem for other, male, loves, Annabella is surprised, the thought being new to her.

He assures her that it is a well-known practice of honourable heritage:

> 'Know then that boys strung old Anacreon's lyre,
> That boys the sober Virgil's lines inspire.
> Catullus pours his elegiac strains,
> Soothed by the portrait of a stripling's reins;
> And'—'Hold', she cried! 'how little had I thought
> Catullus such abominations taught,
> That Virgil's swains beneath the shady beech
> In songs of lewdness dared the muse beseech.
> I oft have heard my venerable sire
> The ancients praise, their doctrines too admire;
> But, sure I am, such things he never read
> To dear mamma, unless it was in bed.'

(1146–57)

It may seem unlikely that a woman of Annabella's intellectual equipment was so ignorant as this; but it is possible. We must not, of course, assume that Colman has all these intimate details exactly right. And now we reach the climax of our drama:

> 'Look, Bell,' I cried; 'yon moon, which just now rose
> Will be the ninth; and your parturient throes
> May soon Lucina's dainty hand require
> To make a nurse of thee, of me a sire.
> I burn to press thee, but I fear to try,
> Lest like an incubus my weight should lie;
> Lest, from the close encounter we should doom
> Thy quickened foetus to an early tomb.
> Thy size repels me, whilst thy charms invite;
> Then, say, how celebrate the marriage rite?'

(1164–73)

An expedient is found, and next, another. Nature has various ways:

> 'But ah! thou little dream'st how wide her hand
> Has spread her gifts o'er Cytherea's land.
> Another path untrodden yet remains,
> Where pleasure in her close recesses reigns.
> The neophyte to that more hallowed spot
> But rarely ventures; 'tis the favourite grot

187

> Where sages, prelates, kings, and bards retire
> To quench the rage of Priapeian fire.
> How many view this grotto from afar,
> Whilst fear and prejudice the entrance bar!
> There fain the pedagogue's lewd glance would reach
> Through the convulsions of a schoolboy's breech.
> There as the youth with tightened pantaloons
> Whirls through the dance in waltz or rigadoons,
> Or misses' haunches wriggle in quadrilles,
> In thought the lecher his libation spills.'
>
> (1192–1207)

At this point our line numerals go wrong, the number 1200 being repeated for line 1210, putting all the rest ten lines out. The error was corrected in the Fortune Press reprint, whose numerals I follow from now on.

To continue—Here, says the poet, the 'pipe-clay'd soldier' is at home, and here, too, 'bishops hold episcopalian courts' (1216–7). Leon suggests they try it. His wife is not unresponsive:

> Who, that has seen a woman wavering lie
> Betwixt her shame and curiosity,
> Knowing her sex's failing, will not deem
> That in the balance shame would kick the beam?
> Ah, fatal hour, that saw my prayer succeed,
> And my fond bride enact the Ganymede!
>
> (1259–64)

The situation resembles that dramatized in the duet 'Shall we?' of Colman's play *Blue Beard or Female Curiosity* (II, iii), when Fatima and Irene are screwing up their courage to enter the mysterious and forbidden 'Blue Room' containing 'Death', on which the plot turns. In both instances female curiosity, as in the story of the Fall in *Genesis*,[1] has its way:

> The Thespian God his rosy pinions beat,
> And laughed to see his victory complete.

[1] We might even ask whether the forbidden Apple in *Genesis* bears any precise relevance to our present study; whether the 'death' which it brings can be related to the question of propagation; whether the adjacent Tree of Life may be brought into the argument; and, finally, whether Christ, often called the 'second Adam', may be regarded as one who knows the secret, and eternal value, of what psychologists would call the 'sublimation' of the instinct in question? See p. 284 below.

'Tis true, that from her lips some murmurs fell—
In joy or anger, 'tis too late to tell;
But this I swear, that not a single sign
Proved that her pleasure did not equal mine.
Ah, fatal hour! for thence my sorrows date:
Thence sprung the source of her undying hate.
Fiends from her breast the sacred secret wrung,
Then called me monster; and, with evil tongue,
Mysterious tales of false Satanic art
Devised, and forced us evermore to part.

(1267–78)

That is the poem's central revelation. For what it may be worth, we must note that Colman supports the view that Byron's wife was no unwilling partner in the act.

Leon next appeals to Moore to 'justify' him, though he fears that he may prove 'a faithless friend' and '*burn*' these confessions (1279–84). If, tempted by some publisher, he writes Leon's life, he is urged, again in true Byronic style (p. 155), to be honest:

Be true to nature; paint me as I am;
Abate no sin I had, no virtue sham.

(1309)

Colman had known the *Memoirs* burned, and had read Moore's *Life*, with its discrete veiling of the crucial issue. *Don Leon* is composed as Byron's reply, as from the grave.

Again we return to Parliament, for the purpose of another prophecy, this time foretelling the social fall of Byron's Cambridge friend, William Bankes. Bankes, incidentally, approved of the destruction of Byron's *Memoirs*, remembering that 'Byron's best friends could always recur to his poetry and conceal his life' (Fox, XVI, 181). He enjoyed an honourable career as member of Parliament until an incident, including the subsequent trial at which Bankes was acquitted, of which 'Note 88 to line 1323' (i.e. line 1333) quotes an account copied from *The Globe* in *Galignani's Messenger* of 'June 11'. Since the year is not named, we may expect the note to have been written in the same year, and this gives us some evidence as to the date of composition. Research shows that the press account appeared in the year 1833. A brief additional statement referring to another incident in 1841 may have been put in subsequently. Checking of the biographical statements in the notes is never easy, since the *Dictionary of National Biography* naturally enough preserves silence on the matters with which *Don Leon* is primarily concerned.

It is, of course, these various *foretellings* of homosexual disaster destined to ruin people after Byron's death that show clearly that no one is expected to believe in Byron's authorship. Bankes, like Byron, had lived in the East and felt 'the subtil venom of their customs' (1326). Again, we see how the poetry, and its main thesis, gains power from use of such negative terms. Conventional morality is *within* the writing, though simultaneously surmounted. We find it again in:

> Then Peel, if conscience be not wholly dumb,
> Within thy bosom shall compunction come.
> How shalt thou sorrow for the moment, when
> A single scratch of thy reforming pen,
> Had from our code erased a peccant lust,
> And left its punishment to men's disgust.
> Nor wilt thou pass that house without a pang,
> Which erst with social joy and revels rang,
> When rendered desolate by his disgrace,
> Whose hand had helped to prop thy tottering place.
>
> (1341-50)

'Disgust'. There is the normal morality within, and a greater morality without, supervening, and this greater morality is next finely expressed in a personal apologia:

> Let my example one great truth unfold!
> And in the mirror of my life behold
> How foulest obloquy attends the good,
> Whose words and deeds are never understood.
> Oh! strange anomaly, that those should wage
> War on my actions, who approve my page.
> Whate'er I write, the town extols my song;
> Whate'er I do, the vulgar finds me wrong.
> Their feelings are not mine; in vain they scoff:
> I hate the vulgar, and I keep them off.
> They've done their worst, and now I heed them not;
> On me long since their farthest bolts were shot.
> Admired and shunned, now courted, now contemned,
> By many eulogized, by more condemned,

I stand a monument, whereby to learn
That reason's light can never strongly burn
Where blear-eyed prejudice erects her throne,
And has no scale for virtue but her own.
  That little spot which constitutes our isle,
Is not the world! Its censure or its smile
Can never reason's fabric overthrow,
And make a crime what is not really so.
The willing maid who plights her marriage vows
Owes blind obedience to her lawful spouse.
Flesh of his flesh, and knitted bone to bone,
As in a crucible two metals thrown,
The ores commixt, but one amalgam form,
And fuse more sure the more their natures warm.
At Hymen's altar mystery presides,
Spreads her dense veil, and in oblivion hides
The sacred orgies of the nuptial bed,
Where timid nymphs to sacrifice are led.
  God of the universe, whose laws shall last,
When Lords and Commons to their graves have past,
Are good and evil just as man opines,
And kens he thy inscrutable designs?
Love, like the worship which to thee is paid,
Has various creeds by various nations made:
One holds as dogmas what the other mocks,
That schism here which there is orthodox.
Some mode of faith finds favour in your eyes,
But must you, therefore, damn my heresies?

(1369–1410)

The reference to 'the vulgar' is not, strictly, Byronic; it was not the vulgar, but high society, against which Byron's anger was levelled. The reference to God's 'laws' is intended to assert once more the natural qualities of the instinct in question.

From here to the poem's conclusion Colman indulges in a gathering and brilliant crescendo of puns too bold for quotation. The conclusion is:

> *Once these were epigrams to raise a laugh:*
> *The world is grown too scrupulous by half.*

191

Deprived through life of fundamental joys,
Things can no longer find their equipoise.
Closed is the Cnidian temple, and we see
Writ on its walls, 'Hic nefas mingere.'

(1460–5)

So ends *Don Leon*.

III

Leon to Annabella is both shorter and simpler, and mainly concerned with recording Byron's agony and mystification at his wife's sudden hostility. He charges her boldly to speak out and accuse him.

The marriage is described, followed by the wedding night, which is rather strangely treated. What 'viands' awaited him, writes Leon, 'I will not say' (64); he tells how he pressed her 'trembling', 'half-resisting' and 'half-yielding', form, and then breaks off with 'but thou know'st the rest' (106); and at last diffidence was gone (113). There may be a suggestion that Leon's unorthodox approach was first used to overcome his wife's reluctance, a custom which our poem later on tells us was usual in ancient Rome. If this reading is correct, our story does not tally with the, probably later, account in *Don Leon*, where it occurs first at the period of pregnancy. We shall return to the question (p. 252).

Nothing is directly said of the marriage-secret until Leon is faced by his wife's desertion, when he starts to wonder, with presumably a reference to the mysterious Mrs. Clermont, if his wife had spoken too freely:

Whilst these reflexions in my brains ferment,
Sudden their course assumed another bent.
What! if by thoughtless indiscretion led,
Thou couldst betray the secrets of our bed?
I know thy unsuspecting soul too well—
All, all thou would'st, interrogated, tell.
Thy sex will often, under friendship's mask,
Shrive a young bride, and such avowals ask,
As pleaders draw from some deluded wench,
Who brings her Tarquin to the judge's bench.
Then, foul-mouthed, forth their specious venom spout,
And try to put the torch of Hymen out.

Accursed be those of man or womankind,
Who could thy duty and affections blind!
Some serpent she, perhaps, whose jaundiced eye,
Beheld our union with malignity.
It could not be thy mother—she's too wise
To blab these Eleusinian mysteries.
She knows the wife, whose conduct prudence guides,
A threefold aegis for herself provides.
Discretion ever is thy sex's boast:
She moves unseen, and comes, like Banquo's ghost,
The bold assassin's impious tongue to chill,
Who dares a woman's reputation kill.
Oh! would some goblin take thee pick-a-back
From house to house, and draw the curtains back,
Where, sheltered by the mantle of the dark,
Hot with desires which reach high-water mark,
The loving couples play Lampsacian games,
In postures more than Elephantis names;
A sage reserve thou surely had'st maintained,
Nor thought thy chastity nor virtue stained;
Thou had'st not bared my actions to the sun,
Nor scoffers called to mock what we had done.

(171–204)

He wonders more and more whether his wife has been 'false to love's freemasonry' (212). We may recall Colonel Doyle's letter saying that Lady Byron's trouble has been caused by her 'too confiding disposition' (p. 99).

Meanwhile rumours grow, 'monstrous' chimaeras are born, Leon is generally ostracized, and leaves England. Scandal follows him to Italy:

How here I live, let busy fame report;
Men's blame I fear not, nor their praises court.
They tell thee harlots sit upon my knee,
And mask and revel in ebriety:
They tell thee atheists, and men profane,
Mock truths divine, and call God's vengeance vain;
They bid thee mark the ravings of my muse,
And every dirty critic venom spews.

Insensate herd! 'tis their's to triumph now:
But time shall come, when, on my honoured brow,
Posterity shall place a tardy crown,
And truth shall hurl the base detractors down.

(227–238)

The lines recall the Promethean stanzas of *Childe Harold* (IV, 137). 'Atheists' refers to Byron's association with Shelley.

At last, he is certain. She has discussed the intimacies of the marriage with lawyers, and the anger roused by the thought of it elevates him to a claim beyond legality, as one of unique power whose actions are outside the law:

My fears were just! Infatuated maid,
And have their arts your innocence betrayed?
How could'st thou go, opinions vile to beg,
And hang thy conscience on a lawyer's peg?—
Some lisping fool, with empty dictums big,
Proud of his LL.D. and periwig.
His mind was not the crucible to try
The deep arcana of love's alchemy,
Whose highest flight of genius seems to be
To settle squabbles on a belfry key.
Shall dolts like him a husband's rights define?
Say wives may grant him this, must that decline,
Arrest the tide with which our passions flow,
And vainly cry no farther shalt thou go?
No!—common stars their usual course maintain,
That order in the universe may reign.
But, through the path of love's celestial sphere
Erratic comets now and then appear,
And spread their tails. With superstitious eye
The vulgar view, and some fear danger nigh.
Not so the sage: his telescope he draws,
And pierces through those fundamental laws
By which the wise Creator's plans may reach
Perfection, not by order, but its breach.

(239–62)

'Fundamental', as before (p. 192), carries a double meaning, and we have a second example of a powerful pun on the word 'breach'.

The repetition marks no lack of resource, the word lending itself peculiarly to Colman's 'ruling passion'. Considerations of decency have prevented our quotations from doing full justice to Colman's punning.

Following the thought of Byron's *Lines on Hearing that Lady Byron was Ill*, Leon now prophesies a miserable future for his disloyal wife:

> *Oh! lady, had'st thou known what mischief hung*
> *On that one slip of my poor silly tongue,*
> *Thou hadst not thus divulged a harmless freak,*
> *And brought contrition on thy pallid cheek.*
> *For dream not peace will ever be thy lot,*
> *Or Leon's wife will henceforth be forgot.*
> *Approving conscience cannot be thy meed,*
> *Fly where thou wilt, thy heart is doomed to bleed,*
> *Through life for thee remains no safe retreat;*
> *Man's finger shall point at thee in the street;*
> *Or, left awhile upon thy thoughts to brood,*
> *Regret shall make a hell of solitude.*

(263–74)

'Tongue' is used as a synonym for *penis* as in the very similar indecencies in *The Taming of the Shrew* (e.g. 'your tongue in my tail'; see II, i, 196–217). The truth of Leon's prophecy may be assessed by our study of Lady Byron's subsequent actions; she was never to be really at peace; and, as we shall see (pp. 278–9), her later life was often bitterly lonely and unhappy.

What infuriates Leon most, Colman certainly and probably Byron too, was the lady's recourse to legality. This anger blazes yet again, with 'Themis' as goddess of Law:

> *And live we then in some Boeotian land,*
> *That love and Themis should go hand in hand?*
> *Fools! take her balance and her sword away;*
> *The sighs of lovers were not made to weigh.*
> *Ah! would you with those manacles repress*
> *The fitful aestus of a warm caress?*
> *Or try Young Hymen's inoffensive sports*
> *By blood-stained statutes and in penal courts?*
> *Hang up the glaive—love does not kill or steal;*
> *He forms no plot against the common weal;*

The playful urchin meditates no sin;
Why sternly rein his wanton gambolling?
His harmless deeds were surely never meant
To be defined by act of parliament;
His code was framed where nymphs in synod sat,
And where his mother wore the Speaker's hat.
Let Paphian casuists expound his laws,
The only proper judges of our cause.

Oh, lovely woman! by your Maker's hand
For man's delight and solace wisely planned.
Thankless is she who nature's bounty mocks,
Nor gives Love entrance wheresoe'er he knocks.
The breechless vagrant has no settled spot,
Now seeks the brook, now nestles in the grot.
Where pleasure offers nectar to the lip,
Anon he steals the honied draught to sip.
Shall priest-born prejudice the draught deny
And send away the thirsty votary?

(275–302)

We are told that Roman matrons were not so unresponsive, and indeed that bashful brides sometimes preferred the more unorthodox approach to start with; and, though today 'salacious lawyers' must 'pry' between our 'sheets' (318), the same desires exist, as in Roman times.

The concluding lines are neat:

Lady, inscribed in characters of gold
This adage—'Truth not always must be told.'
Virtues and vices have no certain dye,
But take the colour of society.
The ore which bears the impress of the crown,
Is passed as standard money through the town;
But what we fashion into private plate,
We keep at home and never circulate.

(323–30)

The error existed simply in the lady's too rash confidence to a friend. This again exactly bears out Colonel Doyle's remark on Lady Byron's 'too confiding disposition' (p. 99).

The two *Don Leon* poems together constitute a text of considerable importance. They are scholarly works, buttressed with notes, presumably by Colman, quoting from Plato, Plutarch, Horace, Catullus, Suetonius, Ausonius, Ovid, Martial, Juvenal, Cicero, Seneca and Lactantius; and other classics, of later date, particularly, and inevitably, Sterne's *Tristram Shandy*. And in manner at least they are themselves, in the best sense, classic. On a literary judgment alone there is surely nothing of the kind of so sustained a mastery outside Byron's favourite, Pope; throughout it is, as Byron said of Pope's, 'poetry without fault' (Murray, 18 May, 1819; LJ, IV, 304). Indeed, it is just such a poetry as Byron himself, as I have shown at length in my *Laureate of Peace* (IV), would have wished to write and for which he cried out to reform the age; and in writing it Colman met Byron's wishes in a deeper than the obvious sense.

The open references to scandals of high life must have made Colman's lines a terror to many families other than Byron's; and we need not be surprised that they have been so fiercely suppressed. But the time for that is passed, and the challenge must be faced. In direct line with the liberal morality of Colman's plays, and handling now in deadly earnest substances both *risqué* and satiric which can be felt behind the themes of his humorous poetry, the *Don Leon* poems blend indecency of reference with moral valuations of the noblest kind. After all, their main satiric attack, levelled against the use of the death-penalty as a deterrent to homosexuality, is one to which we can all, today, subscribe. For the rest their moral valuation scarcely goes beyond that recently suggested by so wise a Christian apologist as Mr. C. S. Lewis (*Surprised by Joy*; VII, 107–8). Even so, the lower morality of convention is not slighted, the phraseology bearing witness throughout to an awareness of it and, in part, an acceptance; but it is surmounted by a wider sympathy and understanding. The psychology is profound, and well before the science of Colman's day. Even the vigorous punning of the more obscene passages, in the manner of Petrucio's wooing of Katharine, marks no relaxation of high seriousness.

The *Don Leon* poems have remained too long in obscurity. They are, it is true, disturbing; some might call them dangerous; but they are great. A new planet swims into our ken.

VI
SUPPORTING EVIDENCE

VI. SUPPORTING EVIDENCE

I

CAN we then assume that Colman was telling the truth? Is there, we may ask, any other, corroborating, evidence? There is, though without *Don Leon* it would have been difficult, perhaps impossible, to focus it. Once, however, we know what to look for, we find a whole sequence of neglected hints, or more than hints, staring at us. And these serve to throw our scattered and contradictory records into a reasonable and significant design.

We shall now look briefly for evidence of (i) homosexuality and (ii) the illicit intercourse between Byron and his wife.

In this section we shall draw on a valuable source of evidence which has only come to light in our time. Sir Harold Nicolson possesses a copy of Moore's *Life of Byron* previously owned by Hobhouse, who has written in it a number of telling comments. Some of these Sir Harold has printed, with annotations, in a 'Supplementary Chapter' to the 1940, but which does not appear in the 1948, edition of his study *Byron: The Last Journey*. For some of Hobhouse's notes which are not included by Sir Harold, I rely on Quennell, who has seen the volume.

We need not suppose that Byron's school friendships went to a dangerous extreme, but they were, as he himself tells us, 'passions' (*Detached Thoughts*, 91; LJ, v, 455). *Childish Recollections* (1807) shows melancholy, but no sense of guilt: 'Not crimes I mourn but happiness gone by' (Suppressed lines, P, 1, 104, note). Guilt is to gain emphasis later, but there was probably anxiety, and we know that there was criticism from others (pp. 5, 29–30 above). Hobhouse's marginal note on Moore's handling of this period runs:

'Moore knows nothing, or will tell nothing, of the principal cause and motive of all these boyish friendships.'

(Quoted from Hobhouse's Marginalia,
Quennell, IV, 118)

Years later, in discussion of her husband's temperament, Lady Byron told Mrs. Beecher Stowe 'that there was everything in the classical course of the schools to develop an unhealthy growth of passion, and no moral influence of any kind to restrain it' (Stowe, II, 164): we may remember the emphasis on classical poetry in *Don Leon* (p. 174). Byron told Medwin that, before leaving for the Levant, he had been his own master at an age when he 'most required a guide', and had been left to the 'dominion' of his 'passions' at a time when they were 'the strongest' (Medwin, 69).

Such phrases remain vague, and may not mean so very much. But there appears to have been a more important incident concerning Lord Grey de Ruthyn, a young nobleman who from 1803 to 1808 was tenant of Newstead while Byron and his mother were living at Southwell. Moore tells us that Byron, when on his holidays from Harrow, often visited Newstead and lodged at a small outlying cottage, until Lord Grey offered him accommodation in the Abbey. But one day Byron, then aged sixteen, returned to his mother, and for ever after refused to visit or even speak to Lord Grey. He described this severance to Augusta on 26 March, 1804:

'I am not reconciled to Lord Grey, *and I never will*. He was once my *Greatest Friend*. My reasons for ceasing that Friendship are such as I cannot explain, not even to you, my Dear Sister (although were they to be made known to anybody, you would be the first), but they will ever remain hidden in my own breast.'

(LJ, I, 23)

Byron's subsequent correspondence with Augusta shows that he refused, despite pressure from his mother, to have anything to do with Lord Grey. She would agree if she knew his reasons, but nothing will make him speak; Lord Grey may claim to 'love' him, but he is 'detestable'; and he refuses to return to Nottinghamshire whilst he remains at Newstead (Augusta, 26 March; 2, 11 and 21 Nov.; 1804; LJ, I, 23, 43, 46, 52). Sir Harold Nicolson tells us that Hobhouse's margin notes comment on the incident:

'This episode has always been something of a mystery to Byron scholars. Hobhouse only increases the puzzle. "A circumstance occurred", he scribbles cryptically regarding Byron's visit to Lord

Grey, "during the intimacy which certainly had much effect upon his future morals". We are left guessing.'

(Nicolson, 1840, Supplementary Chapter, 300)

Does this explain 'what was once his bliss appears his bane' in the early poem *Damaetus* (P, 1, 128)? After 1804 Byron's whole temperament changed (*Detached Thoughts*, 34; LJ, v, 427).

During their travels in Albania in 1809 Byron showed Hobhouse an 'exact' journal of his youthful experiences and thoughts, which his friend at once persuaded him to destroy, thus robbing the world, in Byron's words, of a 'treat' (George Finlay, quoted Edgcumbe, 1, 102). Hobhouse, who disapproved of so much of Byron's poetry, regularly plays the part of grand suppressor, if not vandal, in our story. He was not at all, from our modern standpoint, a prude in sexual relationship of a *normal* kind, but rather, as Peter Quennell puts it, ' a man of the world, conventional alike in his pleasures and his sense of propriety'; and we are not surprised to hear from Quennell that his marginal jottings show that he was less affected than was Byron by the 'Levantine charm' of Nicolo Giraud at Athens (Quennell, 1, 41).

It was, indeed, not until after Hobhouse had left for home that Byron's affair with Nicolo really developed. Moore had noted that Byron was relieved at his departure, and Byron's own letters home show, indeed, that he was. 'Who has not known', writes Vulliamy, with his usual pithiness, 'the inconveniences of a Hobhouse'? Hobhouse was a man of 'cultured insular respectability', and his absence certainly 'made all the difference in the world' (Vulliamy, v, 73-4). But Hobhouse could scarcely be expected to enjoy Moore's biographical honesty and jots down in some wrath:

'What authority has Tom got for saying this? He has not the remotest guess at the real reason which induced Lord Byron at that time to prefer having no Englishman immediately or constantly near him.'

(Nicolson, 1940, Supplementary Chapter, 301)

'Again' writes Sir Harold, 'we are left guessing.' We can hardly suppose that Moore, to whom Byron would have been far more confidential on such matters than to Hobhouse, did not know. But on this particular question the conspiracy of silence observed by everyone always somehow seems to deceive everyone. So we have

Byron writing in his Journal on 10 March, 1814: 'Um! people some-times hit near the truth; but never the whole truth. H. don't know what I was about the year after he left the Levant, nor does anyone —nor—nor—nor—however, it is a lie' (LJ, ii, 399). But Hobhouse probably *did* know, and prided himself on it, once, during a discus-sion on the *Memoirs*, saying to Moore, 'I know more of Byron than any one else, and much more than I should wish anybody else to know' (Moore's *Memoirs, etc.*, 29 April, 1822; iii, 347). What is so strange is the way Hobhouse both regularly tried to suppress, and yet, as in this remark and his marginal jottings, most effectively hints at, this strain in Byron's life.

How far Byron's affair with Nicolo went, we cannot know. In his Will of 12 August, 1811, made directly after his return, Byron left him £7,000 (LJ, i, 328). *Don Leon* may, or may not, have the facts right. But it is clear that Byron's stay in the Levant gave him a freedom he could not enjoy in England. He wrote to Murray on 9 August, 1819, that his life had known adventures 'more extra-ordinary and perilous and pleasant' than anything recorded in his poetry (LJ, iv, 339), and told Trelawny that Greece was the only place he was 'ever contented in' (Trelawny, 15 June, 1823; LJ, vi, 224). His reminiscences included both pleasure and guilt: 'I have had my share', he writes, 'of what are called the pleasures of this life, and have seen more of the European and Asiatic world than I have made good use of' (Journal, 14 November, 1813; LJ, ii, 313). Though no specific actions can be deduced from such veiled phrases, we can at least sum up his *impressions* by quoting one of his compact minia-tures describing a Turkish bath as 'that marble paradise of sherbet and Sodomy' (Murray, 12 August, 1819; LJ, iv, 342). The attraction persisted. After his return he thought continually of again visiting the Levant, sometimes planning to settle there for life (e.g., Hodg-son, 16 Feb., 1812; LJ, ii, 100); and eventually died in Greece.

Byron was cautious in his published work. We have already seen how his early poems, many of which concentrated on themes of friendship, bear evidence of the 'censure' he incurred for his ten-dencies; and how he regularly suppressed his more bold revelations and sometimes tried, as, pre-eminently, with regard to the stanzas in *Childe Harold* on Edleston, to veil the facts (pp. 5, 29–30, 36).

From then, until certain poems to Loukas at Missolonghi, his poetry offers nothing directly relevant. But it is likely that much at least of the strong sense of sin in it, the 'Ishmael' complex, from

Childe Harold on, together with his tales of bloodshed, incest, and remorse, relate to the unorthodox instincts we are discussing. The use of subsidiary crimes as a mask is probably a general poetic process: most great poets appear to have known homosexual instincts, but society demands their transmission through fictions of the more respectable, because less infectious, varieties of sin. There is, for example a very great difference in 'respectability' between the dramatic works of Shakespeare and Colman and the purely *personal* implications of the Sonnets and Colman's poetry. Certainly Byron's work assumes a new biographical coherence if read with such thoughts in mind, since there is little else in his life to account for his insistence on the 'uneradicable taint of sin' (*Childe Harold*, IV, 126), his heterosexual irregularities being normal in that period; and indeed, he was a stricter moralist than most. Whether any of the mysterious troubles adumbrated by the asterisks and innuendoes of his 1813–1814 Journal, or the heavy rows of asterisks in his letter to Moore of 10 February, 1814 (LJ, III, 33), relate to a homosexual engagement, we cannot say; but it is necessary at this point to suggest the possibility.

The years after Byron's return to England show little that is definite. One can, perhaps, point to Lady Caroline Lamb's regular attempts to win his love in the guise of a page, and group them with Byron's mistress in male attire of the year 1808 and the girl Kaled in *Lara*; and he may have finally rebuffed Caroline by an insistence on the abnormality of his instincts (p. 44). Byron's hurtling from one to another of his feminine *liaisons* can be regarded as attempts, like his poetry (p. 251), to escape from himself; and it is probable that when Lady Melbourne and Augusta urged him to marry, they had the alternative in view. After his marriage, Augusta wrote on 15 February, 1815, to Hodgson, saying that she hoped it would prove a solution, and 'will own to you, what I would not scarcely to any other person, that I had *many fears* and much anxiety *founded upon many causes and circumstances* of which I cannot *write*' (Edgcumbe, III, 332).

Our various accounts continually bring us up against a wall of secrecy. Mrs. Beecher Stowe tells us that a certain Mrs. Minns, formerly one of Lady Byron's maids, who was with her during the honeymoon at Halnaby, said, years later, that Lady Byron was already then troubled by Byron's 'irregularities', though even at the age of ninety Mrs. Minns would not disclose their nature, since she had given Lady Byron a solemn promise not to do so. Mrs. Minns had advised Lady Byron to tell her father, but she did not (Stowe, I, 39). Byron is also reported to have spoken to Lady Byron 'always with strong but contained emotion' of 'Thyrza', showing her a lock of the loved-one's hair, but refusing to reveal the real name (Lovelace, II, 42, note; P, III, 31, note). It is, indeed, probable that Byron did let Lady Byron know more than was wise, and if it be true that directly after the marriage he told his wife that 'she would find she had married a devil' (Stowe, II, 158), this was probably his meaning. If so, it was spoken in bitterness and self-criticism rather than in cruelty, in the mood of these lines from his *Epistle to Augusta*:

> *Mine were my faults and mine be their reward.*
> *My whole life was a contest, since the day*
> *That gave me being gave me that which marred*
> *The gift—a fate, or will, that walked astray;*
> *And I at times have found the struggle hard,*
> *And thought of shaking off my bonds of clay . . .*
>
> (P, IV, 58)

The struggle was, indeed, if the poem *Damaetus* be a self-portrait, a torment. In *Childe Harold* he asserts that, having been 'untaught in youth' to 'tame' his 'heart', his 'springs of life', or sexual energies, 'were poison'd' (III, 7).

II

And so we come to the Separation. Our study is making it much clearer, probably helping us to see why Lady Byron disliked Byron's association with Drury Lane. This Augusta had at first thought would be good for Byron, 'but', she wrote to Hobhouse, 'as in other good things one may discover objections' (5 July, 1815; Hobhouse, II, App. A, 358). Moore, while denying any sexual irregularities of a normal kind, nevertheless guardedly admitted that the association led him 'into a line of acquaintance and converse unbefitting, if not dangerous to, the steadiness of married life' (Moore, xxv, 297). It certainly helps us to understand Lady Byron's disapproval of his indulging in drinking parties with, to quote Byron's letter to Moore of 31 October, 1815, 'Sheridan and Colman, Harry Harris of Covent Garden and his brother, Sir Gilbert Heathcote, Douglas Kinnaird, and others, of note and notoriety' (LJ, III, 242). 'Notoriety' fits

Colman well. When she talked to Mrs. Stowe in 1856 Lady Byron still bitterly remembered these parties, of which there were a number during the autumn of 1815 (Stowe, II, 181–2): Colman must have been the last person she wished her husband to associate with. We have it on Hobhouse's authority that she suspected Byron's friends to be of a character unsuited to the converse of 'married men', and, indeed, 'the associates of wickedness' (Hobhouse, II; xv, 231). Soon after the Separation she appears to have accused Byron to Lady Anne Barnard of visiting 'the haunts of vice', while simultaneously representing Augusta 'as exercising a purifying and restraining influence over her brother' (*Blackwood's*; Jan, 1870; Vol. 107; *130*). One version of her Woburn letter of 15 January, 1816, her first letter after leaving her husband, runs:

'The child is quite well and the best of travellers. I hope you are *good* and remember my medical prayers and injunctions. Don't give yourself up to the abominable trade of versifying—nor to brandy—nor to anything or anybody that is not *lawful* and *right*. Though *I* disobey in writing to you, let me hear of *your* obedience at Kirkby. Ada's love to you with mine.

Pip.'

This version, given by Sir John Fox from the Lovelace papers (Fox, XII, 98), may be compared with that given us by Hobhouse (p. 57). The longer version, which is probably Lady Byron's subsequent reconstruction of the letter Hobhouse saw, changes the mysterious 'nau' to 'not lawful and right'. On 17 January, 1816, she wrote to Captain George Byron that a change of scene to a place 'with which no diseased associations are connected' was of vital importance to Byron's health (Fox, XII, 100).

Byron's talk to his wife had probably been foolishly free, and what Lady Byron reported to Mrs. Stowe as confessions of incest had probably a different basis; or perhaps Mrs. Stowe was at fault. John Robertson, who knew Lady Byron well, said that towards the end of her life she used to refer to *two* 'crimes' (*Quarterly*, Oct., 1869; Vol. 127; *426*); and it certainly seems that either she or Mrs. Stowe was capable of confusing them. That Byron could scarcely have confessed to incest and threatened its continuance, we have already (p. 114) shown; but all this might be true of homosexuality. Again and again we are aware of this particular transference. Hobhouse admits that he used to promulgate paradoxical 'doctrines', showing a 'singular love of the marvellous in morals', and pretending that his 'principles' were deduced from 'practice' (Hobhouse, II; xv, 283); and Lady Byron told Mrs. Stowe that he used to assert 'the right of every human being to follow what he called "the impulses of nature"' (Stowe, III, 289). Had these 'impulses' been impulses of homosexuality, that would, indeed, account for Sir Ralph Noel's objection to his 'opinions' (p. 59); for Lady Noel's assertion that it was not fit such men should live (Hobhouse, II; xv, 207); for Augusta's talk of his being given over to 'all that is wrong' (to Hodgson, 9 Feb., 1816; LJ, III, 305); for many, though not all (see pp. 269–70 below), of the various phrases of Lady Byron's moral condemnation; and Lovelace's assertion—though he says, and, as we shall see, *would say*, nothing of homosexuality—that the cause of Byron's unpopularity in England included his 'rejection of law and restraint for himself' (Lovelace, II, 43). We may, I think, assume that Lady Byron's, or Mrs. Clermont's, searching among Byron's books, one of which he afterwards admitted did not do 'much credit' to his 'taste in literature' (Medwin, 42), for evidence of 'that particular insanity under which he laboured', and his wife's horror at his markings of passages concerned with 'depravity' (Hobhouse, II; xv, 250, 283), have now been placed. And we may probably make a close guess as to what she told her parents.

We have already (p. 202) quoted Mrs. Stowe's report of Lady Byron's comment on the dangers of a classical education. This, she said, prepared him for 'the evil hour when he fell into the sin which shaded his whole life'. This Mrs. Stowe took to be incest, but Lady Byron cannot have meant that, since Byron's life-pattern was fixed before 1813; if she did, she was consciously or unconsciously effecting a transference from truth to falsehood. There may be here a reference to the incident concerning Lord Grey de Ruthyn. 'All the rest', she said, 'was a struggle with its consequence—sinning more and more to conceal the sin of the past' (Stowe, II, 164–5). We have, indeed, good reason for our reading. On 24 February 1816, during the Separation proceedings, Lady Byron wrote to Francis Hodgson a most revealing letter which shows very clearly that she did not dispute Byron's general goodness, but was concentrating only on the one, central, sin:

'I believe the nature of Lord B's mind to be most benevolent; but there may have been circumstances (I would hope the *consequences*, not the *causes*, of mental disorder) which would render an original tenderness of conscience the motive of desperation, even of guilt, when self-esteem had been forfeited too far. No *external* motive can be so strong. I entrust this to you under the most absolute secrecy. Goodness of heart, when there are impetuous passions and no principles, is a frail security.'

(LJ, III, 316)

That is, Byron's own conscience, tormented by a single lapse, had forced him on—like Macbeth—to desperation and a life of sin. Lady Byron was an acute thinker. We have another, even clearer, letter which she wrote to Augusta on 30 July, 1816. It runs:

'You seem to have understood from the anxiety I retain that he should become more fit for another world, that I have yet some idea of assisting that end personally. No—Such hope is as far from me as from you—and it would only be in one circumstance that I would ever consent to see him again. Alas—my dear A—you do not, I believe, know him. The selfishness of *strong passions*, and when *Romance* is made the colouring and the mask of Vice, is not so easily perceived as the selfishness of a calmer temper and less fascinating imagination—and the *arts* of a character naturally open and in-genuous, till it was changed and taught to deceive at an early age by the dreadful necessity of concealment—is not as *obvious* as the duplicity of one whose heart was less formed for confidence. Such, as I once told you, are the fatal effects of a Solitary Secret—it chills and hardens and absorbs—and the heart which it does not break must become depraved—if Religious feelings do not save it.'

(Lovelace, x, 248)

'Early age', 'concealment', 'solitary secret' are all valuable pointers, to be grouped with Byron's Calvinist sense of predestined damnation (CV, VI, 246–8) and view of himself as an Ishmael (Miss Milbanke, 26 Sept.; Journal, 22 Nov.; 1813; LJ, III, 402; II, 330); and with *Damaetus* (P, I, 128). Others, from other viewpoints, have recognized that Byron's heart was 'open and ingenuous', but forced by society to assume an apparent hardness. *The Corsair* and *Lara* offer relevant descriptions, and the thought recurs throughout the Blessington *Conversations*, and elsewhere (CV, II, 66–7, 83, 97–8, etc.). Here Lady Byron tells Augusta that she does not know her brother. And yet Augusta had, as we have seen, for long been anxious. Ethel Colburn Mayne (*Lady Byron*, xvii, 248) reports her as having told Lady Byron that from the time that he was sixteen he had been a source of misery to her 'on that account'; and, though Miss Mayne's context means, so far as I can see, to suggest incest, this is surely but another peculiarly clear example of the usual transposition, since the statement could not possibly mean that Byron had been in danger of incest at that age! Indeed, we know that he had not; they had barely met before the year 1813, though he had *at the age of sixteen* corresponded with her frequently about Lord Grey de Ruthyn (p. 202).

Augusta once shows some anxiety to justify herself to Hobhouse for having 'communicated freely' with Lady Byron about her brother's state of mind (Augusta to Hobhouse, 21 May, 1816; Hobhouse, ii, App. H, 364). Elsewhere Lady Byron appears to be blaming her for too easily accepting Byron's vices, and Augusta is perhaps defending herself against this charge in her letter of 15 July, 1816 (p. 95), saying:

'I felt it as my only consolation to do *all* I could, and indeed to the best of my judgment I *did* it. Many a time I should have felt it one to have confided unreservedly in you—but concealment appeared a duty under such circumstances—and you know I am of a sanguine disposition and to the very last had hopes of better for you—and for him. I lament from my heart all the *un*intentional errors to which you allude.'

(Lovelace, x, 232)

As usual, it is hopelessly vague, but it may be the clearer from a letter from Lady Byron to Augusta of 21 September, 1816. She is writing of her parents:

'After they became acquainted with what had been *his* habits of life, and decided propensities, previous to my marriage, and during a time when his general proceedings must have been known to you (and indeed he made it clear that they *were* known), it was their opinion'——

that, in short, Augusta should not have allowed the marriage to go forward (LJ, iii, 328). Augusta is being blamed as Byron's *accomplice*; and we may have here a hint as to the meaning of at least some of those many occasions when she appears to be defending herself less against any incest of her own than against having in some other way

wronged, or been disloyal to, Lady Byron. There is indeed some
evidence that one of Lady Byron's original complaints arose from
Augusta's having acted as an accomplice in helping Byron to hide
a love-affair from his wife; and though the affair is given as one with
a 'mistress', it is possible that the word is being used as a euphemism
(Drinkwater, quoting Colonel Godfrey Massey; 1, 71, note).

We begin to understand the real significance of Augusta in Byron's
story. She functioned as a *sympathetic* counsellor and guardian; and
that is why, on 3 January, 1816, we find her writing to Hobhouse
with a sister's gratitude to him for his 'forbearance' towards Byron's
'infirmities' (Hobhouse, II; App. B, 359). The usual view of her as a
soft and muddled-headed half-wit is probably quite wrong. She is
not to be judged by her correspondence with Byron and Lady
Byron after the Separation, which may even be, in part, *intentionally*
confused, as indeed Richard Edgcumbe's argument would imply.
We can perhaps best understand her actions if we see them from
Byron's own viewpoint, as recorded by Lady Blessington:

'To my sister, who, incapable of wrong herself, suspected no wrong
in others, I owe the little good of which I can boast; and had I earlier
known her, it might have influenced my destiny. Augusta has great
strength of mind, which is displayed not only in her own conduct,
but to support the weak and infirm of purpose. To me she was, in
the hour of need, as a tower of strength. Her affection was my last
rallying point, and is now the only bright spot that the horizon of
England offers to my view. Augusta knew all my weaknesses, but
she had love enough to bear with them. I value not the false sentiment of affection that adheres to one while we believe him faultless;
not to love him would then be difficult; but give me the love that,
with perception to view the errors, has sufficient force to pardon
them,—who can "love the offender, yet detest the offence"; and this
my sister had. She has given me such good advice, and yet, finding
me incapable of following it, loved and pitied me but the more,
because I was erring. This is true affection, and, above all, true
Christian feeling; but how rarely is it to be met with in England!'

(Blessington, 349)

Again:

'Poor Lady —— had just such a sister as mine, who, faultless herself,
could pardon and weep over the errors of one less pure, and almost
redeem them by her own excellence. Had Lady ——'s sister or mine

been less good and irreproachable, they could not have afforded to be so forbearing; but, being unsullied, they could show mercy without fear of drawing attention to their own misdemeanors.'

(Blessington, 351)

These statements, which correspond precisely to Teresa Guiccioli's account of Byron 'as a Brother' (Teresa, i; vii), harmonize also with Byron's known views on moral charity and reproduce in general the content of the lines to Zuleika which we have quoted from *The Bride of Abydos* (p. 43) and of Byron's verses to Augusta (p. 119). Here we have the key to much of the mystery of Augusta's behaviour; and perhaps, too, to the scandal of 'incest'; for it may be that Augusta, of set purpose, set her own powers against the other, appalling, danger; and in so doing she may have run grave risks of misunderstanding and misrepresentation. But those who mattered would have known the truth.

To return to our story. Our evidence suggests that on her arrival at Kirkby Mallory in January, 1816, Lady Byron told her parents that Byron had at some time been guilty of homosexual practices, and was still, in certain moods, a supporter of them in theory; and that it was this which sent Lady Noel in haste to town. Meanwhile, Byron's friends were grievously afraid of what might follow.

We have it on Byron's own authority that Lady Byron had, directly or indirectly, caused him to be accused of homosexuality. Writing to Hobhouse on 17 May, 1819, he quotes a speech, which he also quoted in his letter to Lady Byron of 3 April, 1820 (p. 151), from Dante's *Inferno* (xvi, 43), in which Jacopo Rusticucci complains of the suffering he has endured from a proud wife. To this Byron adds:

'And was it not owing to (her) that they tried to expose me upon earth to the same stigma which the said Jacopo is saddled with in hell?'

(Fox, xiv, 139)

The stigma is homosexuality. Byron does not say that he is not guilty, but merely that they tried to set the 'stigma' of it on him.

And here we may place the extraordinary assumption of Byron's supporters that a separation would necessarily mean his moral ruin. Augusta could see 'only ruin and destruction' ahead; and Francis Hodgson urged that 'to a man so peculiarly constituted' it might mean 'absolute and utter destruction' (Augusta to Hodgson, 7 Feb.; Hodgson to Lady Byron, Feb.; 1816; LJ, III, 304, 307).

After leaving England, despite his assurance to the anxious Augusta regarding 'pages' (p. 130), he seems to have proved true to Hodgson's fears in Venice. No one has explained how, considering his great output of work and the evidence we have of his athletic prowess at the time (CV, III, 108), Byron could have led the dissipated life at Venice with which people have charged him. But if a worse sin than heterosexual licence were involved, even a little might have aroused the scandal. And surely his comic letter to Hobhouse purporting to come from Fletcher at his supposed death, and talking of his 'nine whores' (June, 1818; LJ, IV, 234), is not the letter of a man who *had* nine whores; but it *is* the letter of a man whose real guilt lay elsewhere.

Shelley, we know, was shocked, and in his letter to Peacock of 22 December, 1818 (LJ, IV, 259–60, note), refers to Byron's association with persons 'who do not scruple to avow practices which are not only not named, but I believe seldom even conceived in England'. It surely, too, appears strange, as I have observed elsewhere (CV, v, 255), that Shelley should, as he does, seem to read the Promethean curses against London society in the fourth canto of *Childe Harold* as in any way connected with Byron's disgust at his Venetian experiences; but if both Byron's rejection at home and experiences in Venice were concerned with homosexuality, there is, at least, an association. And when Shelley attributes to Byron a 'wicked and mischievous insanity' he merely repeats Lady Byron's thoughts of madness and pride. We, today, should describe what they meant as 'a pathological state dangerously supported by theory'.

And yet Byron was himself simultaneously shocked. 'He says he disapproves, but he endures,' writes Shelley in the same letter (LJ, IV, 260, note). *Marino Faliero* concludes with a denunciation of Venetian vice containing the fine line, 'Gehenna of the waters! thou Sea-Sodom!' (v, iii, 99), the second phrase being also applied to Venice in a letter to Hoppner (31 Dec., 1819; LJ, IV, 393). We need not be surprised to find Lord Lovelace denying that Byron had anything to do with the 'repulsive abominations' at which Shelley hints (Lovelace, VI, 124), since the exponents of incest are for the most part driving home their charge *in order to cloud all suggestion of the other trouble.*

Here we may consider the ill-fated *Memoirs*. The first part of these, like that earlier journal which Hobhouse had persuaded him to destroy (p. 203), started from his childhood (Medwin, 35) and went up to the Separation; and the second dealt with Byron's subsequent life. This first part, says Moore, contained nothing beyond 'three of four lines' that was objectionable, though the second was 'full or very coarse things' (Moore's Memoirs, etc., 15 May, 1824; IV, 188), and 'some of its details could never have been published at all' (Moore, LVII, 655). Gifford is reported to have said that they, meaning presumably the second part, were of 'a low pot-house description' (Murray to Wilmot Horton, 25 March, 1850; Lovelace, VI, 120, and note). Byron has left us a hint or two. He tells Moore on 9 December 1820 that 'over these latter sheets' he allows him a 'discretionary power', since they contain perhaps 'a thing or two which is too sincere for the public'; but there is a possibility that, in the future, 'tastes may change' (LJ, V, 131). He told Medwin:

'The second part will prove a good lesson to young men; for it treats of the irregular life I led at one period, and the fatal consequences of dissipation. There are few parts that may not, and none that will not, be read by women . . .'

(Medwin, 35)

Referring to his life in Venice, he said that he sought to 'distract' his mind from the thought of the degradation of Venice and his own 'solitude' by plunging into 'a vortex that was anything but pleasure':

'When you read my Memoirs you will learn the evils, moral and physical, of true dissipation. I assure you my life is very entertaining and very instructive.'

(Medwin, 52)

So, too, after the loss of Mary Anne Chaworth, he had tried to 'drown the remembrance of it and her' in 'the most depraving dissipation', but 'the poison was in the cup'; and after that we get two rows of asterisks (Medwin, 63). Here 'poison' exactly recalls Shakespeare's use of the word in Sonnet 118 to describe a similar experience (p. 283 below). In his Detached Thoughts (74–6), after observing that he cannot reveal the 'real causes' of the melancholy for which he is famous without doing much 'mischief', Byron refers to the strangeness of some of the earlier parts of his life, and then says of his Memoirs:

'I sometimes think that I should have written the whole as a lesson,

but it might have proved a *lesson* to be *learnt* rather than *avoided*;
for *passion* is a whirlpool, which is not to be viewed nearly without
attraction from its Vortex.

'I must not go on with these reflections, or I shall be letting out
some secret or other to paralyze posterity.'

(LJ, v, 446–7)

Which suggests that the *Memoirs* themselves did not tell the whole
truth.

But they told enough of it to disturb his friends and help seal
their own fate. It was thought necessary to Byron's good name, his
'fame', to destroy them. Lord John Russell says that both Moore
and Hobhouse, in agreeing to the destruction, 'desired to do what
was most honourable to Lord Byron's memory' (Moore's *Memoirs,
etc.*, IV, 192). 'Such regard have I', said Murray, 'for Lord Byron's
fame and honour'—that he was in favour of destruction (Hobhouse,
III, App. I, 339); Hobhouse himself was certain that 'there was but
one line for a man of honour and for a friend of Lord Byron to
take' (Hobhouse, III, App. I, 338); and it was, says Moore, 'a measure
considered essential to the reputation of my friend' (Moore's
Memoirs, etc., 21 May, 1824, IV, 196). All this was, of course, no new
thing for Hobhouse. After all, he had got Byron to destroy his youthful memoirs in Albania (p. 203); he had expected the worst, and on
the news of Byron's death had immediately told Murray to look
through all Byron papers in his possession and 'destroy whatever
might be unfit afterwards to get abroad' (Hobhouse, III, App. I, 334),
presumably naming the subject he feared. What is so strange, is Hobhouse's way of consistently suggesting the worst whilst apparently
intending to serve Byron's interests. In a statement dated 18 July,
1825, he writes:

'I should certainly have thought it my duty to have disabused the
public, and to have corrected the statements which have been put
forth relative to the destruction of Lord Byron's *Memoirs*, if I could
have done so without compromising the character of my friend, by
telling what I know of the nature of those memoirs . . .'

(Hobhouse, III, App. I, 327)

One would have thought that that, together with his marginalia in
his copy of Moore's *Life*, was sufficiently compromising to leave to
an inquisitive posterity. He might better have left us the *Memoirs*.

After the Venetian period it is probable that Byron's life, with Teresa Guiccioli beside him, was more orthodox. It is, however, interesting to find him writing on 10 June, 1822, to Isaac D'Israeli a long letter about his book *The Literary Character*, which he says 'has often been to me a consolation, and always a pleasure'; and he goes on to suggest that D'Israeli should look at his own memoirs (LJ, VI, 84–5). *The Literary Character* is a study of the trials of men of genius, and contains a section (XIX) on the importance to such men of 'romantic friendship' and the ability 'to feel friendship like a passion'. This is regarded wholly as a virtue, and no darker suggestions are adumbrated.

During Byron's campaign in Greece, the old tendency re-asserted itself. From Cephalonia he took with him Loukas Chalandritsanos, a boy aged fifteen of considerable beauty. He belonged to a family in trouble which Byron had been maintaining at his own expense in Cephalonia, and had come from the Morea, or Peloponnese, to serve Byron (Nicolson, VIII, 183–4, and see Gamba, I, 28; Capt. Knox, 26 Aug., 1823; LJ, VI, 256; Hobhouse, 11 Sept., 1823; C, II, 275, and note). Loukas caused, according to Peter Quennell, 'some stir among the members of his suite' (Quennell, IV, 84). On the voyage to Missolonghi they were in danger from a Turkish battleship, and Byron was most anxious on the boy's account, writing at the time, 'I would sooner cut him in pieces, and myself too, than have him taken out by those barbarians' (Stanhope, 31 Dec., 1823; LJ, VI, 297); but he managed to land the boy with a sailor and send him to Missolonghi (Muir, also Hancock, 2 January, 1824; LJ, VI, 298–9, 302–3). His references show that his thoughts were mainly on Loukas, 'the boy from the Morea' (LJ, VI, 302), at this juncture. Later Byron's ship, after sailing to Dragomestri and back, was in danger of running on the rocks near Missolonghi, and he prepared to save what seems at first to be another Greek boy, whom he calls 'the brother of the Greek girls in Argostoli', by diving with him on his own shoulders (Hancock, 13 Jan., 1824; LJ, VI, 304). Sir Harold Nicolson, however, refers this 'diving' to the previous incident, with Loukas as the boy concerned, and indeed appears in general to have telescoped two separate incidents (Nicolson, VIII, 184–5). But there were certainly two sisters in Loukas' family (Moore, LII, 596), and that family was indeed supported by Byron in Argostoli (Journal, 28 Sept., 1823; LJ, VI, 245). If there was only one boy, then Loukas could not have been actually dispatched across country, as Byron reported, perhaps prematurely. The matter is of some interest, since, if two different boys are involved, an important poem of Byron's *also identifies them*. But there was probably only one.

Loukas was with Byron at Missolonghi. At one time he was struck by fever (Nicolson, IX, 213; Hancock, 5 Feb., 1824; LJ, VI, 315), and soon after Byron had a seizure and there was a terrific earthquake (Murray, 25 Feb., 1824; LJ, VI, 334–5). Now both the two incidents of the voyage and these later anxieties are in sequence exactly incorporated in a poem to which Hobhouse gives two notes. The first says: 'The last he ever wrote. From a rough copy found amongst his papers at the back of the *Song of Suli*. Copied November, 1824'. The other tells us that 'a note attached to the verses by Lord Byron states they were addressed to no one in particular, and were a mere poetical Scherzo' (P, VII, 85, notes).[1] Here is the poem, to which Hartley Coleridge gives a bracketed title *Love and Death*:

> *I watched thee when the foe was at our side,*
> *   Ready to strike at him—or thee and me,*
> *Were safety hopeless—rather than divide*
> *   Aught with one loved, save love and liberty.*

> *I watched thee on the breakers, when the rock*
> *   Received our prow, and all was storm and fear,*
> *And bade thee cling to me through every shock;*
> *   This arm would be thy bark, or breast thy bier.*

> *I watched thee when the fever glazed thine eyes,*
> *   Yielding my couch, and stretched me on the ground,*
> *When overworn with watching, ne'er to rise*
> *   From thence, if thou an early grave hadst found.*

> *The earthquake came, and rocked the quivering wall,*
> *   And men and nature reeled as if with wine.*
> *Whom did I seek around the tottering hall?*
> *   For thee. Whose safety first provide for? Thine.*

[1] A manuscript copy of this poem, together with these two notes, all in Hobhouse's handwriting, is lodged in the Brotherton Collection at the University of Leeds. There is also a copy of *Last Words on Greece*, discussed below.

And when convulsive throes denied my breath
  The faintest utterance to my fading thought,
To thee—to thee—e'en in the gasp of death
  My spirit turned, oh! oftener than it ought.

Thus much and more; and yet thou lov'st me not,
  And never wilt! Love dwells not in our will.
Nor can I blame thee, though it be my lot
  To strongly, wrongly, vainly love thee still.

(P, VII, 84)

This last line is the most explicit, perhaps the only explicit, confession by Byron which is left us. Another poem called *Last Words on Greece* contrasts this personal passion with his national task:

What are to me those honours or renown
  Past or to come, a new-born people's cry?
Albeit for such I could despise a crown
  Of aught save laurel, or for such could die.
I am a fool of passion, and a frown
  Of thine to me is as an adder's eye
To the poor bird whose pinion fluttering down
  Wafts unto death the breast it bore so high;
Such is this maddening fascination grown,
  So strong thy magic or so weak am I.

(P, VII, 85)

The use of the word 'maddening' may be compared with its use in a similar context in *Childish Recollections* (p. 6). Neither of these two Missolonghi pieces were included in the early editions of Byron's poetry; probably Murray and Hobhouse agreed to withhold them. They appeared first in *Murray's Magazine*, February, 1887 (Vol. I, 145–6).

It seems that at the last Byron was impelled to speak out as never before, and we may suppose that there were other such poems. Colonel Stanhope tells us of one:

'No man ever chose a nobler friend. Mr. Hobhouse has given many proofs of this, and among others I saw him, from motives of high honour, destroy a beautiful poem of Lord Byron's, and, perhaps, the last he ever composed. The same reason that induced Mr. H. to tear this fine manuscript will, of course, prevent him or me from ever divulging its contents.'

(Leicester Stanhope, quoted Edgcumbe, I, 208)

Whether or not there is a touch of irony in Stanhope's words, I do not know. After all, he was a disciple of Jeremy Bentham.

The longer of the two poems which we have quoted does not rank high as poetry. Like the various lines to Augusta, it has perhaps the weakness of a too-personal emotion. The second, though only a fragment, is more powerful, partly because a larger, more impersonal, context, involving Greece, is surveyed. And once during these last weeks Byron, thinking clearly of both Loukas and his national task, transmuted his personal suffering into a sustained poem carrying the accents of great art. I refer to the famous lines *On this Day I Complete my Thirty-Sixth Year* (P, VII, 86). Our recent quotations enable us to understand them afresh.

The poem opens with complaint of loneliness and ill-success in love, for indeed he seems to have felt, or imagined, that Loukas was unresponsive. 'The worm, the canker and the grief', he writes, 'are mine alone.' But he wills to surmount his weakness:

> *Tread those reviving passions down*
> *Unworthy manhood!—unto thee*
> *Indifferent should the smile or frown*
> *Of beauty be.*

'Reviving'—it was a life-long torment. But, just as Byron's life, as a whole, witnesses the will, and the ability, to transmute these dangerous, and often futile, tendencies into great endeavour for men and nations, so our poem moves to thoughts of heroic death, for Greece, the land whose ancient culture found place for instincts such as his:

> *If thou regret'st thy youth, why live?*
> *The land of honourable death*
> *Is here:—up to the field, and give*
> *Away thy breath!*

> *Seek out—less often sought than found*
> *A soldier's grave, for thee the best;*
> *Then look around, and choose thy ground,*
> *And take thy rest.*

The 'ground' was, indeed, well chosen. This poem, though it must have preceded at least the longer of the two others, holds, as that does not, the accents of self-surmounting, and therefore of great poetry.

III

We have now good reason to suppose that after leaving her husband Lady Byron told her parents what she knew, mostly it seems from Byron's own confessions, of this the central torment of his life. But this was not what finally turned the scales. There was also the secret which she did not tell her parents, but revealed later, in strict confidence, to Dr. Lushington on her own visit to London (p. 75). This is presumably the sin which Hobhouse calls 'even more enormous' than incest and Brougham designates as 'something too horrid to mention' (p. 78). We may expect it to be the sin of which we are told in *Don Leon*. Colman might well have heard of it from Byron at one of the parties to which Byron went at the time of his wife's pregnancy, when it is supposed to have occurred. Also he is likely to have seen the *Memoirs*, or to have talked with those who had.

This would certainly account for all the flurry and turmoil. 'Even my cousin George', Byron told Medwin, 'who had been brought up with me and whom I loved as a brother, took my wife's part' (Medwin, 47). Both George Byron and Mrs. Clermont seem to have been involved; and indeed it is likely that, as *Don Leon* hints, Mrs. Clermont was in some way and for some reason responsible, perhaps just giving one of her 'harassing displays of character' (p. 59), for forcing the issue. Byron calls her a 'spy' of Lady Noel's and 'very much the occult cause of our late domestic discrepancies' (Moore, 29 Feb., 1815; LJ, III, 268), and Jeaffreson says that Byron regarded her as responsible for Lady Byron's additional, and crucial, statement to Dr. Lushington (Jeaffreson, XVI, 208). After Byron's denunciation of her in his *Sketch*, she replied: 'The little I have said is *strictly true*, and what more I *may be compelled* to say shall be equally so' (Hobhouse, II; XV, 326). We have already seen how Sir Ralph Noel appears to have been prevented from any weakening in decision by this lady (p. 74). Some time in February Augusta wrote to Francis Hodgson:

'Yesterday Captain B. was summoned to Mrs. Clermont's. It

appeared to me they either wished to frighten or coax B. into an amicable arrangement. From what passed, however, *now*, if *they* choose it, it must come into Court! God alone knows the consequences. I think all you do of poor Lady B., and alas! of my dearest B.'

(LJ, III, 314)

Mrs. Clermont's 'summons' is reported by Hobhouse (II; xv, 271), who says that she was urging a quiet arrangement. In a second letter a couple of days later Augusta wrote:

'It strikes me that if their pecuniary proposals are favourable he will be too happy to escape the exposure.'

(*Athenaeum*, 18 Aug., 1883, 208; Jeaffreson, App. II, 481)[1]

Mrs. Clermont plays the part of revealer, and Augusta, who told Hobhouse on 21 May, 1816, that she had made it a rule to be 'silent' regarding Byron as long as she could (Hobhouse, II; xv, 365), is fearful of the revelation. The pattern begins to get clear, and we understand the facts behind Lady Byron's perhaps exaggerated statement to Francis Hodgson that her 'security' depended on 'the total abandonment of every moral and religious principle' (15 Feb., 1816; LJ, III, 313). Much later, according to Michael Joyce, she wrote, and again we must allow for exaggeration:

'He required of a woman's attachment—to use an expressive Scotch phrase—not *heart to heart*, but *heart at his feet*—and mine was laid before him. But this was not enough. I must have prostrated every sacred duty—*even the duty of a wife*, and have gratified his pride by the very guilt which would eventually have disgraced himself, whilst I was to thank him for subverting my only power and protection—Innocence . . . There is *no* vice with which he has not endeavoured to familiarise me.'

(Joyce, VIII, 100; no ref.)

This presumably comes from Lady Byron's private papers: the dots may, or may not, be significant. Lady Byron's statements *after the parting*, are, of course, in themselves, and by themselves, useless as

[1] These two letters were first printed in *The Athenaeum* of 18 August, 1883, and given as addressed to Wilmot Horton. The second is not printed in *Letters and Journals*. The text of the first in *Letters and Journals* shows variants from the version in *The Athenaeum*.

evidence. If she could feel like this, why did she not show it earlier? It is strange that, as Hanson and Hobhouse saw, she had lived con- jugally with Byron up to the last, and parted on terms of 'affection' with a man who had committed a crime 'too horrid to mention' (Hobhouse, II; xv, 215, 350). One can only conclude that she had somehow been newly *forced* into this position, perhaps by the in- sistence of Mrs. Clermont in whom, as *Leon to Annabella* as good as suggests (p. 193), she had confided, and who was now threatening a revelation if the marriage was not broken; or perhaps Lady Byron had never realized that what had happened was accounted a great sin until Mrs. Clermont enlightened her. It may all have started, as the *Don Leon* poems suggest, from Lady Byron's mistake of con- fiding in a dangerous woman; and this would then be the point of Colonel Doyle's remark that her appalling position had been brought about by her 'too confiding disposition' (p. 99).

But was the trouble that indicated in *Don Leon*, or something else? Here we again turn to Hobhouse's Marginalia (p. 201), where we find, beside Moore's suggestion that Byron's own self-accusations might be at the root of the trouble, this shattering comment:

'Something of this sort, certainly, unless, as Lord Holland told me, he tried to —— her.'

I quote from Michael Joyce's *My Friend H* (VIII, 101), which gives a fuller version than Sir Harold Nicolson. The dash is Hobhouse's. Lord Holland was a friend of Lushington, and may have been told by him. Exactly when this information was given to Hobhouse remains uncertain: it may have been on the occasion of Campbell's defence of Lady Byron (p. 227 below). Hobhouse's letter of 18 March 1816 to Lady Byron suggests that he was still at that time not con- scious of it (Hobhouse, II; xv, 314); and so indeed does his whole account, written down in May, 1816, especially his insistence that the charge 'too horrid to mention' *should* be mentioned (p. 78), and his annoyance at Lady Byron's refusing to repeat the formal 'Dis- avowal' on which the Separation had been based (Hobhouse, II; xv, 351). Indeed Sir Harold Nicolson deduces from his margin-note 'that Hobhouse, the closest of Byron's friends', really '*did not know*' the truth of it (Nicolson, 1940, Supplementary Chapter, 303). That is possible, though unlikely; but he certainly did not know that it was false.

The information must have come originally from Lady Byron,

and her evidence is not, as we have seen, reliable. But there is more. Our next witness is Shelley.

We have already had cause to refer to Shelley's visits to Byron at Venice in the year 1818. After one of these visits he wrote a poem *Julian and Maddalo* about himself and Byron. But there is a third person called 'the Maniac', who has usually, at the cost of utter confusion, been regarded by commentators as an aspect of Shelley himself. This is quite unsatisfactory; the lines do not fit Shelley at all; and anyway the poem, as its preface clearly shows, is conceived as a poem about Byron. The error arose from a wrong view of Byron: it seemed impossible to equate the Maniac's gentler qualities with the robust and wicked figure of popular conception. But that they do indeed suit Byron I have demonstrated at length in my former study, where the problems of *Julian and Maddalo* are discussed at length (CV, v, 251–4). There it is shown that, whereas Maddalo represents the bluff, manly, caustic, exterior which Byron, pre-eminently in his letters, presented to the world, the Maniac is his underself, his gentler, emotionally tormented, poetic, self, or parts of his sterner self sympathetically and inwardly viewed.

The Maniac's characteristics precisely suit Byron. There are correspondences to all his gentler qualities and also to his liberal ardour, wit, anger, pride and scorn; also to Augusta, Allegra, and to his rejection by Lady Byron, together with her accusation of 'pride' (408; see p. 269). His sufferings are caused by her rejection. The marriage-secret is hinted. He speaks:

> *That you had never seen me—never heard*
> *My voice, and more than all had ne'er endured*
> *The deep pollution of my loathed embrace—*
> *That your eyes ne'er had lied love in my face—*
> *That, like some maniac monk, I had torn out*
> *The nerves of manhood by their bleeding root*
> *With mine own quivering fingers, so that ne'er*
> *Our hearts had for a moment mingled there*
> *To disunite in horror.*

(420)

The passage continues with some obscurities, and the use of dots. We have here, it seems, a clear correspondence to 'that one slip of my poor silly tongue' in *Leon to Annabella* (264)—'there' recalling the use of 'hic' at the conclusion to *Don Leon*. There has been a

223

'deadly change in love' from 'one vowed deeply' (527–8), and the lady is now said to rain 'plagues of blistering agony' (453) on him. The secret is finally divulged by Maddalo's daughter at the poem's conclusion, which reads:

> *I urged and questioned still; she told me how*
> *All happened—but the cold world shall not know.*

(616)

The important word is 'how'.

When Maddalo is spoken of as putting his woes into poetry, this corresponds to Byron's reading of the fourth canto of *Childe Harold*, with its denunciation of the society which had rejected him, to Shelley (CV, v, 253). The reading made a deep impression on Shelley, and in the letter we have already discussed (p. 213) he denounced these stanzas to Peacock as a 'pernicious' form of 'insanity', and referred to Byron's associates at Venice. The Maniac, the Separation, London and Venetian society, homosexual and related practices, are all one complex, differently viewed by Byron and by Shelley, and variously treated in *Childe Harold*, *Julian and Maddalo*, and Shelley's letter to Peacock. We may here particularly observe how Byron in *Childe Harold* asserts that his destruction was not compassed with 'a just weapon' (*Childe Harold*, IV, 133). He seems to believe that the sexual crime had been *used* for ulterior purposes, and that may well be true. He may also mean that defence had been rendered impossible, since all considerations of honour and good taste prevented him from making public reference to it. That is why both he and Lady Byron were at an *impasse*.

How Shelley can have supposed that his meaning in *Julian and Maddalo* was sufficiently veiled is not clear; but it remains true that it has not until now been read.

There is nothing more to record until the destruction of the *Memoirs*, which we have already handled. How far, we may ask, are we to suppose that they dealt with any really intimate marriage secrets? Certainly they would not have been so outspoken as *Don Leon*. Thinking of the marriage Moore, whose word on such a matter cannot, however, be wholly trusted, tells us:

'Frank, as usual, throughout, in his avowals of his own errors, and generously just towards her who was his fellow-sufferer in the strife, the impression his recital left on the minds of all who perused it was, to say the least, favourable to him;—though, upon the whole, leading to a persuasion, which I have already intimated to be my own, that neither in kind nor degree, did the causes of disunion between the parties much differ from those that loosen the links of most such marriages.'

(Moore, xxv, 298)

That may be true of the *real* causes, since no one will believe that the sin in question would have disrupted a perfect marriage. Moore goes on to hint that there were details which no purpose would be served in revealing. Elsewhere he says that 'on the mysterious cause of the Separation it afforded no light whatever' (LVII, 654–5). This, in view of Byron's own statement (p. 150) that they were written to explain it, is scarcely believable. As we have seen, Moore tells us in his diary that the first part, leading up to the Separation, contained only some 'three or four lines' which made objectionable reading (Moore's *Memoirs, etc.*, 15 May, 1824; IV, 188); and we hazard the thought that these 'three or four lines' may have hinted just enough for those sufficiently initiated to understand how it all happened, though not enough to explain things to the general public. This would make good sense of Byron's remark to Lady Blessington that he often thought of adding notes 'in which *the whole truth* should be declared of, for, and against himself and others' (Blessington, 260).

But why did the *whole* script have to be destroyed? Moore strongly disapproved and in a letter to *The Times* of 26 May, 1824, said he had been willing to acquiesce 'with the sole reservation of a protest against its total destruction—at least without previous perusal and consultation amongst the parties' (Hobhouse, III, App. I, 356). Lord John Russell gives a brief note of the destruction, saying that he omits any 'long account' of the arguments and that the scene at Murray's was a very 'unpleasant' one, but that only 'three or four pages' in the whole were 'too gross and indelicate for publication' (Moore's *Memoirs, etc.*, IV, 191–2). Nevertheless those three or four pages of, presumably, the second part, together with any homosexual hints elsewhere, suggested too much. Even were they excluded, it could be argued that the exclusion might suggest more mischief than was suggested by the destruction, and this argument seems eventually to have convinced even Moore (Moore's *Memoirs, etc.*, 15 Dec., 1824; IV, 257). Murray agreed to the destruction because he understood that they were likely to be 'injurious' to Byron and 'painful' to the 'surviving family' (Murray to Wilmot Horton, 19 May, 1824; *Quarterly*, June, 1853; Vol. 93; *314*). Quite apart from the general horror of the subject, the homosexual emphasis in the second part, even if there had previously been no hints—and there probably had been—regarding the cause of the Separation, came *too near to the marriage-secret* for publication to be safe from Lady Byron's view, and even omitting it might only draw attention to what was being omitted; for it is clear that, whatever part she had originally played in it, the central secret quickly became a terror to her, to be suppressed at all costs; and that is why she was so anxious to get evidence of incest, as simultaneously a weapon and an alternative. Lady Byron herself wrote that Augusta said she agreed to the burning 'for Lady Byron's sake' (Lovelace, VI, 123); and it was probably for her sake that Hobhouse refused to allow a general perusal.

The destruction of the *Memoirs* did not escape criticism. Scott wrote in his Diary: 'It was a pity that nothing save the total destruction of Byron's *Memoirs* would satisfy his executors; but there was a reason—*Premat nox alta*' (Scott's Diary, 22 Nov., 1825; quoted Russell, preface to Moore's *Memoirs, etc.*, I, xvii). Directly after the destruction, there was an outcry in various quarters, particularly from John Wilson. Wilson was Professor of Moral Philosophy at Edinburgh University, and on the editorial staff of *Blackwood's*, and Byron had written what I call his '*Blackwood's* Defence' for him and others to read. From then on *Blackwood's*, previously hostile, was sympathetic to Byron. 'He took Wilson's heart', wrote Mrs. Stowe bitterly, 'by flattering messages, and a beautifully written letter' (Stowe, I, 55). Wilson was one of those to whom Byron wished Moore to show his *Memoirs* (Murray, 10 Dec., 1819; LJ, IV, 385; p. 149 above), and he had presumably done so. Now in the year 1824, in one of the series of 'Noctes Ambrosianae' dialogues in *Blackwood's*, Wilson, writing under the pseudonym 'Christopher North', speaks of the Separation: 'You have heard of the very last thing which preceded their valediction'—what this was is not stated—and then, he says, we are supposed to believe that Lady Byron's first letters were written 'to soothe a madman'. He continues:

'I think, since the Memoirs were burnt by these people, these people are bound to put us in possession of the best evidence which they still have the power of producing, in order that we may come to a just conclusion as to a subject upon which, by their act, at least as much as by any other people's act, we are compelled to consider it as our duty to make up our deliberate opinion—deliberate and decisive. Woe be to those who provoke this curiosity, and will not allay it!—Woe to them! say I.—Woe to them, says the world.'

(*Blackwood's*, 24 Nov., 1824; Vol. 16; *593-4*)

Wilson may talk rhetoric, but he talks sense too. *Blackwood's* itself states that Byron 'expressly' aimed to submit the manuscript to the perusal of Lady Byron and Wilson (July, 1869; Vol. 106; *33*). So this is written by a man who had, we have every reason to think, seen the *Memoirs*, whom we know to have had Byron's interests at heart, and who was a Professor of Moral Philosophy. We may accordingly suppose that the *Memoirs* told, on the whole, in Byron's favour.

And now there arose the problem of writing Byron's life. Moore had the offer and consulted Hobhouse, who was against it. Moore admitted that there were serious objections to such an undertaking, thinking with Hobhouse that 'there were no materials' for it, though he probably meant that there were rather too much. However, he took it on, and Hobhouse helpfully suggested, as a way out, that there might be enough original writing of Byron to save Moore the worry of doing more than 'a light prefatory sketch'. At one point (275) Moore's discussion with Hobhouse is broken off with asterisks (Moore's *Memoirs, etc.*, 17 Jan., 1826–11 April, 1828; v, 40, 41, 66, 185, 275).

Moore's account, which covered the Separation, appeared in 1830 and roused Lady Byron to publish her *Remarks* (p. xiii), in which she denied Moore's imputation that her parents had been responsible for her decision, attempted to explain her first kindly letters before the break, and appended the letter from Dr. Lushington of 31 January, 1830, which for the first time told the reading public of her personal visit to him, the mysterious revelation, and the final and irrevocable decision which followed (p. 75 above). These 'remarks' aroused a considerable controversy.

Thomas Campbell entered the arena in defence of Lady Byron with an article in the *New Monthly Magazine and Literary Journal* of April, 1830 (Vol. 28; *377–82*). Campbell said that his knowledge was drawn not from Lady Byron, but from a 'perfectly authentic' source, where he learned the facts, though his readers need not fear that he would 'inflict them on their delicacy'. He goes on:

'To plenary explanation she ought not—she never *shall*—be driven. Mr. Moore is too much a gentleman not to shudder at the threat of that, but if other Byronists, of a far different stamp, were to force the savage ordeal, it is her enemies, and not she, that would have to dread the burning ploughshares.'

There may be a hit there at Colman, whose *Leon to Annabella* might have already appeared. The trouble, though not specifically named, is made reasonably clear:

'It concerns morality and the most sacred rights of the sex, that she should (and that, too, without more special explanations) be acquitted out and out, and honourably acquitted, in this business of all share in the blame, which is one and indivisible.'

The reference to 'share' is vague, but most important. There was apparently a belief that Lady Byron had, as *Don Leon* suggests, been no unwilling partner; and there may have been more to it than that (p. 252 below). Campbell insists that the responsibility must be regarded as wholly Byron's. There is clearly a doubt, as his next words indicate:

'It is more for Lord Byron's sake than for his widow's, that I resort not to a more special examination of Mr. Moore's misconceptions. The subject would lead me insensibly into hateful disclosures against poor Lord Byron, who is more unfortunate in his rash defenders than his reluctant accusers.'

His general conclusion is fair enough. What we should do, he says, is 'acknowledge frankly this one, and perhaps the only one, great error of his life'. That done, 'what a space is still left in our minds for allowance and charity and even for admiration of him'. Frank acknowledgment is, he says, best:

'But pay the due homage to moral principle, frankly own that the child of genius is, in this particular, not to be defended—abstain from absolving Byron on false grounds, and you will do him more good than by idle attempts at justification.'

That sounds eminently just. But how Campbell's readers are to do this without having knowledge of the crime 'inflicted on their delicacy' is hard to see.

Moore, who had been blamed in Campbell's article for suppressing, or remaining wantonly ignorant of, the truth, made no reply, but merely wrote off the article in his diary as 'rash' (Moore's *Memoirs, etc.,* 5–7 July, 1844; VII, 373). And so it was. Campbell did not seem to realize that no one was less anxious for a disclosure than Lady Byron, who called his article 'injudicious' (Moore's *Memoirs, etc.,* 1 April, 1830; VI, 113). She wrote to him saying that her 'principles and feelings' prevented her from exposing Moore's misrepresentations, and that she could not let the world know the true causes of the trouble (Mayne II; I, 20–21, note). Campbell had, says Ethel Colburn Mayne, been clearly referring to the sin described in *Don Leon,* which she calls a 'filthy brochure'; but he later protested that such insinuations had never been in his mind, and that 'he did not know what he was about when he published the paper' (Mayne, II; I, 20–I; and see Chew, XII, 226, note). Pressure had, presumably, been brought to bear on him. One cannot help supposing that Lady Byron by now hoped and expected people to relate the mystery to Augusta. That is, if my reading be not unjust, what she had been working for, and silence on the true facts was essential.

Hobhouse records on 5 April, 1830, that, when he consulted Lord Holland as to whether he should make a public reply to Campbell's aspersions, he was advised not to do so, and accordingly remained content with having left for publication 'if necessary', 'a full and scrupulously accurate account' of the Separation; that is, the account from which we have already quoted at length (Hobhouse, IV; IX, 17). We must note that he still maintained, six years after the destruction of the *Memoirs,* that his first account was 'scrupulously accurate'; nor have we found it at any point *factually* at fault.

Campbell was, however, quite clear about it all in his own mind, and as late as 2 January, 1831, wrote to Moore apologizing for his rudeness, but claiming in guarded terms that he still regarded the 'cause' as 'just' (Beattie, III, 73). In a letter to his sister of 27 May, 1830, he was too outspoken for print. It goes:

'I have received your letter, my dearest sister, for which I thank you cordially. The defence of Lady B. was a bold step on my part; and I do most gladly rejoice that I meet with your approbation. If all the world were of a different opinion, I should still feel and think that I had done the right thing, and the best thing for the cause of truth and humanity; and that right and best thing was only to be done with bold and blunt earnestness . . .

'I do assure you I am not affecting indifference, but really *feel* entire indifference about the opinion of the worse half of the world. The abuse of part of the press I take rather as a compliment. What I have now to say, I don't give you in absolute confidence; but as it *will* be out one day, I give it to repeat with discretion.

*   *   *   *   *'

(Beattie, III, 64)

Asterisks play a large part in our study. We run up against them continually, in Moore's *Memoirs* and elsewhere, at the more important parts.

This controversy too was discussed in *Blackwood's*, in the issue of May, 1830, where John Wilson comes out firmly but judicially on Byron's side. He argues that in quoting Dr. Lushington's letter in her *Remarks* Lady Byron had now made a public pronouncement to the effect that her husband had been guilty of some extreme offence. A wife, he says, should not, whatever her husband's sins, continue to suggest them after his death (*Blackwood's*, May, 1830; Vol. 27; *825*). Now he believes that plain speaking would be best. At one point (828) he urges that she should from the start have told her legal adviser everything and shown him 'unashamed' the 'records', if such there were, of 'uttermost pollution'. The dialogue continues, with Wilson speaking as 'Christopher North':

SHEPHERD: And what think ye, sir, that a' this pollution could hae been, that sae electrified Dr. Lushington?

NORTH: Bad—bad—bad, James. Nameless, it is horrible—named, it might leave Byron's memory yet within the range of pity and forgiveness—and where they are, their sister affections will not be far—though, like weeping seraphs, standing aloof, and veiling their eyes with their wings.

SHEPHERD: She should indeed have been silent—till the grave had closed on her sorrows as on his sins.

NORTH: Even now she should speak—or someone else for her— say her father or her mother (are they alive?)—and a few words will suffice. Worse the condition of the dead man's name cannot be—far, far better it might—I believe it would be—were all the truth, somehow or other, declared—and declared it must be, not for Byron's sake only, but for the sake of humanity itself—and then a mitigated sentence—or eternal silence.

(*Blackwood's*, May, 1830; Vol. 27, *828*)

This is most important. Wilson had, almost certainly, seen the *Memoirs* (p. 149; John Fox, author of *Vindication of Lady Byron*, to be discussed presently, says unequivocally that he had; II, 99); and he had deplored their burning. Now he states that were '*all*' the truth declared for *Byron's* 'sake', it would lead either to 'a mitigated sentence' or to 'eternal silence'. That is, the whole truth was less blameworthy than the bare fact suggests—remember Shelley's use of 'how' (p. 224)—and might eventually leave nothing to be said. Wilson's plea may have prompted Colman to write *Don Leon*.

We have one more contemporary witness—E. J. Trelawny. He, too, had seen the *Memoirs*, and had said that they were 'truer than such works usually are', and that he considered that a great wrong was done Byron by their destruction (Trelawny, XVIII, 182–3). Now I owe to Professor Oswald Doughty two important references from the unpublished diary of W. M. Rosetti. The first is dated 30 January 1872:

'Called on Trelawny . . . Trelawny disbelieves Mrs. Stowe's story about Byron, and considers that he knows the real reason of the separation from Lady Byron. He has some thought of publishing it before his death, or at any rate leaving it on record: it would vindicate Byron against that grave imputation, but would have shown him to have fallen into "other weaknesses".'

The 'grave imputation' is, of course, incest. Our next is dated 27 February, 1872:

'Called again on Trelawny . . . Trelawny says the book about Medora Leigh is true, but not that she was Byron's daughter: the belief that she was so, however, was the compelling cause of Lady Byron's separation.'

There is an awkward contradiction: Trelawny was an old man in 1872. There is no reason to suppose that he ever knew anything of the intricacies of the Separation, but the main points made, concerning 'other weaknesses' and his denial of the charge of incest, are of interest.

IV

The final version of Colman's *Don Leon*, which seems to have been stimulated by the controversies regarding the *Memoirs* and Lady Byron's *Remarks*, appears to have been composed some time about 1833–1836. There was probably an edition, perhaps done on the Continent, about 1842, and there was the undated edition of *Leon to Annabella* which may have been early (p. 160). Our first external reference occurs in a long letter on *Don Leon* to *Notes and Queries* of 15 January, 1853 (1st Series, vII, 66), in which 'I.W.' speaks of it as having been 'printed abroad many years since'. The letter was probably written with the intention of publicizing the poem. He describes it, and then:

'Is the writer known? I am somewhat surprised that not one of Byron's friends has, so far as I know, hinted a denial of the authorship; for, scarce as the work may be, I suppose some of them must have seen it; and, under existing circumstances, it is possible that a copy might get into the hands of a desperate creature, who would hope to make a profit by republishing it with Byron's and Moore's names on the title-page.'

Neither Lady Byron nor Hobhouse replied.

When either of the *Don Leon* poems was first circulated in England is not known, but one, and perhaps both, seem to have been out fairly early, and Lady Byron must have known of them. This at last explains her continued unrest and otherwise extraordinary desire to keep alive and spread the scandal of incest, both in her various conversations of the 50's and in her private, but abortive, memoirs. After her death, as we have seen, *Leon to Annabella* appeared in 1865, was reprinted in 1866 as 'The Great Secret Revealed', and re-issued in the same year bound up with *Don Leon*. In his *Index Librorum Prohibitorum* H. S. Ashbee prints a note by a gentleman 'acquainted with the publisher' who says that W. Dugdale had bought the manuscript of *Don Leon*, thinking it by Byron; and 'wanted me to advise him as to how he could best approach Lady Byron, from whom he expected to get a large sum to suppress the publication'. This was 'about the year 1860'. He warned Dugdale of the legal dangers of such a course. Lady Byron, who was far from strong at that time, died on 16 May, 1860.

The poems appeared together in the year 1866. In *Notes and*

Queries of 15 June, 1867 (3rd Series, XI, 477), S. Jackson, perhaps, like 'I.W.', really meaning to draw attention to the book, enquired as to its authenticity; and soon after wrote that he had received a letter from a—perhaps fictional—friend who believed that 'owing to some interference' the poem had been 'burked'; a statement which, since all the advertisements had been withdrawn, he assumed to be correct (*Notes and Queries*, 17 Aug., 1867; 3rd Series, XII, 137). When in reporting these letters Ethel Colburn Mayne erroneously adds after the word 'interference' the words 'of the Byron family' (Mayne, II; App. I, 319), the error probably ariscs from her own, inside, knowledge of what had happened. The 1865–1866 editions must, indeed, have caused that family considerable anxiety, and they may have paid Dugdale well for the suppression. Dugdale seems to have known his business.[1]

These 1865–1866 publications of the *Don Leon* poems were also probably, in part at least, the deep though unacknowledged cause of the great controversy soon to break out; for the years 1869–1871 were to see a torrent of Byronic defences and attacks.

Some time before July in the year 1869 came the English translation of the Countess Guiccioli's study of Byron, entitled *My Recollections of Lord Byron and Those of Eye-Witnesses of his Life*. In June appeared the first of some important anonymous articles on Byron's married life in *Temple Bar* by a certain John Fox, hostile to Byron. In July *Blackwood's* printed a review of the *Recollections*, from which we have quoted (p. 82), attacking Lady Byron and her advisers. In September Mrs. Beecher Stowe published Lady Byron's disclosures to her in an article (p. 114) in *Macmillan's Magazine* and in October *The Quarterly* replied with a lengthy attack. October also saw the publication of Byron's *La Mira* Statement (p. 146) and John Murray's letter concerning the destruction of the *Memoirs*, both in the first issue of *The Academy*. This year also saw Alfred Austin's *A Vindication of Lord Byron* and *Medora Leigh*, edited by C. Mackay, a biography of Augusta's daughter. In January, 1870, Mrs. Stowe, whose article had aroused much opposition, brought out her book *Lady Byron Vindicated*, which was met by another long article in *The Quarterly* exposing its fallacies. In 1870 part of Hobhouse's *Recollections of a Long Life*, giving his account of the marriage separation and the destruction of the *Memoirs*, was privately printed;

[1] I am following Ashbee's account in taking W. Dugdale to be the publisher. See p. 160 above.

and, in reply to a review of other Hobhouse papers in *The Edinburgh Review* for April, 1871, Fox in that year included his *Temple Bar* articles in a book, but still anonymously, under the title *Vindication of Lady Byron*.

Of Mrs. Stowe's book we have already spoken, and no more need here be said, except to suggest that it may have been prompted by the recent 1865–1866 publications of the *Don Leon* poems. According to John Robertson, who knew Lady Byron well, she had talked to her friends for years of one crime, which he does not name, but which may have been homosexuality, but later added the charge of incest; 'six or seven' friends were told; and these communications were given 'as facts to be used for the defence of her conduct, character, and memory' (*Quarterly*, quoting Robertson, Oct., 1869; Vol. 127, *426*). She may sometimes have mentioned homosexuality; parts of Mrs. Stowe's book suggest, as we have seen, that she did; but we can be sure that she never wanted the marriage-secret divulged. It is possible that, having seen earlier issues of the *Don Leon* poems, she had briefed Mrs. Stowe to build up the incest-revelation were they to appear again. The book's confusions may, or may not, be Lady Byron's fault. John Robertson tells us that her stories used to differ, and people thought her mind unsound (*Quarterly*, as above). How exactly it happened we cannot say, but the result certainly serves to overlay thoughts of incest on material that had nothing to do with it.

Fox's *Vindication* is of considerable importance. The author seems to have been directly inspired by *Don Leon*, though he does not mention it. Denying that Mrs. Stowe's revelations tell us the cause of the Separation, he concentrates instead, as Mayne (II, App. I, 319) realizes, on that hinted by Campbell and described in *Don Leon*. He does not actually *name* the cause, and says that it would not 'avail' Lady Byron's memory to speculate too exactly (I, 21; III, 205); but his meaning throughout is clear.

Against Byron he is wholly hostile. Everything possible is called as evidence against him—his leaving England; his never having actually published his defences nor insisted on a public hearing; his failure to attack Lushington openly and his only attacking Romilly after his death. It sounds convincing, but every point has its answer. Sometimes the objections cancel out: it is just because his enemies and his friends together burned it that Byron has not left us the 'plain tale' of defence which the author blames him for not daring to leave (II, 88). Nor is it any solution to insist next that the *Memoirs* are irrelevant since Byron would not have divulged the secret to convict himself (II, 91), particularly when we hear soon after that they cannot have denied the truth of it or Hobhouse would never have sanctioned their destruction (II, 106)! Perhaps the worst absurdity occurs whenever Byron's having praised (pp. 59, 67, 78) his wife's truth and other virtues at the time of the Separation is used (I, 11–12, 34, 43; II, 82; III, 145) to leave him miserably and shamefully condemned 'out of his own mouth' under her charges (III, 221). Such are the confusions which spring from a failure in impartiality. There is some poetic justice in the book's having been first issued bearing the Byron arms with the motto '*Crede Biron*'.

Nevertheless, the author's diagnosis of what may actually have happened is extraordinarily penetrating. He quotes (I, 13; III, 147) Byron's letter to Murray of 3 January 1816 saying that his wife would copy anything he desired 'in all the ignorance of innocence' (LJ, III, 251; p. 54): Lady Byron may accordingly have been 'ignorantly innocent' (II, 121) of any guilt in the offence, and that may be why 'she did not revolt until after her arrival at Kirkby Mallory' (III, 147–8). Who enlightened her? Not Lady Noel—*Leon to Annabella* as good as tells us that (p. 193)—but rather Mrs. Clermont, who counselled her to tell Lushington, with the result that henceforth her 'duty both to God and man' forced her actions (III, 145). Lady Byron is highly honoured for the 'ignorance of innocence' and 'serene purity' (III, 145) which enabled her to endure this sin without disquiet. Meanwhile, Byron's denunciation of Mrs. Clermont in *A Sketch* is exactly placed (II, 116), and it is recalled that when sealing the deed of Separation, he said, 'This is Mrs. Clermont's act and deed' (III, 148).

Other possibilities are surveyed. Fox admits that Byron may at first in all honesty not have realized that this was the cause of his wife's antipathy, acutely suggesting that 'of the real offence he might think lightly, if at all, not dreaming that it could be known beyond the cover of the roof under which he had shivered his household gods' (I, 22). This reads like a direct transcription from *Leon to Annabella*. Byron may later have thought that the offence was no more 'rank' to her than to him, and that she had merely *used* it as a pretext (I, 35). This he would have regarded as a piece of 'treachery' leading to his ruin (I, 43). The pattern is reasonable.

But why then did Lady Byron talk to Mrs. Stowe about incest?

Fox believes the incest charge, but says that it is necessary for Lady
Byron's vindication to show that she never said, as Mrs. Stowe said
that she said, that it was the cause of the Separation, since it had been
shown that it was not (IV, 222–3). But he admits that Lady Byron
left such an impression, and it is recognized that she was working to
preserve her reputation for posterity (IV, 238). Her suppression of the
truth is accepted as follows:

'When she spoke of the misery of her married life, she would dwell
upon that cause which she mentioned to Mrs. Stowe, for two reasons.
Hateful as it was, it was less hateful than that other cause of which the
Quarterly Review speaks as too repulsive to be translated into words,
and of which Campbell declared that Moore must shudder at the
thought of her being driven to speak out to the world.'

(IV, 238)

Besides, he says, suspicion of incest might have been the main cause
of her misery, though not of the Separation, since 'in her innocence
she had been ignorant of any other guilt' (IV, 238). The impression
left on Mrs. Stowe is regarded as understandable. But it is a complete
falsification, none the less, and a falsification which Lady Byron
appears to have desired, and worked for.

Fox well insists on the danger of confusing the two charges, noting
that the Quarterly had been showing itself unaware of the distinction
(III, 140). He discusses Mrs. Stowe's confusions at some length, and
indicates how her book started people on Byron's side busily showing that incest could not have been the cause of the Separation
without facing 'the charge that could not be met' (IV, 221). Yes, and,
still more, it was to start those hostile to Byron busily proving incest;
for what Fox, like Thomas Campbell earlier, never seems to realize
is that Lady Byron's supporters had been equally, or more, anxious
to suppress the truth, and that it was apparently Lady Byron's desire
that this very confusion should arise. What her descendants thought
of Fox's book, I do not know. They cannot have liked it, pursuing
as it does the story of the Don Leon poems with such incisive
penetration.

And yet it has so far had little effect. The smokescreen of incest
worked, and has left both parties happily quarrelling for half a
century about an irrelevance.

This development was considerably assisted by Lord Lovelace's
Astarte in 1905. Lovelace's purpose was simple: to prove that incest

had occurred *before the marriage*. He does not argue that it occurred since, leaves it clear that it was not the cause of the Separation, insists that Byron's sexual life was not unduly licentious, deplores the 'crass and egregious suggestions' of Shelley regarding his life at Venice (VI, 124, note), does not believe that the *Memoirs* contained anything disreputable (IV, 120), and strongly urges that incest, in this particular instance, was no serious sin (p. 115).

As for the other charge, he is at some pains to obscure it. He wonders a little querulously why the opposers of the incest theory should try to disprove a sin so 'far less repulsive than some exaggerations and inventions about him which human imbecility and infatuation forged out of infinitely little knowledge' (VII, 152). Again, apparently quite forgetting Lady Byron's March 1816 statement (p. 89) and Dr. Lushington's assertion—'there was nothing else at this time'—that incest was not the important issue at the time of the Separation, both of which Lovelace himself is the first, in this very book, to put before the public (Lovelace, II, 46-8; VII, 159), he at one point naïvely argues that, since there must have been some peculiarly strong reason to influence men like Wilmot Horton, Doyle, and Lushington in insisting on a separation, we should realize that 'all alternative explanations' are 'more heinous and repulsive' than incest with a half-sister:

'His memory has less than nothing to gain from all the possible degrading and disgusting suppositions that might be invented and decoy prospective purchasers, in the event of a high tide of Byronese folly, curiosity, and ill-nature.'

(VIII, 182)

He seems to be fearing a re-issue of the *Don Leon* poems. He certainly is *not* thinking of truth for truth's sake, but rather of a family's reputation. He next falsifies in spirit, if not in fact, what he knows perfectly well to be the truth:

'It is right to state most distinctly that the Separation papers leave no possible place for other charges besides the two commonplace ones of adultery and cruelty, and that connected with Mrs. Leigh.'

(VIII, 182)

They do not of course *name* the other charge; but 'leave no possible place'? Besides, his own family papers contained a document, which we shall soon (p. 238) be quoting, which is not properly used in

237

Astarte, and which indicates that there was indeed a graver charge; and of this paper Lovelace must have known, since he refers to it (II, 49, note).

The book is thoroughly untrustworthy. And why, we may ask, were Lady Byron's own memoir-notes never published? Was it known that they falsify what may one day be proved to be the truth? And might be shown to be doing so?

In 1909 Richard Edgcumbe published his *Byron: the Last Phase*, with a long section developing his theory concerning Medora Leigh. Though his theory is unacceptable, his challenging of the opposition is often sound and suggestive. In 1924 came Professor Samuel Chew's *Byron in England*, with some relevant judgments.

The year 1924 also saw the publication of *The Byron Mystery* by Sir John Fox, son of the John Fox who wrote the anonymous *Vindication*, and himself a man of standing designated as 'Late Senior Master of the Supreme Court, Chancery Division'. He supports Lady Byron and the charge of incest, but, though his book is dedicated to his father, he appears to be ignorant of his father's arguments. Though it is a valuable and scholarly work, with a welcome use of exact references for all its material, the author gets into considerable confusion in boldly producing evidence which he is simultaneously unwilling to face, and indeed distorts.

Here is his main contribution. He asks 'what was the additional communication made by Lady Byron to Dr. Lushington,' and 'was it true?' In answer he prints a document from the Lovelace papers, 'not before published', by one Henry Allen Bathurst, Registrar of the Admiralty Court from 1879 to 1890, 'the surviving trustee of Lady Noel Byron's sealed papers'. This is the paper to which Lovelace refers while suppressing its contents. It is a memorandum of a conversation with Dr. Lushington on 27 January 1870, when the 1869–71 controversy was at its height. Dr. Lushington is reported as saying that it would be a relief to him at this juncture to speak out. This is what he said:

'That he was first consulted by Lady Noel, Lady Byron's mother, and that she did not know all or the most serious of the causes of Lady Byron's complaints against her husband. He (Dr. L.) only learnt them at a subsequent period from Lady Byron herself (referred to his letter in the *Remarks*).

'He considers that the real cause of Lady Byron's separation, when

238

it was ascertained that there was no adequate ground in the opinion of the medical men for supposing him insane, was his brutally indecent conduct and language to her * * *

'Dr. L., speaking with much feeling and emotion, described Lord B's conduct as most foul and gross, but of this there could hardly have been any evidence; and I gathered that Lady B. would have been most reluctant or positively unwilling to charge him with such offences if legal proceedings became necessary—she would naturally shrink from doing so.

'At the time of her leaving his house she was not convinced of any incest having taken place.'

(Fox, IX, 57–8)

The memorandum goes on to state that Mrs. Leigh subsequently confessed to incest, but this, if correctly reported, presumably refers only to Lady Byron's assertion (p. 97), and we must suppose that Augusta herself would have strongly denied any such confession if, as Lovelace tells us, she left at her death some carefully selected papers intended to rebut the charge (Lovelace, VII, 146). However, it is necessary to record that Dr. Lushington appears to have believed in the confession.

The statement points directly to the *Don Leon* secret. We must not, of course, be led astray by the words 'brutally' and 'most foul and gross', since these would inevitably be applied to the action, however it happened. The asterisks leave it undefined, Fox's footnote to them merely telling us: 'A specific instance is referred to in no way connected with the charge of incest.' Once again, we see how the charge of incest blurs the issue: it is being assumed that nothing else is relevant, whereas it is in fact the incest that is irrelevant.

This document was not known to Fox's father, who had reached his conclusions without it. Sir John Fox notes that no one knew of Dr. Lushington's denial that incest caused the Separation until the publication of Lovelace's *Astarte* in 1905 (Fox, XVI, 193); and as for this new document, it had never been published before.

Sir John Fox himself asseverates, again and again, that incest was not the cause of the Separation (IX, 61). All the later evidence, he says, proves 'that incest was not and could not have been' the cause (XVI, 161; and see XII, 109; XIX, 211). He is in no doubt, and could not have been. And yet, by some strange mental action he also clouds the issue by saying of the 'brutally indecent conduct and language' that it is 'more than probable that this included his attempts to corrupt Mrs. Leigh after his marriage' (IX, 61–2). Later in the book he says that 'we now know' that 'cruelty'—just that word alone—was the cause that weighed with Dr. Lushington (XVI, 194). He has apparently by now forgotten the Bathurst statement which he was the first to print. But he does not even stop here. Towards the end of his book he can write of his father's study:

'The author of the *Vindication* believes that the cause of the Separation was some undisclosed offence apart from the grave charge alleged. Literally, this was the case; the two offences were distinct. The later evidence shows that the cause of the Separation was a form of cruelty in the legal sense, namely, conduct in Lady Byron's presence in relation to the sister which made it impossible that the wife should return to the husband.'

(XIX, 211)

Was ever a qualified lawyer, and one presumes that he must have been that, guilty of more muddled thinking? He is merely fabricating an imaginary type of cruelty based on Lady Byron's later and untrustworthy reminiscences, and in doing so contradicts blankly the whole tenour of his father's, Dr. Lushington's, and his own firm assertions running simultaneously throughout that the cause was *not* incest, while apparently quite forgetting, or wishing us to forget, the Bathurst statement, with its definition of the 'real cause' as something which Fox has already told us was 'in no way connected with the charge of incest' (p. 239). This is a usual process with writers on Byron: while knowing perfectly well that incest is not the point, they find it easier, as though by a process similar to that George Orwell named 'double-think', to pretend simultaneously that it is.

In a footnote commenting on Byron's complaint that people have tried to set on him the 'stigma' of 'homosexuality' (p. 212), Sir John Fox writes:

'The stigma was never suggested by Lady Byron or her advisers. The letter points to the nature of the second of the two reports mentioned in the "Disavowal" . . . No evidence in support of the charge indicated, which, it will be observed, was only based on rumour, has ever been put forward.'

(XIV, 139, note)

He equates the 'crime more enormous' than incest of the 'Disavowal' (pp. 77–8) with homosexuality, but pretends not to believe in it. Does he not suspect any relation between this and the 'specific instance' of 'indecent conduct' towards his wife in the Bathurst statement for which he prints asterisks (IV, 57, and note; p. 239)? What was that 'specific act' of which he prefers not to speak? And why does he never refer to the main arguments of his father's book, which he is simultaneously at pains to advertise, dedicating his own work to his father's memory, and printing his father's portrait as a frontispiece?

That was the last full-length work to concentrate on the Separation. Numerous general studies have, however, appeared during our century, and some of them mention the *Don Leon* poems, though, as in T. J. Wise's bibliography of Byron (1933; II, 103), contenting themselves by ruling them off as 'spurious', as though the question of Byron's authorship were the only thing that mattered. In 1912 Ethel Colburn Mayne brought out her life of Byron. We are told that, since her views were acceptable to the family, she was allowed sight of Lady Byron's notes among the Lovelace papers. She does, nevertheless, mention the *Don Leon* poems in connection with both Campbell's article and the *Vindication of Lady Byron*. They are placed under the heading of 'little filthy contraband brochures purported to be "Letters from Lord to Lady Byron",' which 'told of things unspeakable in villainous alexandrines'. She does not, she says, for one moment believe them to be 'genuine', but they serve to show the forms taken by 'rumour' (II; I, I; App. I, 319). How she avoids seeing a significant grouping here, quite apart from all questions of authorship, I cannot say. But, after all, she does not actually say that she does not believe them to be '*true*'; merely that they are not 'genuine'.

In 1922 appeared the two volumes *Lord Byron's Correspondence* containing letters to Lady Melbourne which helped to reawaken interest and belief in the incest. This was followed in 1924 by Professor Samuel C. Chew's valuable storehouse *Byron in England*, which gives the first bibliographical account, so far as one can be made, of the *Don Leon* poems. Drinkwater's *The Pilgrim of Eternity*, appearing in 1925, has a good critical analysis of the weaknesses of Lovelace's *Astarte*, but shows no awareness at all of *Don Leon* or the *Vindication*; nor even of Byron's passionate friendships, Edleston and

Nicolo Giraud being ignored; and one can only suppose, since he claims to have read widely in Byronic material, and is ready to point out one of the confusions into which Sir John Fox is reduced (I, 36-7), that he of set purpose preferred to leave the subject alone, with no more than a hint that a 'yet more obscure secret than is commonly allowed' (I, 70)—'allowed' is a neat touch—might be involved. In 1930 André Maurois, though he had seen Sir Harold Nicolson's copy of Moore's *Life* with Hobhouse's marginalia, and is aware of Byron's tendency to passionate friendship, makes no great use of either, and leaves the theory of incest, together with Lady Byron's quite untrustworthy unpublished notes, which he was privileged to see, to describe the inner workings of Byron's marriage; which is necessarily disastrous. Not until Peter Quennell's *The Years of Fame* in 1935 is there any adequate emphasis on Byron's homo-sexual, or bisexual, propensities. Quennell makes good use of Hob-house's marginalia, and refers in passing to a rumour that Byron 'had been guilty of an unnatural attempt' (XII, 362). To the 1940 re-issue of Nicolson's *Byron: The Last Journey* was appended the 'Supple-mentary Chapter' containing extracts from Hobhouse's margin notes, with Sir Harold's comments. Vulliamy's *Byron* in 1948 is a lively study, but it leaves the heart of the problem untouched.

The same year, 1948, saw the publication by John Murray of Michael Joyce's *My Friend H.*, a biography of Hobhouse, which con-tains, so far as I know, the first explicit support in this century of the main fact, if fact it was, revealed in *Don Leon*. Joyce bases his con-clusion on Hobhouse's margin note, already discussed (p. 222), which he takes to mean 'an unorthodox sexual approach' (VIII, 101). This he is apparently ready to accept, without further evidence, writing:

'Hundreds of pages have since been written on the cause of the Separation, and the issue has been confused by vanity, rancour, family pride, and defects of intellect, candour, and historic sense. The more judicious writers have been hampered, at first by lack of evidence, and latterly by mistaken notions of decency—mistaken because, when once such a problem has arisen, the cause of decency is better served by putting all the known facts on record than by suggest-ing gross misconduct and leaving its precise enormity to guess-work.'

(VIII, 100)

It is hard to see why Joyce so readily accepts the theory on this single piece of evidence, which, after all, merely gives us Hobhouse's private reminiscence, not intended for publication, of a remark of Lord Holland, based presumably on what Dr. Lushington, or some other, had told him that Lady Byron had said. Hobhouse's note is not only, standing alone, poor evidence, but, as Sir Harold Nicolson observes (p. 222), he himself appears to be uncertain. However, as we know, there is more evidence, and in its light we can regard Joyce's comments as judicious.

As for the *Don Leon* poems, Joyce admits having seen what he rather ungratefully designates 'these obscene squibs', but only after forming his own conclusions (Notes, 357–8). And yet without them his own conclusions could be no more than tentative. It is necessary to have evidence from trustworthy and sympathetic authorities who had learned the facts from Byron himself, or deduced them from his *Memoirs*; and of these there are three only: Colman pre-eminently, Shelley, and John Wilson. Besides, without the *Don Leon* poems it is probable that much of the evidence we have been reviewing would never have appeared at all. They were known to exist, circulated on the Continent, and in 1866 had appeared together in England, functioning as a sword of Damocles, always ready to strike. No one knew when or how they would again appear; we still do not know when next the complete text may be—to use Campbell's happy phrase—'inflicted on our delicacy'; and hitherto, directly or indirectly, they may be supposed to have been surreptitiously goading people into print, on one side or the other; as they have, indeed, forced the writing of this book, for I would never have searched for, or been ready myself to focus, the evidence here collected, without the authority of the *Don Leon* poems in mind. They were re-issued together in 1934 by the Fortune Press and, after being ruled as spurious, were seized by the police. Since the quality of the writing shows the integrity of great poetry, I inserted a respectful reference to them, which must be the first they have ever received, in the preface to *Lord Byron: Christian Virtues*, in 1952; and in July of 1954 my article *Who Wrote Don Leon*, outlining the gist of my present study, appeared in *The Twentieth Century*, followed by *Colman and Don Leon* in June, 1956.

The importance of the *Don Leon* poems in this investigation cannot be exaggerated. They still remain the only firm evidence as yet available; the rest is mainly ancillary, and, if not directly inspired by them, must be regarded as of supporting and cumulative, rather than intrinsic, value.

VII
CONCLUSIONS

VII. CONCLUSIONS

I

We must not, of course, suppose that our analyses have given us the exact truth and certainly they have not given us the whole truth. Nevertheless, I shall next offer a brief account of what they suggest, stating it, for simplicity, as a factual narrative.

First, we turn to Lady Byron. Soon after the marriage Byron told her of his homosexual propensities, sometimes regarding them as sinful, at others defending them; and among the troubles of 1815 she was disturbed by his association with the theatre, and in particular with Colman and others of 'notoriety' (p. 206). She had also become involved—why we do not know—in the illicit relationship with her husband. She may have been herself in part responsible, for it would be a grave error in human insight to suppose, just because she was outwardly a woman of strict morality, that she was not capable of a passionate abandon. It did not prevent her living 'conjugally' with him up to the last (p. 56), and she left him in the mood of her facetious letters. But she was genuinely anxious concerning his mental state, and told her people of it, saying something of his homosexual theories; and since the doctor could not regard his state as pathological, the Noels decided on a separation. But it was not until her own visit to Dr. Lushington that she revealed the marriage secret. This she may have done as a means to force the separation which she desired for other reasons; or because she had only now learned its wickedness; or because Mrs. Clermont, whom she had in her 'too confiding disposition' (p. 99) told of it, was threatening to make it known were the marriage not disrupted. Perhaps, too, Mrs. Clermont had told her that she had been made to 'enact the Ganymede' (p. 188) as a *substitute*; and her pride was involved. Pressure on all sides, pride and morality, all forced her, though the agony was severe, to part.

247

And now she began to fabricate reasons, convincing herself retrospectively (p. 65) that Byron's various abnormalities sprang from a consistent course of 'revenge' directed against herself. She rationalized her actions wholly in terms of 'principle', using such phrases as 'the strictest principle of duty', 'determination to be wicked', 'the *total* dereliction of principle' and 'duty to God', saying that her 'security' with Byron 'depended on the total abandonment of every moral and religious principle' (to Augusta, 20 Jan; to Byron, 13 Feb.; to Augusta 14 and 15 Feb.; 1816; LJ, III, 299, 310, 311, 313). Sir Ralph Noel's condemnation of Byron's 'opinions' (pp. 59, 68) is readily placed.

But more was involved than moral principle. Lady Byron's fear of the further revelation of what she had herself too incautiously revealed caused her to implore Byron for a quiet arrangement and, after getting it, to work on Augusta under false pretences in order to get proof of incest, *which had not hitherto been a serious consideration at all* (pp. 88–9), as a means of enforcing Byron's silence. For some reason she still felt insecure, if not guilty; her advisers were well aware that her position was dangerous and justification needed (pp. 98–9); and we must assume that the facts were complex. On hearing of Byron's proposed defence in the *Memoirs*, she replied by a threat; and after they had been burned, suggested that she and Hobhouse should concoct a spurious version of their own (p. 109); her *Remarks* in 1830 falsified the facts (p. 76), and in making public her revelation to Dr. Lushington in these *Remarks* she very likely hoped that people would understand it in terms of incest. *Don Leon* appeared soon after, printed abroad (p. 160); she composed various papers for posterity, which have never been published, but have been freely used by biographers; she tried to get a confession from Augusta at Reigate; she set herself assiduously to spreading the scandal of incest, and seems to have told various friends (p. 114), including Mrs. Stowe, that it was the cause of the Separation. She may have mentioned homosexuality also, since traces of it appear beneath the surface of Mrs. Stowe's account, though whether Lady Byron intended the confusion cannot be known. It seems that the threat in 1860 of an English edition of *Don Leon* may have precipitated her death (p. 232).

It will be clear that nothing coming from Lady Byron or her supporters after the break, no reminiscences, *nor letters in any but the original text*, can be regarded as trustworthy. We have accordingly no reason to suppose that Byron was ever deliberately unkind to his wife, in word or deed. As Hobhouse tells us, 'there was nothing fierce about Lord Byron' (Nicolson, 1940; Supplementary Chapter, 298).

Augusta's behaviour is less easy to explain. Whatever may have happened between her and Byron, our study leads us to conclude that the part she played in his story was one not of tempter, but of guardian angel. That during the period of her early correspondence with Byron starting in the year 1804 she regarded herself almost in the light of a foster-mother to the boy, showing a fine sense of responsibility, may be seen from her letters to John Hanson of 18 November, 1804, and 7 March, 1806 (LJ, 1, 45, 97, notes). Later she seems to have incurred risks and scandal on her own account. She had for long known, perhaps from John Hanson, Byron's lawyer and semi-guardian, of Byron's homosexual propensities and done all she could to save him from danger; she had even, perhaps, acted on occasion as an accomplice rather than leave him to himself (p. 210). She was, for his sake, ready to say she thought him insane (to Hobhouse, 21 May, 1816; Hobhouse, II; App. H, 364). Lady Noel reports her as saying: 'I had rather think it malady than depravity of heart' (Fox, XII, 107). She defended herself again and again against some rather obscure form of disloyalty to Lady Byron; as for Byron himself, 'I have made it a rule to be silent as long as I can' (to Hobhouse, 21 May, 1816; Hobhouse, II; App. H, 365).

After Byron's departure she for some reason allowed Lady Byron to dominate her. Either she was genuinely afraid of the incest-scandal; or, being fearful lest his wife would openly charge her loved 'baby Byron' with either the marriage-secret or homosexuality, she was deliberately playing up to her suspicions of the lesser evil, incest, by fencing with letters of an unnatural obscurity, which continually appear to deflect the charge, or innuendoes, of incest into questions of loyalty, in order to keep this powerful woman at bay. She had never herself seen the *Memoirs*, but when told by Hobhouse—and probably by Lady Byron too—that their references to homosexuality and perhaps also to the marriage-secret would do harm to all concerned, including Byron's posthumous reputation, she gave her assent to their destruction, being the more willing to do so since Hobhouse, rather unfairly—since no one could contradict him—and probably inaccurately, insisted that Byron had regretted them (Augusta's Statement, p. 106 above). It is significant that after Byron's death her fear of Lady Byron appears to have subsided; the friendship was ruptured and Augusta 'used to proclaim that nothing could justify Lady Byron in abandoning her husband' (Lovelace, I, 29). The sharp and angry tone of the letters written by her to Lady Byron from 15 January to 24 February, 1830 (Jeaffreson, App. II, 488–91) contrast vividly with her earlier obsequious and obscure effusions. At Reigate in 1851 (p. 112) she had nothing to say, beyond again defending herself against some form of disloyalty to Lady Byron, who had loved her passionately before turning against her. To this strange passion we shall return (p. 276).

And what of Byron himself? How far have we explained his extraordinary behaviour?

From childhood the key to his character is 'affection' (pp. 4, 282–3); and this was, again and again, thwarted. He grew up with a tendency to passionate friendships, for which he was reproved (pp. 5, 30). His first public collection of poems, *Hours of Idleness*, which concentrated mainly on his friendships and the, to him, closely related themes of virtue, honour and nobility, were publicly scorned. As he told Lady Blessington, his work might have been one 'unbroken blaze of light' (Blessington, 304), by which he meant as much ethical fervour as poetic glamour, had he not been embittered by opposition; the point being, though it is not, naturally, stated, that all his finest poetical and moral aspirations were rooted in an instinct regarded by society as anathema. He may have been introduced to physical vice by Lord Grey de Ruthyn; but on the other side were many virtues. Throughout his life, the pattern recurs: an idealized and passionate love of youth, both sexual and maternal, accompanied by instincts of protection and education, and widening out to human service in general, support of the oppressed, and liberation of young nations.

His loves for Edleston and Nicolo are primary examples; and it may be that the affair with Nicolo went, as *Don Leon* asserts, to the limit. In the Levant he found a moral atmosphere more congenial than England, and that may, as *Don Leon* states, have been why he went there.

He was henceforward tugged apart by his more passionate instincts on the one side and his respect for society on the other. He felt himself an 'Ishmael', or a 'fallen spirit' (pp. 209, 45), and yet he could not deny the central instinct. From this torment, he tried various escapes: he 'plunged amidst mankind' (*Manfred*, II, ii, 145), allowing himself to be seduced into various heterosexual entanglements; he compounded with his troubled conscience by deliberately arousing suspicions of such lesser evils as murder (p. 41) and incest; he wrote poetry pre-eminently to escape from himself (Journal, 27 Nov., and 6 Dec.; Miss Milbanke, 10 Nov.; 1813; LJ, II, 351, 369; III, 405), choosing tales of piracy and incest; he expanded his tormenting instincts into social and national aspirations; and from time to time thought of returning to the Levant.

The two *positive* values in his story are: (i) romantic friendship, with its accompaniment of poetical idealization, protection, education, and in general, responsibility; and (ii) service to men, especially the relief and release of those who had been, as he from youth had felt himself to be, oppressed. These two 'positives' are really the same; where we find one the other is not far off.

The *negatives* are found in his general sense of guilt, caused by his, in Lady Byron's words, 'solitary secret' (p. 209), which may have been increased by the Lord Grey de Ruthyn incident and his recollections of the Levant; and also by his horror of heterosexual engagements after, as so often happened, they had gone wrong and he felt his soul being violated by feminine pursuit.

These points remembered, and if in addition we never forget that Byron was both a man of moral fervour and a humorist, much of the mystification with which he and others have clouded his personality will be found to dissolve. We have what Pope would have called his 'ruling passion', and the rest immediately assumes coherence. We can now place his recurring horror at the lack of moral charity in the religious thought of his time, together with his *will* towards repudiation of the doctrines of Hell and Damnation. In these doctrines his *mind* half believed; but from his *soul* he denounced them (CV, II, 96).

In marrying a woman of a bisexual temperament like himself he probably knew what he was doing, and it might have succeeded, as it succeeded with the Brownings. But it did not. Many troubles, including financial difficulties and ill health on both sides, were against it; and so, still more, was Byron's almost terrifying concern with international affairs. June of 1815 saw Napoleon's final downfall followed by the re-instatement of Louis XVIII; and to understand Byron we must recognize that these great events were to him personal matters, closely related to his central instincts. At this period those central instincts were, it seems, aroused, perhaps through his association with Drury Lane, or with Colman; and, though how and why we do not know, nor whether this was the first time that it had happened, they even, it would appear, invaded the marriage-bed.

How much Byron told Hobhouse cannot be known. It seems that everyone, including Byron, agreed to make the most of his bad moods and erratic behaviour; but even had he told Hobhouse more, we can be sure that it would not have been recorded. Byron himself could never speak out boldly since the honour of a lady was at stake, but he was ready to go to court ('I never shrank'; p. 135), if need be. If she were willing to speak, well and good; but if not, why go to the lawyers? Nor could Byron be certain that this *was* the cause, since on this issue there had at first been, so far as one can see, a perfect understanding between them, while his wife would not now charge him, even in private, fearing, presumably, that he might answer in public. The *impasse* was absolute; and we must beware of assuming that we know exactly what had happened, and who was to blame. There are possible reasons on grounds of frigidity; and we know that Byron wanted children, even if Lady Byron, as we have some reason to suppose (p. 276 below), was less interested. We have already (p. 192) seen that the bridal night passage in *Leon to Annabella* may contain a hint to this effect, and it certainly tells us that reluctant brides in ancient times preferred to start that way (311–16). Perhaps it started that way with the Byrons. The first issue of *The John Bull Magazine and Literary Reviewer* (July, 1824; Vol. I, 19–21) printed what purported to be the gist of a section of Byron's destroyed *Memoirs* which describes the breaking down of his wife's coldness into loving warmth on the bridal night; and the author of the *Vindication of Lady Byron* observes that *Blackwood's*, of which John Wilson, who, he says, had read the *Memoirs*, was part editor, rebuked the writer, while allowing the piece to be a genuine report (*Vindication*, II, 99; the reference is to a poem addressed to the editor of *John Bull* by 'Timothy Tickler'; *Blackwood's*, July, 1824; Vol. 16, 115–16).[1] There is a poem, which is listed in *Registrum Librorum Eroticorum* (compiled by Rolf S. Reade; London, 1936) and supposed to be by Byron, called *The Bride's Confession, or The Bridal Night*, which purports to be a letter from a bride to her friend Bella. The

---

[1] The contents of the article are repeated in a section purporting to reproduce Byron's *Memoirs* in *The Life, Writings, Opinions and Times of the Rt. Hon. George Gordon Noel Byron* by 'an English Gentleman in the Greek Military Service and Comrade of his Lordship'; London, 3 vols., 1825. The relevant passage occurs at II, 278–84.

poem is obviously spurious and contains nothing relevant, but it certainly seems that the *bridal night* may have held some peculiar importance in our story. The *Memoirs* had been widely, if privately, read. Though Moore signed a document directly after they had been burned stating that 'to the best of his belief' no copies had been made (Hobhouse, III, App. I, 342), this was obviously done as a necessary step towards invalidating any future publications; and it seems clear both from his own diary and a statement in *Blackwood's* that copies could be and had been freely taken by those to whom they were shown (Moore's *Memoirs, etc.*, 24 Nov., 1819; III, 80; *Blackwood's*, June, 1824; Vol. 15; 709). Our 'bridal night' pieces may accordingly be giving us a hint as to the meaning of Wilson's statement (p. 231) that, were '*all* the truth' revealed, it would be a good thing for Byron's 'sake', and the result either a 'mitigated sentence' or 'eternal silence'.

As it is we do *not* know 'all the truth'. Had it been simply a coarse but ineffectual 'attempt' on Byron's part, as we are sometimes asked to believe, we may be sure that Lady Byron and her advisers would never have acted as they did. There was far more in it than that; and in view of the secretive way in which the nameless charge was first made, the refusal to allow Byron any chance of answering it during his life, the criminal burning of his defence, the *Memoirs*—that 'precious life-blood of a master-spirit'—after his death; together with Lady Byron's record of blackmail, suppression, and falsification —the verdict of posterity cannot, as things stand, remain in question.

Byron probably thought that most of the hostility towards him, perhaps even that of the Noels and Lady Byron, was really based on other, probably political, considerations and that the marriage-secret was being used as an unjust (*Childe Harold*, IV, 133) weapon.

After his rejection, he was in the torment of unrest written into *Childe Harold* (III, 42–3) and *Manfred*. At Venice he enjoyed a normal relationship with Marianna Segati, but there was worse. Once again, and this time more reprehensibly, he 'plunged amidst mankind' (*Manfred*, II, ii, 145). He had married, it seems, in order to save himself from this, but, despite all the efforts of his friends, the uncompromising severity of the adverse party had now, in effect, condemned him to the worst. His conscience was, however, always awake, calling 'life' a 'false nature', deeply aware of the 'uneradicable taint of sin' in man (*Childe Harold*, IV, 126), and seeing Venice as a 'sea-Sodom' (p. 213). Soon after, he swerved back to the alternative of national liberation with the Italian Carbonari. The period of dissipation was no pleasure, nor indeed undertaken as such (pp. 213-15). It was probably undertaken rather as A. C. Bradley read Macbeth's engagement in murder; that is, as 'an appalling duty'.

As for the Separation, he continued to resent it. On the main issue —if indeed it was the main issue, and he was never sure—he could not, in honour, speak out. But he must have told Shelley of it (p. 223), and perhaps Medwin, though the printed text of Medwin's book does not actually report it. It must be remembered that all our source-books come down to us heavily bowdlerized: Medwin's is full of asterisks (p. 214).

With Teresa Guiccioli Byron was for some years happy. The exact nature of the relationship is uncertain, and we cannot even be sure that Teresa was guilty of anything beyond exaggeration when in later life she pretended that it was purely Platonic (Origo, x, 415-16). Her claim may be untrue, but it is probably less so than has been supposed. This may sound fantastic; but Byron's story is fantastic.

It also shows artistic form, with a good conclusion. For in Greece at last the two *positive powers* of Byron's life were together, with Loukas at his side, and death in the perfect cause, that of Greece, the land which understood him, and which he and Wilde alone of the more famous figures in English literature have visited.[1] And here, for the first time, he leaves us, in those last three poignant poems (pp. 217-20), direct statements of his life-long torment, though now the only conflict left is that between the two positive powers covered by Loukas and Greece.

What, we may ask, will be the effect of our investigations on Byronic biography? The answer is simple. We shall be reduced to charging Byron with one, and really only one, failing: homosexuality, together with its extension into the marriage-relationship, which was in Campbell's view perhaps the only real error of his life (p. 228). For the rest, we shall be left free to enjoy that amazing record of magnanimous acts and superlative endeavour unworthily summarized in Lord Byron: Christian Virtues. It is reasonably certain that every page of that study will, within the compass of another century, appear so obvious as scarcely to merit the setting down.

With this will come a proper appreciation of Byron as a moralist, and an understanding of his admiration for Pope (*Laureate of Peace*,

[1] This interesting fact was brought to my attention by Mr. F. Kinchin Smith.

iv). But the morality he aimed at was, whether he knew it or not, one using, and not denying, his instincts; and that is why he so exactly responded to Pope whose poetry was directed less at precept than by the aim to 'set the passions on the side of truth' (*Imitations of Horace*, To Augustus, II, i, 218). It is therefore appropriate that Byron's own justification in the *Don Leon* poems should have been written in couplets recalling Pope's. Nor is this merely a lucky chance, for the poise and perfection of Pope and Colman at their best were needed to sound the note to which Byron's life—for it was his destiny to *live* what others *wrote*—was aspiring. Nor is it a matter of chance that the remarkable *expertise* in the use of the couplet throughout the *Don Leon* poems should have accompanied the outspoken treatment of an instinct lying so near the heart of poetic composition.

II

Byron's best virtue was inclusive. We cannot write off the homosexual impulse as no more than an unfortunate blot, since his greatest accomplishments flower from it. This Moore, perhaps the only biographer, except for Teresa, to do intellectual justice to his stature, saw clearly. True, he could write depreciatingly of Byron's lapses, as a concession to convention. But he also tells us:

'It is invariably to be borne in mind that his very defects were among the elements of his greatness, and that it was out of the struggle between the good and evil principles of his nature that his mighty genius drew its strength.'

(Moore, XIII, 149)

Since his 'defects' were 'among the sources of his greatness', to require of him 'the one without the other' would be unreasonable; since 'an impetuous temperament, and passions untamed' were 'indispensable to the conformation' of such a poet (Moore, XXV; 298). Moore is, of course, silent as to the real nature of these passions, and he underrates the extent to which Byron battled with them; but his remarks are sound pointers.

We are accordingly faced by a man of genius whose great qualities appear to be based on what society regards as a criminal instinct. Are there, we may ask, any analogies to such a phenomenon?

The answer is, of course, that analogies abound. I have elsewhere

CONCLUSIONS

discussed at some length the sexual peculiarities of genius (*Christ and Nietzsche*, IV; *The Mutual Flame*, II), and have already (pp. 11, 38) shown how closely the Byronic and Shakespearian patterns correspond.

In such men the female elements of the psyche are strongly developed. Sometimes this may, probably most in youth, look like effeminacy, as when we find Mary Russell Mitford, in a letter of 22 February, 1847, to Charles Boner, recalling 'how exactly' Browning resembled 'a girl dressed in boy's clothes', and continuing: 'I met him once as I told you when he had long ringlets and no neckcloth—and when he seemed to me about the height and size of a boy of twelve years old—Femmelette is a word made for him. A strange sort of person to carry such a woman as Elizabeth Barrett off her feet' (*Elizabeth Barrett to Miss Mitford*, London, 1954; Int., xiii). And yet not so strange, really, since femininity is in such instances no sign of weakness, and may well develop into a frightening spiritual power. After all, Milton was known in youth as 'the lady of Christ's'; and Byron was not only regularly regarded by his friends as an half-feminine type, but has left us as his two last heroes Sardanapalus and Don Juan, both in part feminine, and the latter at one point given the disguise of a girl (CV, II, 81; *Don Juan*, V, 73–80).

The term 'bisexual' is confusing. It may signify either simply a person of homosexual instincts or one whose sexual instincts are at home with either sex. But without distinguishing too exactly, we can observe both bisexual and homosexual qualities in the lives and works of genius. Ancient literature, as *Don Leon* reminds us, is full of them. In English we find Shakespeare, Marlowe, Gray, Shelley (*The Mutual Flame*, V, 211–14), Tennyson, Wilde, Housman and Lawrence, directly or indirectly implicated; and probably Marvell, in *The Definition of Love*, and Browning in *Saul*. Marvell and Milton were once accused (*Andrew Marvell*, Bradbrook and Thomas; I, 19). Both Ruskin and Swinburne were sexually abnormal. The greatest American poet, Walt Whitman, was a striking example of homosexuality, and Herman Melville shows many of the symptoms. Sometimes the thought of bisexuality is explicit. The loved person may be imagined as bisexual, as pre-eminently in Shelley's *Fragments Connected with Epipsychidion* (*The Starlit Dome*, III, 242; *The Mutual Flame*, V, 213–15); or when *Don Leon* describes the appearance of Nicolo Giraud as raising 'pleasing doubts' as to his 'gender' (567–70); or Tennyson, whose *In Memoriam* disturbed his contemporaries,

256

praises Hallam as one in whom he found 'manhood fused with female grace' (*In Memoriam*, CIX); and both Byron and Eliot use the bisexual figure of Tiresias as a symbol of a comprehensive human understanding (*Don Juan*, XIV, 73; *The Waste Land*, notes).

Men of poetic genius are often unhappy, as Moore (XXIII, 267–71) argues at length, with especial emphasis on Dante, in their marriages; they may show a strong anti-feminine bias, as do Shakespeare, in his 'Dark Lady' Sonnets, Milton, Swift, Strindberg, and others; but also, being in part feminine themselves, they can create exquisite women, and especially love-poetry from the woman's view, as do Shakespeare with his many heroines, and Pope in *Eloisa to Abelard*. An all but excessive male idealization is the key to D. H. Lawrence's novels; and within the far greater range of John Cowper Powys' comprehensive understanding, it is nevertheless interesting to observe how powerfully the feminine element asserts itself. Powys deliberately insists on his own, as well as Shakespeare's and Dostoievsky's, experience of *becoming a woman*; and in his work offers an insight into the nature of feminine love of a precision perhaps hitherto unequalled (*Autobiography*, X, 528; *A Glastonbury Romance*, 'Consummation'; I, XI).

On 8 November 1842 Elizabeth Barrett reported to Miss Mitford an interesting remark of Coleridge:

'He said that Coleridge said that every great man he ever knew had something of the woman in him, with one exception: and the exception was Wordsworth. Now, mind! The observation was intended as no reproach to great men generally, but praise—and the subject defined had no relation to *effeminacy* (strictly speaking) but to softness, tenderness!'

(*Elizabeth Barrett to Miss Mitford*, London, 1954; 141)

Wordsworth did, indeed, once as good as admit the lack, claiming that his sister served to fill it for him. But his theoretical emphasis on the importance of the feminine element in the process of integration is as strong as anyone's (*The Prelude*, XIV, 206–75).

We are being pointed towards an integration or wholeness beyond normality; towards an androgynous state. Though themselves often appearing as neurotics and misfits, these men of genius are in reality enjoying, or suffering from, an abnormally full and rich consciousness which inevitably involves them in contradictions to which their fellows are blind. For example, we find the typical pillar of society, statesman, bishop or judge, striking by day a figure of convention-alized dignity, but by night allowing a very different man who, if publicly expressed, might ruin his professional status, to take control. This we agree to forget, civilization having worked out a com-promise fitting man's divided nature. But some people cannot do this. They insist on full consciousness and a free interplay, bringing, as Moore tells us (*Moore*, XXIII, 268), their ideals into marriage, and even, perhaps—and how D. H. Lawrence worried about it—into the most secret intimacies of nocturnal passion, while simultaneously shocking their community, as Byron shocked his in *Don Juan*, with Rabelaisian reminders by day. We shall, of course, relate the nocturnal and daylight modes to the female and male principles, Nietzsche's Dionysian and Apollonian.

This adventurous honesty may lead to the queerest extravagances, and to gross behaviour too, by day or by night, working under a compulsion not easy to explain. Byron's own honesty is well expressed in his comment on the extraordinary compound of 'dirt and deity' in Burns' letters which, he says, is nevertheless not just licentiousness: 'It seems strange; a true voluptuary will never abandon his mind to the grossness of reality. It is by exalting the earthly, the material, the *physique* of our pleasures, by veiling these ideas, by forgetting them altogether, or, at least, never naming them hardly to one's self, that we alone can prevent them from disgusting' (Journal, 13 Dec., 1813; LJ, II, 377). Byron knew both directions; both the will to idealize, and the compulsion to face, and this remark witnesses his full consciousness of it all. If such as he appear confused, that is only because they refuse to veil those confusions basic to human nature which they are themselves trying to surmount.

Whether this is worth the labour may be questioned. Hugh Ross Williamson observes that the safeguarding of such abnormal pro-pensities as we are discussing is necessary if human life is to exploit itself on any plane beyond the biological (*The Arrow and the Sword*, v, 81). In practice such men have little choice. And they have their reward. If it be all a disease, it is at least a disease which proves more vital than health, leading to works and reputations which survive beyond death. Indeed, death and eternity inevitably come into the picture, as may be seen from the regular tendency, descending from the ancients, to write elegies on male themes. Shakespeare's sonnets are tragically toned; and we have *Lycidas*, Gray's *Elegy*, *Adonais*, *In Memoriam*, Arnold's *Thyrsis*, *A Shropshire*

Lad; with, in Byron's story, the *Thyrza* poems. The value glimpsed is somehow inbound with death; possibly the attraction of young male forms blending strength with grace is really, as Plato tells us, a shadowing, an earthly reflection, of eternal types; or, shall we say, of 'seraph-forms' (*The Mutual Flame*, v, 210–20); and indeed the Fair Youth of the Sonnets was Shakespeare's 'better angel' (Sonnet 144), angels were regularly pictured by him as young men (*The Wheel of Fire*, 1948; App. B), Edleston was to Byron as 'a dream of Heaven', (p. 35), and he called Nicolo and the other boys at Athens 'sylphs' (Hobhouse, 23 Aug., 1810; C, 1, 14).

We need not therefore be surprised to find Dante noting the many 'great scholars and of great renown' (*Inferno*, xv, 106) in Hell who have been guilty of homosexual tendencies; nor by the emphasis in *Don Leon* on figures of ecclesiastical and academic distinction. After all, many important elements in the religious and educational traditions of the West can trace their origin to Plato, for whom this esoteric love was, at its best, the central pathway to the heights. Indeed, we all but reach the conclusion that sexual abnormality is a normal characteristic of human greatness, and the first source of wisdom.

Both homosexuality and incest may be symptoms of a state which approaches self-sufficiency and integration, and so looks for affection less to an opposite than to a replica, as when Byron in *The Adieu* says of Edleston 'our souls were equal'; or Shakespeare writes of 'one respect' in Sonnet 36; or Marvell speaks of two souls running *parallel* in *The Definition of Love*. That is why incest, though it probably occurs rarely in life, is, as Shelley once said, though his reasons were superficial, 'like many other incorrect things, a very poetical circumstance' (to Mrs. Gisborne, 16 Nov., 1819; quoted P, IV, 100, note); 'circumstance' being a vile phrase inexactly but continually used in Shelley's period in such circumstances. Both Wordsworth and Shelley have been accused of incestuous tendencies. Poetical, or any other artistic, labour is, by its very nature, incestuous, growing from an inward coition, a union of faculties within the personality, as in the meditations of Shakespeare's Richard (*Richard II*; v, v, 1–11: see *The Mutual Flame*, vi, 138). Themes of incest are handled in Ford's *'Tis Pity She's a Whore*, Dryden's *Don Sebastian*, Shelley's *The Cenci* and *The Revolt of Islam*, Byron's *The Bride of Abydos, Parisina* and perhaps *Manfred*, and in the drama of ancient Greece. It appears in ancient mythology, Jupiter being Juno's sister, and was the rule among the royal houses of the Pharoahs of Egypt and the Incas of Peru. Such 'familial' love may be related to a fear of mixing with lower castes, or beings, not unlike that of Byron's Manfred when he feels himself 'degraded back' to the level of normal humanity and talks of again becoming 'clay' (*Manfred*, II, ii, 78). Incest is not our main theme; but it is interesting to find Byron, like Wordsworth and Herman Melville, enjoying emotional sustenance from a sister's love. He has been accused of incest; and whether it happened or not, the suspicion contributes to our pattern, since it was Byron's unenviable destiny to live what others write.

Despite his efforts Byron could never disguise himself; or, if he did, the disguise was no less vivid than the reality. Oscar Wilde's claim to have put merely his talent into his 'work', but his 'genius' into his 'life', may be applied with equal truth to Byron, though what Byron had to offer in both was immeasurably the greater.

The name of Oscar Wilde, is, of course, likely to arouse a sense of un-ease, if not of revulsion; [1] and many who would admit the high value of homosexual instincts in their expanded or sublimated form, or even, if kept within bounds, within a personal relationship, will nevertheless react in, as *Don Leon* has it—though the word was less strong in his day than in ours—'disgust' (*Don Leon*, 1346), at thought of the extreme of vice. But, while we may well repudiate such vice on moral grounds, it seems to have had so strange a hold over certain otherwise enlightened personalities that it should at least be susceptible to a metaphysical, or mystical, interpretation. Though both Colman and Shelley (in *Fragments Connected with Epipsychidion*, 29–37; see *The Mutual Flame*, V, 212) emphasize its natural origin, all perversion appears, on the plane of biology, to be meaningless, and from the view of propagation dangerous; but can it hold significance on any other plane? [2]

The 'disgust' is mainly aroused by thoughts of excretion. We may, however, recall that certain saints were at great pains to assimilate without disgust what is biologically repulsive; and we must never forget that from a non-human, non-biological, view the repulsion

---

[1] It is a pleasure in this connection to draw attention to Mr. John Furnell's sensitive dramatic handling of Wilde's story in *The Stringed Lute* (1955).

[2] The distinction is important. Moral judgment is not here my purpose; nor do I regard myself as competent in that field. But it may be observed that probably as good an indictment as one could wish from the moral standpoint, written, as such an indictment to be effective must be, from personal experience, was lost to us when Byron's *Memoirs* were burned by the guardians of convention. See pp. 214–15 above.

would not exist; nor does it when any high or engrossing purpose, such as a doctor's, takes control. We may suggest that all physical love is, in its way, a victory over physical secrecies and physical repulsions, and that this victory is constituent to the ecstasy and the value; and if so, the form we are discussing pushes it to the limit.

The forbidden area and its forbidding functionings are regularly accepted in broad comedy: you find examples in Aristophanes, Chaucer, Rabelais and Shakespeare. Swift was simultaneously fascinated and repelled; Sterne has his contribution (see *Don Leon*, Note 64 to line 993); Colman is a specialist, and drives home the relevant thoughts more firmly than any predecessor; and James Joyce dares the fortress. But why, we must ask, should such fine minds as these dally with such indecencies at all?

What is biologically rejected, or excreted, is a poison, and so a form of death; and there may be some *kathartic* process at work, not unlike that of tragedy. As for the great sin, it is not only a mingling of life with life, but a mingling of life with death. It is a marriage of life and death, of good and evil, and so makes, in sharp physical terms, a concentration of tragedy; it is a tragic act. Such loves, with or without the sin, may be variously spiritual, tragic or transcendental. In one form or the other, transcendental categories continually invade our discussion.

The problem is obscure, and goes very far beyond my own understanding. At such an *impasse*, only the most profound sources of wisdom can serve our turn, and I accordingly fall back on some relevant, if difficult, words of John Cowper Powys, surely the greatest literary seer of our time. He is writing in the foreword to the new edition of *A Glastonbury Romance:*

'The Grail has its counterpart in the mythology of Greece and in the oldest heathen legends of Wales and Ireland. There are intimate correspondences between it and the traditions that reach us from both the extreme East and the extreme West. It changes its shape. It changes its contents. It changes its aura. It changes its atmosphere. But its essential nature remains unchanged; and even that nature is only the nature of a symbol. It refers us to things beyond itself and to things beyond words. Only those who have caught the secret which Rabelais more than anyone else reveals to us, the secret of the conjunction of the particular and extreme grossness of our excremental functions in connection with our sexual functions, are on the right track to encompass this receding horizon where the beyond-thought loses itself in the beyond-words.'

(Preface, xv)

This is followed by a reference to 'that incongruous and disgustingly humorous intermingling of the excremental with the sacramental of which Rabelais makes so much' (xvi): other relevant thoughts are found in the concluding sections of Mr. Powys' *Rabelais*.

This balance is also struck in the Chapter named 'The Grail' of the main story of *A Glastonbury Romance*. At a high point in the narrative Sam's devoted and saintly life is crowned by a vision of the Holy Grail accompanied by the inrush of the transcendental felt agonisedly as a penetration of his guts from below by a 'gigantic spear' (xxvIII, 938–9). Pursuing his saintly course Sam next ministers to an old man suffering from constipation and piles:

'Sam was not, it must be confessed, a born nurse; but he was a born naturalist and an unfastidious countryman. As he struggled with his task, bending over the old gentleman's rear, the tension of his spirit brought back with a rush the miraculous power of the vision he had seen. The two extremes of his experience, the anus of an aged man and the wavering shaft of an Absolute, piercing his own earthly body, mingled and fused together in his consciousness. Holy Sam felt, as he went on with the business, a strange second sight, an inkling, as to some incredible secret, whereby the whole massed weight of the world's tormented flesh was labouring towards some release.'

(xxvIII, 948)

The reality of the experience is next driven powerfully home for us, the narrative preserving a careful balance of revulsion and revelation.

Whatever this obscure truth beyond words and thought may be, it is clearly germane to our discussion. The great passage of obscene punning at the conclusion of *Don Leon* contains a neat association, involving death:

> Look through the world! whatever mortals do,
> They still must keep their latter end in view—
> Not death; for that let bloated parsons quail:
> Our latter end—what is it, but our tail? [1]

(Don Leon, 1445)

[1] For the more generalized meanings of 'tail', which are today almost forgotten see the *New English Dictionary*.

CONCLUSIONS

As for the morality of it, the disconcerting closeness of the extremes is neatly hit off by a vivid couplet:

> *Or feared the scald of that infectious taint*
> *Which makes a man or sodomite or saint.*

(Don Leon, 872)

The two are recognized as very close. This is not, of course, the same as identifying them.

But, quite apart from vicious actions, and indeed these may not be our real, our main, social problem at all, since comparatively few will be tempted to the worst, and it is the essence rather than any external expressions which is important, we must see that those who endure such emotional directions as we are reviewing are in no easy case. They may attain some degree of integration, and have intimations of eternity. But they cannot be isolated from nature and the community; they still remain part of the biological order, with physical instincts awake, and social and political responsibilities. More than sexual activity is involved; the whole life may feel itself 'out of joint'. They have become conduits down which rushes power from other, and higher, dimensions (*The Mutual Flame*, quoting Wyndham Lewis' shamans and John Cowper Powys' druids; II, 30); and this power has next to be related, expressed, adjusted on the horizontal plane. The task may be almost beyond the frail human animal who has, for no fault of his own, been placed in such a position. This was Byron's lot in the years 1815–1816.

III

We have seen how Byron's life reveals the dual positive impulses of (i) homosexual passion and (ii) human service. It seems that at this period both appeared in extreme, and dangerous, forms. We have reason to suppose that the sexual sin was committed, and there may have been other, related, practices. But the main cause of Byron's unrest appears to have been national, or inter-national.

His 1813–1814 Journal shows how deeply he was involved in the drama of Napoleon; and so does his *Ode to Napoleon*. These bitter passages I have discussed elsewhere (CV, III, 153–60; V, 236–40; DP, 24–7). Now in June 1815, the month of Waterloo, Napoleon had finally fallen. But, though he felt for Napoleon, who since his school-days had been a *personal romance* to him, as a disillusioned lover (CV,

III, 159), there was more involved, for he had for some years been feeling himself a potential leader of Napoleonic stature, who was yet reluctant to make any move, since he would be '*aut Caesar aut nihil*', 'either Caesar or nothing'; whose epitaph was to be 'He might, perhaps, if he would'; and who heard a Shakespearian voice murmuring, 'Brutus, thou sleep'st' (Journal, 23 Nov., 'Tuesday', 1813, and 18 Feb., 1814; LJ, II, 339, 340, 384). But now, in 1815, Napoleon had left the stage. Was Byron himself to enter it? Others, as well as himself, recognized his similarity to Napoleon; he had the same personal magnetism, the same ranging political vision; the comparison was usual enough (CV, V, 238). But it was Napoleon the liberator he admired, deploring the despot. His own assertions were all soft, loving, Promethean rather than Napoleonic. This made it so much the more complicated, and, after all, he was, surely, but an 'insect' in comparison (Journal, 9 April, 1814; LJ, II, 409). What was he to do? It is perhaps significant that it is only after the battle of Waterloo that we find any real evidence of Byron's chafing against his marriage.

Byron's thoughts on Napoleon had always been bold, and after Waterloo he continued to support the revolutionary elements in France. During the separation proceedings poems of his, thinly veiled as 'from the French', were printed in certain sections of the London press (P, III, 427–38). Napoleon the liberator he had always applauded; Napoleon the despot he condemned; but the newly reinstated Bourbon dynasty he detested. On 15 March, 1816, *The Morning Chronicle* published his *Ode from the French*. This is the poem to which, after an off-hand comment on Colman's Caleb Quotem in *The Review or The Wags of Windsor*, Byron refers as 'my Ode on Waterloo' in his letter to Murray of 24 April, 1820 (LJ, V, 19), noting that it was written in 1815, and had since proved prophetic. In it freedom's safety is said to depend not on the success or failure of a Napoleon,

> But in equal rights and laws,
> Hearts and hands in one great cause—
> Freedom, such as God hath given
> Unto all beneath his heaven
> With their breath, and from their birth,
> Though guilt would sweep it from the earth
> With a fierce and lavish hand
> Scattering nations' wealth like sand,

Pouring nations' blood like water,
In imperial seas of slaughter!

(P, III, 434)

Another poem, also 'from the French', called *On the Star of the Legion of Honour*, was printed in *The Examiner* of 7 April, 1816. In it the Tricolor receives a fine poetic encomium:

One tint was of the sunbeam's dyes;
One, the blue depth of Seraph's eyes;
One, the pure Spirit's veil of white
Had robed in radiance of its light:
The three so mingled did beseem
The texture of a heavenly dream.

(P, III, 437)

These colours are blended 'like tints in an immortal gem', a phrase recalling the description of Edleston's Cornelian Heart as a 'sacred gem' in *The Adieu* (P, I, 240). Love of *that* kind was indeed very close to political freedom in Byron's poetic thought, and the 'seraph's eyes' and 'heavenly dream' of the Tricolor is not far from the 'hope in Heaven' and 'dream of Heaven' in the *Thyrza* poetry (pp. 31, 35). The wave-length, so to speak, is the same.

Such political, or inter-national, principles were enough to make Byron, whose authorship was generally recognized, unpopular. More, he was feared. He had even, perhaps, been meditating action of some kind, such as he had at one time thought of in Holland (Journal, 23 Nov., 'Tuesday', 1813; LJ, II, 340) and later took up in Italy and Greece. Just before his engagement he had been thinking of going on the Continent, and had suggested that Hobhouse accompany him (Hobhouse, II; xv, 193). On 25 November 1815 Hobhouse records in his diary that Byron gave him strong advice against marriage and was 'talking of going abroad' (Hobhouse, I; VII, 324). In his discussion of Byron's failings as a husband Hobhouse admits that Byron had continued to think of such a visit, or of living alone in London, and adds that 'he had mentioned other schemes, which those who knew him would never have reflected upon for a moment, but which had a painful effect upon her Ladyship' (Hobhouse, II; xv, 282). It seems that Hobhouse was to go too. He and Byron had been thinking of going abroad together (Jeaffreson, xv, 191).

What were these 'schemes' which Hobhouse prefers not to explain? Byron may have had some plan of going to France with Hobhouse, a man of strong radical sympathies, who had been in the habit of stimulating Byron's admiration for Napoleon (Journal, 18 Feb., 1814; LJ, II, 383-4), and had only recently returned from France, where he had been staying to observe events after Napoleon's return from Elba (see his own relevant entries; Hobhouse, I; VII, 208-318). After Waterloo he came back to England, and on 31 July records that Byron 'confesses he sometimes thinks that nothing is left for it but suicide' (Hobhouse, I; VII, 322; for the reference to Whitbread's death, and the political implications of Byron's words, see Hobhouse, I; VII, 310). Whatever was in the air, it certainly worried Lady Byron. Some time during the latter half of 1815 she had written to Augusta: 'Hobhouse is come—I have great reason to think to encourage a plan for going abroad' (*Quarterly*, Jan., 1870; Vol. 128; *225*). The day of her arrival at Kirkby Mallory, on 16 January 1816, she wrote to Augusta saying that her mother

'has relieved my mind about the foreign scheme by a mode of prevention that appears likely to be effectual against any practices of H's, viz. that if requisite my father and Captain B. should wait upon him, and state as their joint opinion that it would be a measure most injurious to B., after which H. dare not promote it for his own character's sake.'

(LJ, III, 295)

'Scheme' again. Lord Ernle suggests, uncertainly, that 'H' may stand for 'Hanson', Byron's solicitor; but it sounds much more like Hobhouse. That Byron had some 'foreign scheme' in view is evident. Possibly he had been invited by some revolutionary elements in France to come over and join them, lending them, as he later lent Greece, the lustre of his name. There is another suggestive remark in Lady Byron's letter to Augusta of 28 January, 1816: 'The Paris scheme was *very near* executed in the Summer' (LJ, III, 302). Here indeed we may have a hint as to the nature of Byron's first disagreements with his wife and Augusta (p. 64). Such phrases do not fit a pleasure-jaunt, nor any normal, personal, adventure. Besides, when Byron thought of going abroad for personal reasons, it was always Italy or the Levant. France, as France, he never liked, nor its literature: what he liked about France was its stand for freedom, and in particular Napoleon as destroyer of tyrannies, before he himself became a despot. Whatever may have been Byron's purpose in planning to visit Paris, it certainly was not to pay court to Louis XVIII: for his views on that monarch and his chief minister, Talleyrand, see his proposed letter to the press, dated 29 July, 1815 (LJ, III, 209, note).

Having gone so far, what, we may ask, was the real significance of that extraordinary Napoleonic carriage costing five hundred pounds (Hobhouse, I, VII, 334; Maurois, II, XXV, 256) in which Byron eventually left London and travelled across the Continent? But not through France. The French Government would not allow him to set foot on French soil (Maurois, II, XXV, 257). Dr. Lushington wrote to Lady Byron on 30 April, 1816, reporting that Lady Holland had said 'that the ladies of Paris would have received him with open arms had he been allowed to go there' (Lovelace, II, 52). Two months later Hobhouse was also unable to obtain a French passport 'in consequence of his book about the Hundred Days' (Lovelace, II, 52, note; an account of the book is given at Hobhouse I; VII, 319–21; and see Joyce, VII, 91–4).

All this was going on during the Separation, and in Byron's mind it was probably far more important; and probably in others' minds too, though the Separation was a very convenient implement. After Byron had left England there was a violent controversy, carried on on party lines (P, III, 535), John Scott of the Tory *Champion* deliberately coupling Byron's poems 'From the French' with an obvious reference to the *Don Leon* marriage-secret, thereby neatly aligning for his purpose Byron's morals with his politics (P, III, 532–3). Indeed, the whole Separation played so perfectly into the hands of Byron's political enemies that we have good reason to agree with Mr. Perry of *The Morning Chronicle* that 'there had been a conspiracy against the domestic peace of Lord Byron' (Hobhouse, II; XV, 332). John Scott himself later admitted to Byron 'that he, and others, had been greatly misled, and that some pains, and rather extraordinary means, had been taken to excite them' (LJ, V, App. III, 576; Teresa, II; V, 87). During the crisis an unnamed person called on Byron suggesting that the calumnies would be silenced were he to change his political opinions (Teresa, I; Int., 39–40, and note).

Let us enquire more exactly into the queer state of Byron's mind at this period. Our evidence is meagre, but pregnant. He admitted that his poor state of health had been driving him 'into excess' (Moore, 8 March, 1816; LJ, III, 273). 'His mind', wrote Augusta to

Hobhouse on 3 January, 1816, 'makes him the most unhappy of human beings' (Hobhouse, II; App. B, 359). Lady Byron once referred to the trouble as being at its worst after he came home and was alone in his room (p. 55). According to Lovelace he appeared during December and January scarcely responsible for what he said or did.

Was this madness? Not quite. Once Lady Byron defined his state as less a state of deficiency than one of super-abundance: 'I cannot', she wrote to Augusta on 19 January, 1816, 'believe in the loss of memory from the appearances you mention, because they might equally arise, as they often have, from *absorption in deep thought*—and I am sure he is dwelling on *deep* (and perhaps *wild*) projects concerning me' (LJ, III, 297). These words Lord Lovelace may have had in mind when he wrote that Byron was quite capable of making a rash remark, and 'afterwards, being wholly absorbed in his recollections and projects', to forget what he had said (Lovelace, VI, 135). But we may well doubt if Lady Byron was so central as she thought to these 'projects', unless as an obstruction. Both Hobhouse and Byron himself tell us that once, when asked by his wife if she was in his way, he replied, bitterly, that she was; this being the only harsh remark which he recalled ever having made to her (Hobhouse, II; XV, 279; Medwin, 42); and the reference was presumably to the 'projects', which were likely to have been large ones. Byron's state was not madness, though it may have looked like it. Hobhouse tells us that with Byron inspiration regularly appeared to accompany what was, or seemed, ill-health (Hobhouse II; XV, 238-9); and it was Lady Byron's complaint that 'in his best moods he has always wished to be away from me' (to Augusta, 20 Jan., 1816; LJ, III, 298).

Whatever the sexual or homosexual lapses of this period, they were part of a far larger complex, involving public affairs. They may have been merely means of relief from an intolerable pressure leading to what Lady Byron complained of at the time as an 'habitual passion for excitement', such as that which Byron himself once defined in writing of the unrest of genius, in his poetry (Mayne, *Lady Byron*, XIII, 194; *Childe Harold*, III, 42-3). But what of the larger issues? Here some of Lady Byron's first letters after leaving her husband are very helpful, pointing as they do to troubles apparently far outspacing the sexual or the domestic.

Some of these letters may, certainly, refer to sexual matters, and to these we have already referred (pp. 60-3). But more is also involved, with a peculiarly strong emphasis on *power* and *pride*. The first reference appears in her autumn 1815 letter describing Byron's angry mood directed, according to Lady Byron, against both her and Augusta: this we have already (p. 64) noticed. On 19 January, 1816, Lady Byron told Augusta that she regarded 'the *love of power*' as a 'principle feature' of his 'disease or character' (to Augusta, 19 Jan., 1816; LJ, III, 297), and on 25 January she wrote to her:

' "The Thunder" to which you allude would not be so terrible. I it be disease any strong shock will for a time restore reason, though in the end it can make no difference, and as far as a boundless and impious pride may be combined with it, reverses and humiliations would be mercies, indulgence and success more injurious than anything. I have neither forgotten considerations of *justice* or *charity*, and for the latter I have done much since I saw you.'

(LJ, III, 300)

Later on the same day she again wrote to Augusta, saying that she must follow her 'duty', that the Separation would not cause Byron much pain, that she wished to be remembered 'only as a burden', and believed 'feelings' must now be left out of it; she was not bitter, and could say, 'God bless him' (LJ, III, 300–1). But she was now acting as the agent of justice. On 14 February she told Augusta that her 'duty to God' demanded it:

'If Pride be not expiated on earth, but indulged, who may dare to look beyond? The lessons of adversity may be most beneficial when they are most bitter. Not that I would *voluntarily* be the means of chastisement, but I seem to have been made so, and am doomed to participate in the suffering.'

(LJ, III, 311)

She refers to her love for Byron, but cuts in with, 'I must not remember these feelings'. She was now pursuing some duty which *took precedence over a wife's love*. Again, on 15 February:

'Is the present injury to his reputation to be put in competition with the danger of unchecked success to this wicked pride? and may not his actual sufferings . . . expiate a future account?'

(LJ, III, 313)

The emphasis on 'pride' is vivid. So is Lady Byron's deliberate will towards accomplishing Byron's disgrace. She actually *wished*, on principle, to ruin her husband. In so doing, she did not deny his goodness. She was well aware that his mind was 'most benevolent' and of his 'goodness of heart' (pp. 208–9). But she remained firm.

What was the 'boundless and impious pride' (p. 73) in question? Our easiest way to focus it is to turn to *Manfred*, written soon after the Separation, and study the many phrases suggesting that the hero was a greater than his fellows; that he was a Promethean 'enlightener of nations', but refused to be a leader at the price of that time-serving and flattery which is the only way to political power (III, i, 104–7). It is suggested that the protagonist is of a higher *order* than normal humanity: 'I am not of thine order', 'the order which thine own would rise above', 'this man is of no common order', 'there is an order of mortals on the earth' (*Manfred*, II, i, 38; II, ii, 123; II, iv, 51; III, i, 138). The comparison of Napoleon with poetic genius in *Childe Harold* (III, 36–45) may be read as autobiographical; and so may the poem *Prometheus*. But all this has been discussed in my essay 'The New Prometheus' (CV, v).

It is recorded that Byron's mood in 1815–1816 was 'I'll show the world I'm fit for great things' (Lovelace, II, 41, and see Fox, XII, 109). Stendhal, who met him in Italy, records that he both admired and was jealous of Napoleon; that he expressed pleasure in signing his own name 'N.B.' ('Noel Byron'); was 'unceasingly tyrranized by some ruling passion'; and could himself, in certain moods, 'pretend to everything' (LJ, III, App. VII, 439, 444); and the Countess Albrizzi observed that 'his thoughts and feelings' were 'more stupendous and unmeasured than Napoleon's' (LJ, IV. App. II, 442).

We have, naturally enough, little first-hand evidence of the nature of these claims, as little as we have of the psychologically related matter of homosexuality. Byron was unsure of himself; more, he was severely critical of all extravagant ambitions; his natural tendency was to respect tradition and scorn minor prophets. As a revolutionary, he was a revolutionary within the tradition, and accordingly endured a severe conflict. Now we have one really striking hint regarding Byron's Napoleonic instincts and anxieties, given in a bulletin on Byron's mental health sent by Augusta to Lady Byron during January 1816, as reported by Ethel Colburn Mayne:

'He talked of you quite coolly and of his intention of going into a lodging by himself . . . in short looked black and gloomy, nobody could tell why or wherefore, the rest of the night. One of the things he said was ... that he considered himself "the greatest man existing"; G. (George Byron) said laughing, "except Bonaparte". The answer was, "God, I don't know that I do except even him". I was struck previously with a wildness in his eye.'

(Mayne, *Lady Byron*, XIV, 207; Fox, XII, 105)

Byron is reported in no mood of flamboyant exultation, but rather in an agony of knowledge in face of an awe-inspiring truth. Miss Mayne, with exact insight if less than clarity of expression, makes a sound comment regarding the effect Augusta's bulletin must have had on Lady Byron: '*She* knew that Byron was not thinking of his fame, of the poetry that was "not my vocation"; that it was from something "which was in his nature more than in theirs who did not ridicule or deny the Divine" that this belief in his greatness was drawn' (Mayne, *Lady Byron*, XV, 226). Byron was, of course, the last man ever to 'ridicule or deny the Divine'; but too original an expression of it may often appear as a denial. The words are quoted as Lady Byron's, and they mean one thing only: that Byron's self-assertion was levelled against the religious tradition. 'The part of prophet of Antichrist', says Lord Lovelace, 'half in jest, half in earnest, was assumed in his writings'; and we are next told that the spirit of the French Revolution was 'reflected in his formidable laughter and his mystery of lamentation' (Lovelace, VI, 117). That is, anyway, how his contemporaries saw him. They thought that he was threatening to come forward as a Messiah, as Anti-Christ.

This was what everyone had been fearing. For Byron's was a personality of staggering power, and large sections of the community had for long been prepared to seize any opportunity to ruin him. We, today, too readily under-rate the mystery. 'It is only', wrote Augustine Birrell in *William Hazlitt*, 'by reading the lives and letters of his astonished contemporaries and immediate successors that you are able to form some estimate of the power of Byron' (quoted Lovelace, I, 6, note). To Southey his very gentleness reminded him of a tiger softly patting with sheathed talons what had not yet angered it (to Henry Taylor, 3 March, 1830; quoted Lovelace, I, 17). The power of his *eyes*, in beauty of calm or fire of wrath, was noted again and again (CV, v, 278–80). He was generally recognized as a being far outside, probably far above, the normal. To Teresa Guiccioli he was simply 'a man superior to the rest of humanity'

(II; XII, 272); Moore saw him as belonging to 'a class so set apart from the track of ordinary life, so removed, by their very elevation, out of the influence of our common atmosphere', as to be unsuited for matrimony (Moore, XXIII, 270); and the extraordinary range of his genius as man and poet is magnificently handled in one grand chapter at the end of Moore's *Life* (LVII). Of Byron's multitudinous passions Goethe said that 'the like would never come again' (to Crabb Robinson, Aug., 1829; quoted Lovelace, I, 14). The tough 'fire-master' William Parry said that his personality radiated the same sort of power as Napoleon's was said to have done (Parry, II, 24). Lovelace, who tells us (VI, 117) that Byron used to regard himself as a fallen spirit expelled from Heaven, writes: 'It may be that Lord Byron was peculiarly a re-incarnation of cosmic man, similar in this to Napoleon' (Lovelace, I, 3). The term is obscure. I have myself defined Byron as 'Promethean' (CV, v). Whatever our own views, we cannot deny that this is how his contemporaries saw him.

So his 'madness' was not exactly a limitation; it was rather a superabundance. He was enduring that higher, or deeper, madness said to be characteristic of genius in *The Dream*. It was, in its way, an artistic state, rather in the sense in which *Manfred*, though not to be limited by any one strain of autobiographical reference, is nevertheless made of many such strains, fused together (p. 126); and the mind is then too full, or 'absorbed' (p. 268), to attend to details. 'I have no doubt', he told Medwin, with reference to the visit of the lawyer and doctor engaged by his wife to test his sanity, 'that my answers to these emissaries' interrogations was not very rational or consistent, for my imagination was heated by other things' (Medwin, 44). But he could always attend exactly to any details which really demanded his attention. There seems to be no evidence at this time of his ever having really lost control of himself. Though a seething workshop of energies and purposes, he rode them as a liner rides a storm. So, whilst the bailiffs were in his house, his wife worrying about his laudanum bottle and pistols, and his best friends fearing his suicide; during the weeks of near-insanity and bitter torment, whilst all London, press and public, were turning against him, throughout this period he himself is found writing with utmost calmness and clarity to Hunt, Rogers, Murray, and Moore, planning a gift to Godwin, discussing literature and indeed behaving with a cool-headed self-lessness that bears no relation whatever to our drama (CV, II, 62–3).

CONCLUSIONS

His greater self remained completely unruffled. Lady Byron admitted that he was 'particularly acute' (Lovelace, II, 40) in matters of business. We have already watched him functioning as his own dramatist in the affair of Lady Frances Wedderburn Webster; he was now controlling the whole web of passions and purposes to be later reflected in *Manfred;* and though the most violent elements are present within the drama, his greater self could preserve the cool and passionless quality of an art-form.

This is not to say that he was always cool, but merely that he always could be, if occasion demanded; he could rise beyond himself. Nor do I suggest that to others he was easy; indeed, we know that he was, I do not say cruel, but terrifying. As Moore says, genius regularly casts a shadow in proportion to its own greatness (Moore, XXV, 295). Everyone was baffled. 'It seemed fated', wrote Hobhouse, 'that Byron should never take any step without being misrepresented' (Hobhouse II; XV, 316). It is a well-known discrepancy; as Nietzsche tells us, the Superman will always appear, to his contemporaries, as indeed did Christ Himself, to be in league with Satanic forces (*Thus Spake Zarathustra*, II, 21). So much by way of attempt to characterize what Moore calls 'that whole combination' of 'grand but disturbing powers' (XXVIII, 328) which struck fear into London.

Of all this you will find little direct record in Byron's writings. There are the relevant jottings in his Journals (CV, V, 236-7); there is *Manfred*; and a telling line in *Marina Faliero*, a play into which he wrote much of his personal and political compulsions, 'The secret were too mighty for your souls' (V, i, 285); and there is also Shelley's statement that 'the sense that he was greater than his kind' had blinded his 'eagle-spirit' which suffered from 'gazing on its own exceeding light', so driving him to distraction (*Julian and Maddalo*, 50). Byron feared these greater compulsions; and his fear was dramatically expressed in his violence at Cephalonia (CV, V, 275-8). In this matter, as in that of homosexuality, we have to rely on hints, from himself and others.

We begin to see that Byron was not rejected merely for a sexual lapse, or lapses; and yet the marriage-secret was, almost certainly, behind Lady Byron's sudden change and later actions. We have accordingly *two* causes: (i) the fear of Byron as a satanic Messiah, and (ii) homosexuality and the marriage-secret. Which was the real, the motivating cause?

CONCLUSIONS

A possible solution runs as follows. Byron had aroused fear, jealousy and hatred:

> He who surpasses or subdues mankind
> Must look down on the hate of those below.
> *(Childe Harold, III, 45)*

Now his political enemies, who appear not to have been above blackmail (p. 267), may have somehow deliberately availed themselves of Mrs. Clermont's capacity for 'giving harassing displays of character' (p. 59) and so used her as a willing spy (p. 80). She could then have used her own knowledge to terrify Lady Byron, force the Separation, and so bring about Byron's downfall. Such a reading would at least fit: (i) Byron's apparent sense of his own comparative integrity in the matter, together with his repeated assertions that he did not know the *real* charges against him; (ii) his willingness to face court proceedings, since, if some such dishonesty were indeed at work, and if it all came out in public, few would have regarded him as at fault; (iii) Byron's remark on signing the deed of Separation, 'This is Mrs. Clermont's act and deed'; (iv) his strong insistence that his ruin had not been compassed by a 'just weapon' *(Childe Harold, IV, 133)*; (v) the tantalizing asterisks at Medwin, 43; and (vi) Lady Byron's continued sense of insecurity, leading on to fresh lines of blackmail.

It may seem strange that Society should have been so deeply antagonized by one who was, after all, a deeply humane and kindly man of genius. But literature provides many analogies. Shelley was so antagonized by Byron's poetic record of his rejection in *Childe Harold* (IV, 132–7) that he called it 'the most wicked and mischievous insanity that ever was given forth' (to Peacock, 22 Dec., 1818; LJ, IV, 259, note); Moore found in *Cain* 'a deadly chill' (Moore, XLVIII, 554), and Hobhouse, whose record of hostility to his best friend's poetic and autobiographical excursions is throughout remarkable, urged Byron not to publish it as he valued his friendship (Medwin, 126). Hobhouse never much liked *Childe Harold* and tried to suppress *Don Juan* (CV, 1, 32), which, indeed, was considered by much of the press as the work of some new variety of fiend. In such instances it is, of course, the critic, not the man of genius, who is bad and insane; and, gradually, views change, as Byron himself recognized when he planned his *Memoirs* (p. 151). Or perhaps quickly. Soon after his denunciation of the Promethean stanzas in *Childe Harold*, we find

Shelley using them for incorporation into his greatest work, *Prometheus Unbound* (CV, v, 257–8).

Byron's drama is more than literature; it happened, in actual fact. What Shelley found disturbing in literature was precisely that to which Lady Byron, who here deserves our utmost sympathy, was subjected to daily in the intimacies of married life; and just as Shelley reproduced in his own work that which he had rejected as a dangerous insanity in Byron's, so we find Lady Byron, after her husband's death, living out her life in direct conformity with many of Byron's most cherished opinions. The correspondence is remarkable.

Lady Byron has too often been written off as a pallid, self-righteous, and neurotic woman. This is not true. She was a woman of great gifts, both mathematical and imaginative, and possessing, as some of her comments on Byron show, considerable psychological insight. But she put too great a trust in her own intellect. Teresa Guiccioli wrote her off as 'one of those minds that act as if life were a problem in jurisprudence or geometry; who argue, distinguish, and, by dint of syllogisms, *deceive themselves learnedly*' (II; XII, 230). We have, indeed, already seen how readily she engaged in legalistic subtleties. According to Teresa, Byron was extraordinarily tractable if you knew how to handle him: but when he was 'plunged in the delights of Plato's *Banquet*' (i.e. *The Symposium*), 'or conversing with his own ideas, it was folly to interrupt him' (Teresa, II; XII, 245). But then she was in his world; her brother was an associate with him in his work for Italian liberation, and again later in Greece; and she was prepared to regard him as one superior to the rest of mankind (p. 271).

Lady Byron was not. From the start she had been out to reform him. But she was no fool. It is probable that she understood Byron not less well, but better, than Hobhouse, who tried to see him as simply a charming person suffering from a few disturbing faults to be hushed up as effectively as possible. Byron himself reports an acute insight of hers as to his own ingrained melancholy (*Detached Thoughts*, 73; LJ, v, 446). Lady Byron recognized his powers, and found them dangerous. Teresa responded to his genius positively, with the eyes of love; Lady Byron negatively, with the eye of criticism; but it was to his genius that both responded.

And yet much that we have been saying of 'genius' and 'integration' applies to Lady Byron herself. She was, like Byron, a highly-developed and spiritualized personality. Her mother, writing to her on 3 March 1816, remarked on it:

'I neither do or can expect that you should not *feel* and *deeply feel*— but I have sometimes thought (and that not *only lately*) that Your mind is too *high wrought*—too much so for *this* World—only the *grander* objects engage your thoughts. Your Character is like *Proof Spirits*—not fit for common use—I could almost wish the *Tone* of it *lowered* nearer to the level of *us every day people*, and that You would *endeavour* to take *some interest* in *every day concerns*—believe me, *by degrees*, You will find the benefit of it.'

(Lovelace, III, 55)

This is revealing.

Nor was she a normally sexed woman. Mrs. Stowe tells us that she had a 'commanding mind' and the soul 'not only of an angelic woman, but of a strong, reasoning, man' (Stowe, II, 136; III, 290). She lacked maternal instincts, as a child had never liked dolls, and only wanted children herself for the sake of Byron (Mayne, *Lady Byron*, I, 6; XIII, 191), who was, as we know, devoted to them (CV, II, 75-85; and see p. 72). Her emotions were most naturally given, not to men, but to women. She was herself homosexual. Like Byron, she called her friendships 'passions'. Ethel Colburn Mayne writes:

'Her feeling for Augusta was more than sincere; it was, like that which she had felt for other women in her girlhood, impassioned: "These—passions, I must call them." Throughout her life Annabella was strongly attracted by other women; she was much more of a woman's woman than a man's. To none, however, was the attraction so strong as to Augusta.'

(*Lady Byron*, XIII, 186)

Indeed we are told that this passion led to jealousy (Mayne, *Lady Byron*, XIII, 186; XXVI, 411); which would explain much, including Augusta's repeated asseverations of loyalty. Lovelace may even be right in saying that 'the real obstacle between Lord and Lady Byron' was Augusta (Lovelace, I, 29), but if so, it was not in the way that has been generally supposed. Human nature has many surprises. For that matter, it is well known that Hobhouse was possessively jealous of others, especially Moore, in all that concerned his friendship with Byron, which was both protective and possessive. 'Where Byron was concerned', writes Joyce, 'Hobhouse was jealous of the whole world' (Joyce, VIII, 102). He regarded Byron as one would 'a favourite and sometimes froward sister' (quoted from Hobhouse's *Travels in Albania*, CV, II, 95); and the friendship was one to which he could refer as 'the more than brotherly union which had bound us together' (Hobhouse, III; II, 36). If we may suppose that there was, on his side, a romantic element in the association, his behaviour towards Byron during his life and the passionate will to preserve his fame intact after his death, becomes much clearer. More—we can even suggest that his violent antipathy to the homosexual strain in his friend, which made him so insistent for the burning of the *Memoirs*, and afterwards capable of callously referring to the wicked deed as 'that pious work' (to Wilmot Horton, 23 Nov., 1824; Fox, XVI, 181), was perhaps not independent of personal jealousy. It will be seen that our complications are unending, but this is merely because we are probing beneath the surface of conventional biography into a drama of real life, and the ramifications of such a study are likely to be unending.

Byron was probably well aware from the start of the male strain in Annabella, and this may in part have been why he married her; he thought that she would understand him. But unfortunately people do not in practice fail to be shocked in others by qualities which are highly developed in themselves; indeed such people are often the most critical. Our whole study has been impeded by the extraordinary *silences* of all our authorities for the very reason that each either (i) has no homosexual propensities, and is therefore baffled or uninterested, or (ii) has them, and is fearful of committing himself to anything but condemnation or silence: in such instances anger can be very revealing.

Anyway, Lady Byron, who appears at first to have accepted Byron's confidences, at some point, and for some reason, turned against him. In allying herself, broadly speaking, with conventional morality, she acted in a way which many will applaud, but there is a lesson for us in the result. For whenever the critical and moralistic intellect, in any field, attempts to function independently of the greater, dramatic and religious, dimension which is the happy hunting-ground of genius, it is really assuming pretension beyond itself, and quickly degenerates. And this happened to Lady Byron, her morality falling to the level of blackmail and scandalmongering.

More, just as we find Shelley, like so many a literary critic, being himself influenced and creatively pointed by the very work which he had scorned, so Lady Byron was not only for many years subjected to the same kind of ostracism as Byron, being as Lovelace puts it 'condemned unheard' (Lovelace VIII, 184), but she actually became a vigorous exponent of those very Byronic excellences which she had in effect opposed.

I shall now rely on Lord Lovelace's account of her life (Lovelace, VIII, 184–96). She devoted herself much, in both practice and theory, to social works. She was, it is true, severe in her aims and had, says Lovelace, a horror of the flesh, and she was anxious, above all, that boys—she was less worried about girls—should be cut off from all temptation to vice, and 'condemned to the society of the old and wise', their own society being apparently considered dangerous. Traces of her experience with Byron are here very obvious. But Byron too had, in his own way, an equally severe horror of physical degradation, and might well have approved of such a course. Lady Byron reflected her husband's more liberal views very exactly. She was consistently hostile, like Byron, to all 'vindictive oppression, even of crime'; one 'disposed to love all who, like herself, were calumniated or oppressed—Catholics, negro slaves, the poor Irish goaded into rebellion, heretics like the Unitarians'. She was hostile to all religious *dogmas* and religious oppression, desiring liberty even for its enemies. The Old Testament—and here she differs from Byron —she disliked, and was not even 'unreservedly attached to the New', which to her mind hardly ranked above Tacitus, Dante, Pascal, Chateaubriand, Wordsworth, and Shakespeare. But 'Christ was for her the Man of Sorrows, the Poet of the deathbed, who knew what was in man and had compassion upon all.' He was 'the friend of the distressed', and 'remained till the end, when Dante and Shakespeare were powerless to console'. Her own brightest side 'showed itself to those who were in presence of trouble, pain, remorse, or death'. She was deeply interested in suffering. Byron has left us comparatively few references to Christ, but much of the rest is on a Byronic wavelength. Mrs. Beecher Stowe even credits her with a Nietzschean insight into the nature of evil:

'She saw the germs of good in what others regarded only as evil. She expected valuable results to come from what the world looked on only as eccentricities, and she incessantly devoted herself to the task of guarding those whom the world condemned and guiding them to those higher results of which she often thought that even their faults were prophetic.'

(Stowe, II, 147)

Was that drawn from her association with Byron? Was all this a kind of creative purgatory, semi-consciously making amends for what she had done?

Mrs. Stowe's reverential respect for Lady Byron knew no limit. She regarded her as one of the truly great women of the century. 'There was so much', she writes, 'of Christ in her' that even 'to have seen her' drew one 'nearer to Heaven' (Stowe, III, 300). Mrs. Stowe is not alone in her opinion: others felt much the same. Lady Byron's personality had, like Byron's, an unearthly aspect. Soon after the Separation we find Augusta writing to Francis Hodgson:

'I never can describe Lady Byron's appearance to you but by comparing it to what I should imagine a being of another world. She is positively reduced to a skeleton, pale as *ashes*, a deep hollow tone of voice and a *calm* in her manner quite supernatural. She received *me* kindly but that really appeared the only *surviving* feeling—all else was *death-like* calm. I can never forget it, never!'

(Mayne, *Lady Byron*, XIV, 222)

That stands as a record of what she had endured.

As we watch her great husband's spirit descending on the lonely and gifted woman who had rejected him we cannot help wondering what might have happened had the marriage succeeded. Each had what the other lacked, like Duke Vincentio and Isabella in *Measure for Measure*: 'What's mine is yours, and what is yours is mine' (V, i, 539); that is, the mating of profundity with moral fervour. The violence of the later antagonism, Annabella's devotion to the task of suppressing her husband's defence and blackening his name, and his own vitriolic outbursts during the years which followed the Separation against the 'infernal fiend' (Augusta, 19 June, 1817; Lovelace, XI, 288) and 'moral Clytemnestra' (*Lines on Hearing that Lady Byron was Ill*) who had ruined him, merely mark the measure of what might have been. Byron had clearly glimpsed the possibility. He is usually blamed for choosing so unsuitable a wife; but he married Annabella precisely because she possessed what he lacked, what all his life he aimed at; whose symbol was the ethic of Pope's poetry— that is, moral principle. He half *wanted* this 'high Soul', this girl 'serenely purest of her sex that live' (*A Sketch*), to control him, to save him from his destiny. But this was not easy. Pope's aim to 'set the *passions* on the side of truth' (p. 255) was no simple doctrine; and Byron's passions were no less than the Shakespearian universe incarnate.[1]

Lady Byron was, undoubtedly, frightened. She had been fighting a battle, for herself, and still more, for Byron. But her hand was suddenly forced by, probably, Mrs. Clermont, or at least some consideration involving the marriage-secret; and she gave up, at the crucial moment, and so started her accusations of 'revenge' and 'pride'. What, once again, *was* it that so shocked her in actuality and Shelley when recorded in verse? Pride? But many are proud. Lady Byron was far more obviously proud than her husband, suffering, as Byron himself told Lady Blessington, from an exceptional degree of that very self-respect of which the lack was his own 'besetting sin' (Blessington, 316). Byron's was no ordinary pride. It was rather a half-shocked, indeed a miserable, all but pitiable, an *abject*, recognition in himself of powers beyond all normal categories; he was not only greater, he was different. From the days when he meditated on a tomb at Harrow or drank from a skull at Newstead, he was ghost-ridden; he was, to himself as well as to others, fey; he knew himself a thing apart, unclean, an Ishmael, a fallen angel, an anti-Christ, a new Messiah. And what was worst of all, he was right. That was the awful thing, to others and no less, as his fury at Cephalonia witnesses (CV, v, 276–8), to himself. He was as a being from another world, lighted on earth. This Hobhouse would never recognize; Moore glimpsed it; Lady Byron denounced it. Teresa alone both recognized and accepted it; and, when the hour came, she let Byron, with grief it is true, but without bitterness, follow his destiny to the end.

Such 'heavy matters', as the Shepherd in *The Winter's Tale* would say, may appear to bear little relation to our sexual problems. But we must not forget our recent quotation from Powys on the Holy Grail. In Byron was both Falstaff and Hamlet, comedy and tragedy, sex and spirit; and somehow these converge. The most profound spiritual disturbances can be related to sexual experience; and in Byron the greater national compulsions can be seen as an extension of sexual impulse. So, while recognizing the risk of antagonizing

[1] This I hope to show in another study. Meanwhile I would point to the suggestions thrown out in my lecture *Byron's Dramatic Prose*, published by the University of Nottingham (1954)

critics both rationalist and religious by reference to the New Testament, I would, before closing, attempt to drive home and crown our argument, and bring together our themes, in one great, yet simple comparison.

IV

I have talked much, here and elsewhere, of the bisexual integration. Roughly we may note certain conditions and characteristics of such abnormal persons; a type of which as good a description as any occurs in my brother's account of the psychology of Virgil (*Roman Vergil*, IV, III–16). There is, often, a close relationship to the mother, with the father playing a less emphatic part, a well-known condition often associated with the name 'Oedipus'. A strong feminine element is preserved, which is less 'effeminacy' than spiritual insight, and the result is 'bisexual'. Such men are, as Moore notes, ill-attuned for marriage; they may be ascetic, licentious, homosexual, or incestuous in tendency. Friends and disciples are usually male, but there may also be strong devotion from women, such as Swift received, and it may be returned in complete dissociation from sexual action. The result is an expansion into service, artistic, social, political or religious, including scathing satiric attacks on insincerity and convention in the cause of a disturbing and astringent love. The tale is shot through by intimations of eternity.

Now the story of Christ, as it comes to us through literature and dogma, contains many of these elements. Some, as in the dogma of the Virgin Birth and the part played by Mary, Mother of Christ, the Transfiguration and the Resurrection, are raised to an extreme. But the more homely, more 'psychological', more social, elements, are there too; and they are intrinsic to the meaning and value which we receive. Christ himself could not have been the power He is, had He been married; and D. H. Lawrence's attempt in *The Escaped Cock* or *The Man Who Died* to give Him a sexual partner surely marks a failure in understanding. Rather should we turn to the words of Jacob Boehme: 'This champion or lion is no man or woman, but he is both' (*Signatura Rerum*, Everyman ed., XI, 43)[1]. He must have been, in tendency at least, androgynous; for He was complete. Even so, we cannot, at the risk of denying the total humanity of the Incarnation, regard Him as existing independently of sexual impulse. And,

[1] This valuable reference I owe to Mr. Melville Chaning-Pearce.

CONCLUSIONS

once we allow this, we find that *He conforms far more closely to the abnormal psychology of genius than to what might be called the biological psychology of the ordinary man.* It does, indeed, seem that once again, as so often happens, our furthest penetrations are forced to admit that they have all the time been covered by a proper understanding of the Christian revelation.

In such a matter we must move with caution. And yet, if we wish for some human analogy to what Christ may be supposed to have felt for His first followers[1], and feels still for his Church on earth, we cannot surely do better than listen in, as I have already suggested in *The Dynasty of Stowe* (III, 44–5), to the Platonic doctrine of educational and creative love in *The Symposium*; or, to take a concrete example, to Shakespeare's jealous guardianship of his Fair Youth, or Byron's protective and yearning affection for such young lives as Rushton, Edleston, Nicolo and Loukas. Our comparison finds fleeting support in one of those many profundities housed in Byron's epistolary asides, when, after referring to 'Luke', or 'Loukas', he explains off-handedly, 'not the evangelist, but a disciple of mine' (Hancock, 5 Feb., 1824; LJ, VI, 315). If indeed an element of Platonism, in rather more than the academic sense of that well-worn term, has lain, unguessed throughout the centuries, in Christianity, then such men of tormented genius as we have been discussing, the Shakespeares, Miltons, Swifts, Byrons and Nietzsches, are really men who have been compelled to replace the worship of Christ by, however fragmentarily, the imitation of Christ. This is not easy, nor pleasant. Nor do we claim that they have succeeded: they generally cut sorry figures on the stage of life beside the statesmen, soldiers, and ecclesiastics of their time. They would probably choose otherwise, if they could; but, like Luther, they 'can do no other'.

Byron especially makes emotional claims—and this it is perhaps which has most repelled his English readers—on the very wavelength of the New Testament. And here John Cowper Powys is again helpful. Writing of Christ as a divinity on earth he discovers in Him, as a natural characteristic of that divinity, 'Majestic lovableness, and a magnetic passion for being loved' (*The Pleasures of Literature*,

[1] Among the charges levelled against Christopher Marlowe by Richard Baines and Thomas Kyd was that of asserting a passionate relationship between Christ and the disciple John (*The Life of Marlowe, etc.*, C. F. Tucker Brooke, 1930; Apps. IX and XII; 99, 107; and see *Christopher Marlowe*, Paul H. Kocher, University of North Carolina Press, 1946; VIII, 209–11).

63). Now whatever *we* think of Byron, this is, except for the resounding word 'majestic', precisely how Byron's friends saw him, Hobhouse and others insisting that his magnetic appeal was such as no other man, perhaps, has ever possessed (p. 15), and Moore referring, again and again, to his capacity for affection and the yearning for its return as forming 'the dream and torment of his existence'; to 'that intense craving after affection which nature had implanted in him', and which 'mingled with even the least refined of his attachments' (Moore, VIII, 84; XXIII, 269; XXVIII, 328). This yearning reaches a poetic climax in a famous passage:

> But I have lived, and have not lived in vain.
> My mind may lose its force, my blood its fire,
> And my frame perish even in conquering pain;
> But there is that within me which shall tire
> Torture and Time, and breathe when I expire;
> Something unearthly, which they deem not of,
> Like the remember'd tone of a mute lyre,
> Shall on their soften'd spirits sink, and move
> In hearts all rocky now the late remorse of love.
>
> (*Childe Harold*, IV, 137)

As a simple matter of rational and analytic comparison, we cannot deny the New Testament quality of those lines.

And what Byron felt and expressed has been felt, if not so aptly expressed, by other men of his calibre. Such men would attain, or at least announce, what Swift in *The Battle of the Books* called 'sweetness and light'. That is their final end, the purpose of their existence. But it is only by fits and starts achieved, and on the way there is torment, loneliness, misrepresentation, thwarted love, and the insistent, sexual, itch for contact. So, as Shakespeare puts it, they may, being over-full of 'sweetness', be tempted to descend to 'bitter sauces'; in Byron's words, to 'plunge amidst mankind'; or as Nietzsche has it, to crave, by reason of their very repletion of virtue, for 'wickedness', in order to 'touch the souls' of others (Sonnet 118; *Manfred*, II, ii, 145; *Thus Spake Zarathustra*, II, 9; see *Christ and Nietzsche*, V, 179, and *The Mutual Flame*, I, V, 124–7). Of this particular curve in the fortunes of genius Byron's Venetian experiences, of which he himself told Shelley that he *disapproved* whilst *enduring* them, offer a perfect example (see p. 213; also CV, V, 256–7). Two directions are possible: (i) to force sexual love into abnormal channels, or (ii) reach consummation and contact through self-sacrifice. We may, recalling our earlier analysis (p. 261), observe that both involve the concept 'death'. True, Swift and Nietzsche did neither, and went mad; Wilde engaged in sin; Byron probably sinned, and moved on to sacrifice. In Christ we have the perfect, and purposive, Shakespearian sense of letting 'determin'd things to destiny hold, unbewail'd, their course'. The Cross was, for Him, as I have elsewhere (*Christ and Nietzsche*, III, 103–4, V, 179) demonstrated, the one way of universal *contact*.

It would surely be a pity to fear such comparisons. After all, should we wish to feel into the experience of Christ in suffering the transition from popular adulation to scorn and mockery, we do well to study the near-distance experiences of Byron and Wilde. Though there may indeed be great differences, each was anathema—as was Socrates—to the guardians of morality; each endured ignominy; and each suffered for love. Shelley once adduced the teachings of both Socrates and Christ in a similar context to ours (*Fragments Connected with Epipsychidion*, 33–4; *The Mutual Flame*, V, 212–13), and Christ appears to be given as a *solution* to the whole problem in Browning's *Saul*. Wilde was, as we know, aware of the analogy; and so, in a general sense, and most unwillingly, was Byron. He strongly objected to the blasphemy of such a comparison (Medwin, 122); and the only vivid example we possess of violent behaviour on his part sprang precisely from his response to the semi-divine honours paid him at Cephalonia (CV, V, 275–8); and yet once, 'after commenting on his own wrongs', and remarking on the way Shelley too was 'hooted' out of 'his country' like 'a mad dog', he added: 'Man is the same rancorous beast now that he was from the beginning, and if the Christ they profess to worship reappeared they would again crucify Him' (Trelawny, VII, 55; we cannot, of course, be sure that the words are precisely Byron's). Moore, too, seems to have had some such thoughts, and perhaps had Loukas in mind as well, when he wrote of Byron's poem *On This Day I Complete my Thirty-Sixth Year* that 'there is perhaps no production within the range of mere human composition, round which the circumstances and feelings under which it was written cast so touching an interest' (Moore, LIV, 615). That poem contains the cry: 'But, though I cannot be beloved, yet let me love'. Byron was, if nothing else, one of the world's greatest, and most universal, lovers. Lady Blessington saw the truth:

'Byron's heart is running to waste for want of being allowed to expend itself on his fellow-creatures; it is naturally capacious and teeming with affection; but the worldly wisdom he has acquired has checked its course, and it preys on his own happiness by reminding him continually of the aching void in his breast.'

(Blessington, 284)

That is, in their degree, the story too of many a lesser man. Nietzsche once commented on the vast stores of 'kindness and power' that lie hidden, and unused, in mankind (*Thus Spake Zarathustra*, III, 11).

It may be argued that these tragic figures add nothing to the one revelation, and are therefore irrelevant. But, even though they seem like gestures towards the impossible, we may remember that it was St. Paul who said that Christ was to become the 'first-born of a great brotherhood' (Romans, viii, 29); which means more than a community of pious *worshippers*. And perhaps they also do, in their own troubled way, add something. Though sex and politics, which I have elsewhere (CV, 1, 48) called 'those two practical jokers on the soul of man', may indeed be, to a sensitive understanding, covered by the New Testament and Christian Dogma, yet the teaching is not always explicit, nor are its ramifications developed. Of our various men of genius, Milton and Swift engaged strenuously in politics, and Nietzsche philosophized on them; the contribution of others, such as Wilde, may be, if only through our study of their unhappy lives, more personal, more sexual. Byron's life and work show both, raised to the limit of significance. Such men are symbolic, and we learn as much from their failures as from their successes.

As we look back on a century of falsification, fabrication, distortion, and even lying, in Byronic studies, we may well decide that the time has come for more honesty; and the first sign of such an honesty must be *a complete forgiveness of Lady Byron;* for it was simply *fear,* born of morality and social pressure, which forced her actions. And yet there is little to fear from an honest approach to these problems, and only from an honest approach can a true morality mature. We do not, surely, wish to be grouped with those who, as Nietzsche puts it, see the 'sparks' of genius, but enjoy no understanding of the inward mechanisms, the 'anvil' and 'the cruelty of its hammer' (*Thus Spake Zarathustra*, II, 8; and see p. 190 above). Hitherto, fear has ruled. Byron, though perhaps the most daring and honest of our great poets, never, so far as we know, spoke out boldly on homosexuality; and when he saw himself as one forced by power and plenitude to 'live and die unheard', sheathing, 'as a sword', the very 'lightning' of his being, and letting it remain a 'most voiceless thought' (*Childe Harold*, III, 97), the reason was, at least in part, the very prosaic one of 'convention'; prosaic, but powerful, especially to one like Byron who would have agreed with Burke that irrational prejudice is generally worthy of respect, if only because it *is* irrational prejudice, and therefore must have some deeper justification. He deliberately preferred to slander himself with suggestions of murder and incest rather than acknowledge the true nature of the idyllic *Thyrza* poems; and since his day many a young man has been led into actual crime by what Lady Byron called this 'solitary secret' (p. 209). Even so, Byron is more personally honest than other great poets; one hardly likes to hazard how much is veiled by *their* works. Byron at least wanted, and often tried, to speak out, and may indeed have done so, to some extent, in his *Memoirs*. His poetry, too, hints at what it may not say:

> *What from this barren being do we reap?*
> *Our senses narrow, and our reason frail,*
> *Life short, and truth a gem which loves the deep,*
> *And all things weigh'd in custom's falsest scale;*
> *Opinion an omnipotence—whose veil*
> *Mantles the earth with darkness, until right*
> *And wrong are accidents, and men grow pale*
> *Lest their own judgments should become too bright,*
> *And their free thoughts be crimes, and earth have too much light.*
>
> (*Childe Harold*, IV, 93)

The plea is not against morality, but rather for some shift in ethical valuation. As Colman puts it:

> *I stand a monument, whereby to learn*
> *That reason's light can never strongly burn*
> *Where blear-eyed prejudice erects her throne,*
> *And has no scale for virtue but her own.*
>
> (*Don Leon*, 1383)

Again,

> *God of the Universe, whose laws shall last*
> *When Lords and Commons to their graves have past,*
> *Are good and evil just as man opines,*
> *And kens he thy inscrutable designs?*
>
> (*Don Leon*, 1401)

As we study such passages, and remember that all the great political denunciations of *Don Leon* against statesmen who have done nothing to humanize the laws against homosexuality *are supposed to be spoken by Byron*, we are brought up against the thought: did the two positive powers of Byron's life converge, during the years 1815 and 1816, in a more obvious sense than that which we have already, from time to time, stated? Was the 'impious pride' of which Lady Byron spoke connected with both politics *and* the sexual problem? What was the import of those strange words, spoken as from the ecstasy of martyrdom, which he is reported to have uttered: 'Let them come forward, I'll Glory in it!' (Fox, XII, 108). Was his half-formulated, but quickly stifled, pseudo-Napoleonic, or Promethean, programme, message, or gospel concerned, like *Don Leon*, with the urging of some new sexual tolerance? Byron's poetic challenge was throughout levelled against those doctrines of Hell and Damnation, in which, none the less, he half believed; and his primary religious insistence was moral charity. He is also the first really militant anti-militarist in English poetry. Was he perhaps groping after some wider recognition of the powers of love as an alternative to a world distraught by tyranny and slaughter? It is possible.

We should now be in a position to read with a measure of under-standing, and perhaps of sympathy, Byron's separation stanzas to his wife, *Fare thee well, and if for ever*; and to place with some degree of accuracy the lines

> *All my faults perchance thou knowest,*
> *All my madness none can know.*

(P, III, 539)

That is true; for there is necessarily much which remains veiled.

INDEX

Names occurring in references to correspondence are not necessarily all indexed.

L.B.M.—U*

INDEX

Justinian I: 176.
Juvenal: 197.

Kennedy, James: xiii, 79, 149.
Kessel, Marcel: 139.
Kinnaird, Douglas: 54, 79, 108, 152, 154, 206.
Knight, G. Wilson: *Byron's Dramatic Prose*, xv, 80, 263, 280; *Christ and Nietzsche*, 256, 283–4; *The Dynasty of Stowe*, 282; *Laureate of Peace*, 197, 254; *Lord Byron: Christian Virtues*, ix, xiii, xv, 10, 15, 24, 45–6, 68, 72, 128, 131, 147, 209, 213, 223–4, **243**, 251, **254**, 256, 263–4, 270–4, 276–7, 280, 283–5; *The Mutual Flame*, 256, 259–60, 263, 283–4; *The Starlit Dome*, 256; *The Wheel of Fire*, 259.
Knight, W. F. Jackson: 281.
Kocher, Paul H.: 282.
Kyd, Thomas: 282.

Lactantius: 197.
Lamb, Lady Caroline: 15–19, 22, 44–5, 53, 87, 110, 127, 134, 142, 205.
Lamb, The Hon. Mrs. George: 90.
Lansdown, Lord: 152.
Lawrence, D. H.: 256–8; *The Escaped Cock*, or *The Man Who Died*, 281.
Leigh, The Hon. Mrs. (Augusta Mary Byron): x, xii, 3, 7, 19, 24–5, **38–44**, 52–6, 58, 60, 64–5, 68–9, 73–4, 77, 80–1, **87–116**, 123, 125–7, 142, 147–148, 202, 223, 229, 233, 237, 240, 266, 269–71, 279; her goodness, 43, 129, 207, **211–12**, 249; knows Byron's secrets, 93–4, 96, 209–11, 220–1, 249, 267–8; anxiety regarding his instincts, 130, 202, 210; adviser and moral support, 22, 26–7, 42–3, 46, 129–30, 202, 205, 207–8, **211–12**, 249; as accomplice, 96, 210–211, 249; in Byron's poetry, 43, 102, 119–21, 126, 212, 219; question of incest, see under Byron, Lord; submission to Lady Byron, 100–1, 108, 129, 133, 137, 142–3, 249; at cross purposes, 94–5, 111–13, 210–11,

249–50; change of attitude after 1830, 111, 249–50; the Reigate meeting, 112, 248, 250); correspondence with Byron, see Byron, Lord; with Lady Byron, 94–102, 111–13, 135, 142–3; the 'incriminating' letter, see Byron, Lord; her supposed confession, 96–7, 101, 103–4, 111, 140, 239; leaves papers to rebut the charge, 97, 113, 239; epistolary styles, 94, 111, 133–4, 142, 211, 249–250; her part in the destruction of Byron's *Memoirs*, 106–8, 152–4, 249; her official statement, 106, 153–4; recapitulation, 249–50.
Leigh, Elizabeth Medora: 25, 27, 39, 40, 131, 137–8, 231, 233, 238.
Leigh, Colonel George: 38–40, 131.
Leigh, Georgiana: 130.
Le Mann, Dr. Francis: 58, 67, 80, 128, 247, 272; and see Baillie, Dr.
Lewis, C. S.: 197.
Lewis, M. G. ('Monk'): 13, 146–7.
Lewis, Wyndham: 263.
Llangollen, The Ladies of: see Butler and Ponsonby.
Long, Edward Noel: 6, 28.
Longman & Co.: 151.
Louis XVIII and the Bourbon Dynasty: 53, 251, 264, 267.
Loukas: see Chalandritsanos.
Lovelace, Lady, formerly Augusta Ada Byron: see Byron.
Lovelace, Mary, Lady, editress of the second edition of *Astarte*: xiv, 59, 87–8, 91, 111, 115, 129, 142.
Lovelace, Ralph, Lord: xiv, 15, 41–2, **87–116**, 129, 132, 137, 154, 208, **213**, 268, 271–2, 276, 278; his *Astarte*, xiv, 51, 87, 113, **115–16**, 130, 135, 142–3, **236–9**, 241; its untrustworthiness, 115–16, 125, 128, 237–8; other references, 22, 41–2, 52, 56, 59, 77, 123, 129–38, 144–5, 150–1, 206, 209, 214, 250, 267, 270, 273, 279.
Lovelace papers, the: 57, 104, 112–13, 207, 221, **237–8**, 241.
Luke, Saint: 282.